W9-AMZ-963

REGENTS CRITICS SERIES

General Editor: Paul A. Ol...

L

J

DATE DUE			
Aug 17 '72			

Other volumes in the Regents Critics Series are:

Literary Criticism of
James Russell Lowell

Edited by

HERBERT F. SMITH

UNIVERSITY OF NEBRASKA PRESS · LINCOLN

810.9003
L95L
79379
Aug. 1972

MANUFACTURED IN THE UNITED STATES OF AMERICA

Regents Critics Series

The Regents Critics Series provides reading texts of significant literary critics in the Western tradition. The series treats criticism as a useful tool: an introduction to the critic's own poetry and prose if he is a poet or novelist, an introduction to other work in his day if he is more judge than creator. Nowhere is criticism regarded as an end in itself but as what it is—a means to the understanding of the language of art as it has existed and been understood in various periods and societies.

Each volume includes a scholarly introduction which describes how the work collected came to be written, and suggests its uses. All texts are edited in the most conservative fashion consonant with the production of a good reading text; and all translated texts observe the dictum that the letter gives life and the spirit kills when a technical or rigorous passage is being put into English. Other types of passages may be more freely treated. Footnoting and other scholarly paraphernalia are restricted to the essential minimum. Such features as a bibliographical checklist or an index are carried where they are appropriate to the work in hand. If a volume is the first collection of the author's critical writing, this is noted in the bibliographical data.

PAUL A. OLSON

University of Nebraska

Contents

Introduction

Historically, periods of attack upon literature have brought to birth some of the most important works of literary theory and criticism: Plato's strictures on the poet probably suggested Aristotle's famous comparison of the poet's and the historian's representations of truth; Gosson's attack upon the drama, *The School of Abuse*, may have prompted Sidney's magnificent *Defense of Poetry*; Wordsworth's Preface to the *Lyrical Ballads* purports, at least, to be a reaction to an ambiance of rhetoric antithetical to his conceptions of poetry. One could multiply the instances. When the enemies of literature become most hysterical, a champion for art seems always to answer vigorously with an enduring work of criticism. One might admit one exception to this general principle, however. America in the nineteenth century almost literally denied the poet the right of access to its something-less-than-ideal republic; it consistently associated art with immorality in a much more vulgar way than any seventeenth-century Puritan would have; and it called for "plain talk" in no uncertain terms. Yet, who is the American critic who leaped to the defense of literature? Emerson prophesied an ideal poet, but admitted that he looked in vain for the contemporary specimen; Poe defended art, to be sure, but went so far as to defend it for its own sake, an exaggeration that literature is still trying to live down; and the rest of America's critics were either hack journalists elevated to the role of critic by the law of supply and demand, or artists who only rarely became articulate outside their art. And so the defense of poetry in nineteenth-century America came to rest finally on the man who was surely her most tentative and timid—not champion— but *cavaliere servente*, James Russell Lowell.

Lowell was a good deal more than just a critic—which is, of course, often a way of saying that he was something less. Poet, diplomatist, scholar, abolitionist, humanist—his critical writings represent only a small part of the twelve volumes of his collected works. And though all of Lowell's writings are graceful and polished, none are of the highest significance. One might assume, that being the case, that his criticism would, if it were inadequate, merely pass into limbo and be forgotten. But that has not been its fate. Less than thirty years after Lowell's death in 1891, Joseph J. Reilly gave his criticism a full-length study in *James Russell Lowell as a Critic* (New York, 1915), only to conclude that Lowell was *not* a critic; John M. Robertson, reviewing Reilly's book, made the obvious reply by asking, if Lowell is not a critic, who is?[1] The forces gathered, the lines formed, and for the past fifty years Lowell's reputation as a critic has been an esthetic battlefield. The stridence of his debunkers (in general, the Marxist critics and others who insist upon relevance in literature) is matched by the idolatry of his supporters (the New Humanists). Yet, as his critics inevitably admit the range and depth of his criticism, so his defenders hedge and qualify his achievements with talk of his "superlatives," his "impressionism," his divagations. Both sides claim too much or too little for him, must therefore qualify their claims, and somehow reason is lost. The fact of the matter is that Lowell cannot be considered a great critic except by comparison with the relatively low level of other American critics of his time. He is, nevertheless, a critic who must be reckoned with. He wrote too much; he is repetitive; few principles of criticism seem, at first sight, to make his work cohere; he was traditional and con-servative—indeed, he was inconsistent and even self-contradictory in many of his judgments. One may grant him all these faults (though I shall try to show that most of them are vitiated by some basic misconceptions about the nature of his criticism) and yet conclude that the critical writings of a man with such taste, such erudition, and such esthetic sympathies may not be written off either as out-dated or as evidence of the immaturity of the man and his epoch.

Among the misconceptions about Lowell's criticism that have spawned dispute over his reputation, none is more troublesome than the belief that his inclination was toward prescriptive criticism. A few unqualified, usually epigrammatic castigations of one writer or another are taken as Lowell's norm of criticism when the reverse is

1. "Lowell as a Critic," *North American Review*, CCIX (February 1919), 246.

actually true. It would be hard to find a critic more catholic in his taste or humble in his belief in his criticism than James Russell Lowell. One finds among his critical essays, time after time, statements concerning the need for critical objectivity, refusals to damn or to praise in an unqualified manner, and copious extracts intended to allow the reader to make up his own mind. His review of Ward's *Life and Letters of James Gates Percival* opens with a typical statement; contemptuous of Percival himself, Lowell praises Ward for enabling "us to form our own judgment by letting [Percival] so far as possible speak for himself."[2] His own works are strewn with quotations, long and short, from the writers whom he is considering, and this reviewer's habit has probably done more to destroy his reputation than any other fault. Even his friendliest critic, Norman Foerster, remarks: "Instead of regarding quotations as a documentation and illumination of purposeful discourse, he tended to look upon himself as a kind of showman, displaying this, that, and the other, with comments expressing his own pleasure in the objects."[3] Foerster properly takes this predilection as evidence of Lowell's impressionism; so it is. But for him it is not a denial of initial responsibility, but a critical position, arrived at after a good deal of thought. He wrote,

> As my own excursions widened, as I opened new vistas through the crowding growth of my own prejudices and predilections, I was fain to encourage in others that intellectual hospitality which in myself I had found strengthening from an impulse till it became a conviction that the wiser mind should have as many entrances for unbidden guests as was fabled of the Arabian Prince's tent.[4]

However much this statement seems to demean the critic's role, it represents a principle of sanity in criticism. Critics are, of course, not always correct in their criticism; since this is so, the too catholic taste, the tendency to indulgence in criticism, is far less sinister a

2. *The Complete Writings of James Russell Lowell* (Elmwood Edition; Boston and New York: Houghton Mifflin, 1904), II, 103. Hereafter cited as *Works*.

3. *American Criticism* (Boston and New York: Houghton Mifflin, 1928), p. 116.

4. Quoted by Robertson, "Lowell as a Critic," p. 249, who cites Lowell's Apology for a Preface to *The English Poets, Lessing, and Rousseau* (London, 1888).

fault than critical intolerance. Better to have too many poets in the Republic than too few.

A corollary to this principle of catholicity of taste in the critic is Lowell's profession of the need for a unique kind of enthusiasm on the part of the reader and critic. As he says, unless we are "capable of bringing to a work of art some freshness of sensation, and receiving from it in turn some new surprise of sympathy and admiration— some shock even, it may be, of instinctive distaste and repulsion— though we may praise or blame, weighing our *pros* and *cons* in the nicest balances, sealed by proper authority, *yet we shall not criticise in the highest sense*" (italics added).[5] The remark seems to be a dangerous one. It might be read as a justification for the most visceral impressionism, for the Housman-Dickinson school of criticism by the tingling of ganglia. Yet, doubtless that particular thought never entered Lowell's mind; thoroughly trained in the classics, he was always aware, as he wrote of Bryant, "how much grace, strength, and dignity lie in repose." Indeed, on balance, Lowell favors dignity much more often than surprise, as in his comments apropos of Carlyle's fiery style:

> No doubt a great part of our pleasure in reading is unexpectedness, whether in turn of thought or of phrase; but an emphasis out of place, an intensity of expression not founded on sincerity of moral or intellectual conviction, reminds one of the underscorings in young ladies' letters, a wonder even to themselves under the colder north-light of matronage.[6]

Here, as almost always, Lowell may be found in the middle of the road, far from any critical extremity. Therein, probably, lies the reason for the wild swings of Lowell's critical reputation. Firmly located in the center as he is, humble and undemonstrative as he is, he is either looked up to or looked down upon, as the case demands, by modern factionalist critics, as though he were the satellite and they the mother earth. Lowell professes as guide and principle for his criticism only humility and catholicity, taste and erudition; how

---

5. *Works*, III, 247. Lowell immediately qualifies this statement to the effect that "certain principles" must be "fixed," else criticism is only impressionism.

6. *Works*, II, 60.

infuriating that posture must seem to a modern critic with an ax in his hand and grinding to do!

A second series of misapprehensions about Lowell's criticism derives from the form of many of his essays. They seem to be review-essays in the classical manner of, for example, *Revue des Deux Mondes* of a hundred years ago: *X: sa vie, son âme, ses oeuvres.* Insofar as they are of this type, they have perhaps only an antiquarian interest for the modern reader. However, if the reader will only take the time to distinguish between the practical criticism and the theoretical criticism in these essays, they take on a new character. Most of the inconsistencies disappear magically as what ought to be separates itself from what merely is, and the pure gold of Lowell's theoretical criticism is separated from the crude ore of the merely historical and practical. Oddly, none of the commentators on Lowell seem to have performed this basic refinement of his work,[7] even though the guideposts are clearly there—general statements, theoretical principles, are rhetorically isolated from specific analysis. Both kinds of criticism have their interest, but it would be silly to claim that Lowell's practical criticism deserves more than passing mention before one proceeds to the criticism that transcends its own day.

Lowell's practical criticism spans Western literature from the Greeks to the Victorians, with no fewer than thirty authors between Chaucer and Thoreau considered at length in major essays. As one might expect, with such scope, Lowell is uneven in both emphasis and achievement. He is best with writers who have been already canonized—Dante, Chaucer, Shakespeare—and with writers with whom he is in fairly close sympathy—Coleridge, Keats, "Emerson the Lecturer." He is almost totally unsympathetic with writers whose work lies outside of classical forms—Carlyle, Swinburne—and with writers who, as he saw it, perverted classical form into neo-classical formulas—Pope, and to a much lesser extent, Dryden. Much of his specific criticism of writers is not criticism at all; it is a mere gathering of details about the life of the writer interspersed with jejune hypotheses concerning the influences of these barren details

7. An exception may be Richard Harter Fogle, "Organic Form in American Criticism, 1840–1870," in Floyd Stoval (ed.), *The Development of American Literary Criticism* (Chapel Hill: University of North Carolina Press, 1955), pp. 108–111.

upon the writer's character. Often such passages gave Lowell opportunities for displays of erudition, which he seemed to enjoy; in reviewing lives of writers, he would sometimes curse the pedantry of the author reviewed, only to substitute a pedantry of his own. At times this pedantic element of his criticism could be permanently useful, in however limited a manner, as when he excoriates the editors of Elizabethan playwrights for their arbitrary readings. More often, he is himself almost comically inadequate when, for example, he substitutes his own folk etymologies for those of the editors he berates.[8]

When Lowell gets down to the texts of his writers, he fares better. His writings are filled with sudden flashes of insight which one senses are as inspired as they are correct. Who would not gladly read through a good deal of dross on Pope, for instance, to encounter his inspired comment that " Pope's proverbial verse,

> True wit is Nature to advantage drest,

unpleasantly suggests Nature under the hands of a ladies' maid."[9] Again, his consideration of Wordsworth is neatly summed up in his analysis of the following lines from Book IV of *The Prelude*:

> In fine,
> I was a better judge of thoughts than words,
> Misled in estimating words, not only
> By common inexperience of youth,
> But by the trade in classic niceties. . . .

Lowell's comment is perfect: "Though he [Wordsworth] speaks in the preterite tense, this was always true of him, and his thought seems often to lean upon a word too weak to bear its weight. No reader of adequate insight can help regretting that he did not earlier give himself to 'the trade of classic niceties.'"[10]

In both of the instances which we have cited, the critical remark is primarily rhetorical: the connotations of the word "drest" are inappropriate to the serious tone of Pope's line, at least to the

8. See *Works*, III, 227–230, for example.
9. Cited by Foerster, *American Criticism*, p. 117.
10. *Works*, V, 224.

nineteenth-century ear; the more general criticism of Wordsworth fastens upon word choice again, suggesting a more basic poetic inadequacy. Yet both criticisms of word choice also pertain to the world of idea. The critique of Pope suggests that the neoclassical form was inadequate to the expression of the dignity of the concept with which he dealt; the critique of Wordsworth suggests that Wordsworth's poetic technique was too easily satisfied with the vague and general expression of the grand idea. If we are not reading too much into these brief criticisms—and I doubt that we are—they are almost excruciatingly suggestive. We need not agree with them, or with the esthetic and moral perspective behind them, but we are obliged, because of them, to examine their subject from a new viewpoint.

The real problem, in each of the two instances cited and in all of Lowell's practical criticism, is that Lowell's value judgments enter into what should be objective analysis. Here Lowell's theory is not at fault. He quotes Goethe to the effect that "destructive criticism" proceeds from the critic's setting up "in his mind any standard, any model, however narrow," and judging other writing by contrast, while "productive criticism" asks, "What did the author propose to himself? Is what he proposes reasonable and comprehensible? and how far has he succeeded in carrying it out?"[11] Unfortunately, Lowell only rarely managed to follow this dictum himself, and failure to do so led him to such critical monstrosities as his treatment of Rousseau. In the first half of his essay, "Rousseau and the Sentimentalists," Lowell seemed to find nothing valuable in Rousseau's work, simply because Rousseau lacked "character." Then, in the last half of his essay, he resuscitated Rousseau by means of the idea that somehow Rouseau's "genius" managed to compensate for his defects of character.[12] The details of this miraculous transformation are, as we might imagine, hedged about by some extraordinarily foggy rhetoric on Lowell's part.

Indeed, except for a handful of epigrams (a rather large handful, to be sure), Lowell's practical criticism has little to offer the modern

11. *Works*, III, 290. Foerster, p. 119, cites this same passage to show that Lowell was not an expressionistic critic.

12. See "Rousseau and the Sentimentalists," *Works*, IV, 173–217.

reader through nine-tenths of its volume.[13] It is that last tenth
devoted to American writers and the peculiar problems of American
literature in the nineteenth century that is particularly valuable.
His criticism of American writers is far from complete, and it is
embarrassing at times (his treatment of Thoreau illustrates his almost
total lack of sympathy with what were to be the major American
themes; he apparently hardly knew and only once mentioned Mel-
ville in a published work). Yet, his criticism was unique and
thorough, a body of criticism fit to begin the critical education of our
country. *A Fable for Critics* remains a major piece of practical criticism of American literature, the more so because its usual manner is
the epigram, so well suited to Lowell's taste. Other works, like the
review of Percival, "Emerson the Lecturer," and his review of
Henry James's first work, are useful criticism as well as historical
documents. One must remember that Lowell was a Brahmin, a
Bostonian of the well-known three-cornered society that included the
Cabots and God. If one keeps that particular bias in mind, with all
that it suggests about Lowell's attitudes toward his culture's
traditions of morality and literature, he may find much of value in
Lowell's practical criticism.

In his theoretical criticism Lowell examines most of the problems
of literary composition, from the most general to the most specific,
from the nature of the poet to the usefulness of the vernacular. He
is an unabashed eclectic; he seems to have absorbed critical ideas
from every angle and attitude of his voluminous reading. Plato and
Aristotle, Sidney and Dryden, Dr. Johnson and Coleridge were
equally his inspirations. Yet, for all of the direct sources that can be
traced in his writings, there is unquestionably something of Lowell's
unique self present in each work, too. "I never hesitate to say anything I have honestly felt, because someone may have said it
before," he wrote to a friend, "for it will always get a new color from

13. In general, Lowell's historical criticism derives largely from Taine. In his
full-length studies of English writers, he devotes nearly equal space to their lives
and times, often interspersing comments like "there can be no doubt that in order
to understand the motives and conduct of the man we must first make ourselves
intimate with the time in which he lived" (*Works*, V, 249).

the new mind."[14] In a sense, Lowell lived more in the world of books than in "real life," and his ideas, correspondingly, came from this experience-once-removed. Reading was his vice; he complained often about his sloth in preferring to browse among the authors he loved instead of doing the work he should do. He loved old books as artifacts: "We cannot breathe the thin air of that Pepysian self-denial, that Himalayan selectness, which, content with one bookcase, would have no tomes in it but *porphyrogeniti*, books of the bluest blood. . . . There is to us a sacredness in a volume, however dull."[15] Lowell knew, however, that this love of "volumes, however dull," was a fault. "Books are good dry forage," he wrote. "We can keep alive on them; but, after all, men are the only fresh pasture."[16] As a critic, Lowell profited from his erudition, but understood its limitations. However Brahmin he was, he could not wholly deny what he called the "sense of life," and his theory of literature insists on a "living creativeness":

> The higher kinds of literature, the only kinds that live on because they had life at the start, are not, then, it should seem, the fabric of scholarship, of criticism, diligently studying and as diligently copying the best models, but are much rather born of some genetic principle in the character of the people and the age which produced them. One drop of ruddy human blood puts more life into the veins of a poem than all the delusive *aurum potabile* that can be distilled out of the choicest library.[17]

If one pursues Lowell's insights into this "genetic principle" of literature and the age producing it, the distinctions between art and nature tend to fall away. All of the past is implicit in the present, and the artist, in creating his poem, is effectively reshaping both present and past—that is, he creates a new universal. Thus the art object itself, and the tradition it represents, differs not at all from any other creations of nature in its capacity to inspire further reproduction. As Walt Whitman put it, "There was never any more inception than there is now / . . . . Urge and urge and urge, / Always the procreant urge of the world." Although Lowell would find these lines

14. *Works*, XV, 266 (to Charles Eliot Norton, 15 October 1890).
15. *Works*, II, 276.
16. Lowell to Miss Norton, April 6, 1869, *Works*, XV, 200.
17. *Works*, II, 170.

barbarous as poetry, he would agree with them as criticism. The true poet, whether he finds his inspiration in books and tradition or in original insight, must define his own time and must be judged critically by how well he does so and how well his definition is paradigmatic for man's state as a whole. For it is man's state that the poet is always interested in, since, according to Lowell,

> the divine life of nature is more wonderful, more various, more sublime in man than in any other of her works, and the wisdom that is gained by commerce with men, as Montaigne and Shakespeare gained it, or with one's own soul among men, as Dante, is the most delightful as it is the most precious, of all. In outward nature it is still man that interests us, and we care far less for the things seen than the way in which they are seen by poetic eyes like Wordsworth's or Thoreau's, and the reflections they cast there.

In this liberal and humanistic view of mimesis, again, according to Lowell, "the question of originality is not one of form, but of substance, not of cleverness, but of imaginative power."[18] And this substance and power do not appear merely as contemporary forms (although, of course, they must be more than merely appropriate to their age—they must somehow define it), but as an inevitable product of their tradition: "No man can look into the title-deeds of what may be called his personal estate, his faculties, his predilections, his failings—whatever, in short, sets him apart as a capital I— without something like a shock of dread to find how much of him is held in mortmain by those who, though long ago mouldered away to dust, are yet fatally alive and active in him for good or ill."[19]

When he applies these ideas to individual writers, Lowell reaffirms them. Chaucer is "original, not in the sense that he thinks and says what nobody ever thought and said before . . . but . . . because he sets before us the world as it honestly appeared to Geoffrey Chaucer, and not a world as it seemed proper to certain people that it ought to appear."[20] Again, although some men have found that Keats lacked originality, "because his poems take the color of the authors he happened to be reading at the time he wrote them,"

18. *Works*, II, 148, 94.
19. *Works*, II, 211.
20. *Works*, II, 263.

they ought properly, if they understood the workings of tradition, to see that "men have their intellectual ancestry, and the likeness of some one of them is forever unexpectedly flashing out in the features of a descendant, it may be after a gap of several generations."[21] So much for the defense of tradition. The perversion of tradition—abandonment of natural observation and of the "statement of self" for a hackneyed traditional model—is roundly trounced by Lowell's outspoken alter ego, Hosea Biglow:

> Jes' so with poets: wut they've airly read
> Gits kind o' worked into their heart an' head,
> So's 't they can't seem to write but jest on sheers
> With furrin countries or played-out ideers,
> Nor hev a feelin', if it doos n't smack
> O' wut some critter chose to feel 'way back:
>
> .   .   .   .
>
> This makes 'em think our fust o' May is May,
> Which 't ain't, fer all the almanicks can say.[22]

Lowell's artist is a composite of feeling and tradition. He can no more deny the one than he can do without the other, and his mimetic capacity is a result of his integration of both sources.

Just as Lowell sees the perfect artist as a man made up of equal parts of self and tradition, so he, as critic, believed it his duty to analyze the poet's success in achieving that perfection. Therein, of course, lies the origin of Lowell's reputation as an impressionist critic. When one's norms, one's standards, are the same as one's ideals, it is sometimes hard to observe strict comparative principles, simply because the perfection of a type may not indeed exist. When that happens, the critic appears arbitrary; he may, in a positive instance, appear simply to be pointing out beauties; when he criticizes adversely, it may appear that he is being completely subjective. When he is dealing with a period of literature—the neoclassical, for example—he may never be able to do it justice simply

21. *Works*, V, 341. The similarity between this observation and several ideas in T. S. Eliot's "Tradition and the Individual Talent" is noteworthy.

22. *Works*, XI, 209. Lowell seems generally to have spoken out most vigorously as a critic when he could remain anonymous, at least at first, as he did in *A Fable for Critics*, or when he could adopt a persona, as he did in the *Biglow Papers*.

because he is unable to accept its working principles. Thus, Lowell examines all of the faults of the poetic diction of the Augustan age without ever proceeding beyond this superficial criticism to show how Pope managed to produce works of great genius within his tradition. He may be a good, or at least satisfactory, critic of the style and the age, but he is certainly not satisfactory as a critic of Pope. The same problem appears with Lowell's criticism of Romantic writers; never admitting the possibility of a value to egotism as a principle in poetry, Lowell's practical criticism of Carlyle, Rousseau, and the Romantics generally, suffers. His failure as a critic in these two instances is not because he is impressionistic, but because his standards, quite rigorously applied, do not allow him room to maneuver.

These are, however, flaws in his practical criticism only. His theoretical criticism uses "flawed" writing chiefly as a device to identify and distinguish perfect work within the same genre, thus moving from the concrete to the abstract, from what is to what ought to be. What art ought to be is to Lowell always clear: "Art always Platonizes," he says categorically.[23] This is Lowell's touchstone, the one axiom to which all else is corollary. And yet, it is not for him axiomatic in the sense that it is an unexamined principle. On the contrary, the bulk of Lowell's criticism is taken up with extensive examinations of alternatives to this assumption, which are denied one by one, in a kind of critical *reductio ad absurdum*. There are four such alternatives to Platonism in art: the artist weaving his art chiefly from his own feelings, or sentimentalism; the artist instructing his audience in the true and beautiful, or didacticism; the artist facing the dark side of existence, or cynicism; and the artist concerning himself only with what is, denying its correspondence, or realism.[24]

Lowell is most contemptuous of the sentimentalist, finding little in either his art or his personal morality to justify him. The senti-

23. "The Imagination"; see below, p. 23.

24. Lowell only rarely found it necessary to examine the fourth alternative, realism, since he did not live long enough to observe its full impact upon esthetics. He does mention that he thinks Zola the worst of writers (*Works*, VII, 103), but he is tolerant of him just the same. For the range of his ideas on this subject, see his reviews of James and Howells reprinted below, pp. 240, 245.

mentalist poet, he wrote, "always insists on taking his emotion neat, and, as his sense gradually deadens to the stimulus, increases his dose till he ends in a kind of moral deliquium."[25] He is merely amused by the didactic poet, who writes verses which are thrown out of "Olympus's back window," whence they flutter down to earth:

> The verses? Some in ocean swilled,
>   Killed every fish that bit to 'em;
> Some Galen caught, and, when distilled,
>   Found morphine the residuum;
> But some that rotted on the earth
>   Sprang up again in copies,
> And gave two strong narcotics birth,
>   Didactic verse and poppies.[26]

The cynic poet is treated with more respect. His attitude is "congenial to certain moods" and is not "inconsistent with original nobleness of mind," but is finally described as "the intellectual analogue of the truffle; and though it may be very well in giving a relish to thought for certain palates, it cannot supply the substance of it."[27]

Lowell does not merely produce ex cathedra pronouncements on these alternatives to Platonic art. Sentimentalism is the subject of a fifty-page essay, and cynicism and didacticism are among his most usual subjects. Always, his technique is to compare the healthy specimen with the diseased. Shakespeare, he points out, is apparently amoral in his writing, but by "Platonizing" *events* by combining them with *emotions* to suggest *ideas*, in a "Platonic ladder," he achieves a moral insight purified of didacticism.[28] Similarly, he insists that the real power of the imagination consists in assuming the consciousness of "man, beast, rock or tree," an insistence which comes perilously close to a justification of sentimentalism. Yet readers of the essay "The Function of the Poet" will sense the distinction. As Lowell explains it, sentimentalism is produced by the forced substitution of

25. *Works*, IV, 196.
26. *Works*, XIII, 240.
27. *Works*, II, 83–84.
28. See below, "The Function of the Poet," p. 7.

the writer's impression for the emotion itself, while Platonic art naturally assumes the consciousness which is purged of self.[29]

Lowell is a competent analytical critic when, in discussing didacticism, cynicism, and sentimentalism, he points out what literature must *not* be if it is to be most fully great art. The question naturally follows, What does he suggest positively on this issue? The answer, simple as it is, permeates Lowell's criticism and is his one great esthetic axiom: Literature must be organic. Statements to this effect, positive and negative, cloudy and clear, profound and simplistic, may be found throughout his writing. He denies the possibility that a work may be "masterly in parts" but "feeble in design."[30] No element of writing is so inconsiderable that its organic propriety is not an overriding consideration; the rhythm of a poem must be organically, not mechanically, appropriate. The whole is greater than the sum of its parts, and modern critics and modern writers who concentrate their skills upon passages instead of the whole are equally wrong. A passage from *A Fable for Critics* perhaps sums up his ideas as well as anything can:

> Some poems have welled
> From those rare depths of soul that have ne'er been excelled;
> They're not epics, but that doesn't matter a pin,
> In creating, the only hard thing's to begin;
> A grass-blade's no easier to make than an oak;
> If you've once found the way, you've achieved the grand stroke;
> .   .   .   .
> Now it is not one thing or another alone
> Makes a poem, but rather the general tone,
> The something pervading, uniting the whole,
> The before unconceived, unconceivable soul,
> So that just in removing this trifle or that, you
> Take away, as it were, a chief limb of the statue;
> Roots, wood, bark, and leaves singly perfect may be,
> But, clapt hodge-podge together, they don't make a tree.[31]

This bit of doggerel has a most serious intent, as Fogle has noted. It achieves, with remarkable compression, a full catalog of the

29. See below, "The Imagination," p. 25.
30. *Works*, III, 253.
31. *Works*, XII, 37–38.

criteria necessary to judge poetry "in the organic tradition of Herder, Goethe, and Coleridge."[32] Its tone is also perfectly typical of Lowell's criticism in general and may serve to characterize what Lowell added to the Romantic critical tradition—a homely, no-nonsense, democratic attitude to the process of creation which suggests its importance (the parallel with the original divine creation), at the same time that it justifies limited aims ("A grass-blade's no easier to make than an oak"). His conception is further democratic in finding that, though the works in question are "not epics," they well from "rare depths of soul," that is, they are mythic or archetypal creations. Here is the ultimate democratic principle of artistic creation, as announced by the brothers Grimm, "*Volk dichtet,*" or, the people are themselves, en masse, poets. This thought underlies much of Lowell's organicism as a critic.[33]

These democratic arguments for art are the ones that must be made for a society that professed to despise art for its impurity, its insignificance, and its aristocratic tone. One may criticize Lowell's esthetic principles endlessly, but one must finally admit that he was the only American critic for some fifty years who consistently defended art on the Philistine's home grounds—that is, that it had value in a raw democracy. Lowell's "Epistle to the Philistines" on the practical value of art is found most concisely in the two essays placed first in this anthology, "The Function of the Poet" and "The Imagination." Neither was published in Lowell's lifetime, because Lowell, we may doubtless assume, sensed their importance to his critical *raison d'être.*[34] He did, however, work them over carefully

32. Fogle, "Organic Form in American Criticism," 109–110.

33. I am indebted to the editor of this series, Paul A. Olson, for the suggestion that Lowell got this idea from his friend and colleague at Harvard, Francis James Child (1825–1896), the great ballad scholar, who was the foremost proponent of the Grimm theory of ballad origin in America. I know of no proof for this conjecture, but those who are familiar with Child's work and Lowell's criticism and the relationship between the two men must find it a delightful hypothesis.

34. Charles Eliot Norton, in editing "The Function of the Poet" for the *Century* magazine, remarked that "Lowell never printed it because, as his genius matured, he felt that its assertions were too absolute, and that its st/le bore too many marks of haste in composition" (Quoted in Albert Mordell [ed.], *The Function of the Poet and Other Essays* [Boston and New York: Houghton Mifflin, 1920], p. 3). However,

after their first appearance as his lectures before the Lowell Institute
in 1855. "The Function of the Poet" was greatly enlarged from its
first form, especially the parts criticizing nineteenth-century
America's treatment of the poet. "The Imagination" is almost
wholly a new work, developing ideas from a majority of the original
twelve lectures, but going far beyond them in defining the theme as
stated at the beginning of the essay: "Imagination is the wings of the
mind; the understanding, its feet." It is a lyrical, profound, yet far-
ranging essay, covering most of the material I have outlined above
as basic to Lowell's criticism. In it, Lowell attempts to provide a
more finished and inclusive definition of art than he does anywhere
else, and in terms which he might expect would be understood by a
materialistic American, largely unburdened by the wings of imagination. Lowell fails, of course. The essay is unfinished, ending haunt-
ingly with a comparison of some lines of Henry More the Platonist
on the nightingale with the seventh stanza of Keats's "Ode to a
Nightingale." One senses that the conclusion is perhaps not simply
fortuitous, especially if one considers Lowell's own comment on the
quatrain by Gongora (see p. 32, below). Some experiences, especially
esthetic ones, simply cannot be explained.

"The Function of the Poet" is a much less ineffable piece, much
more limited in its objectives, and therefore more finished and comprehensible. Lowell begins with a cliché which he might hope would
be understood by the veriest clod in his audience—the concept of
progress—then moves ahead to justify poetry to his suspicious
audience in the only way possible: "After all, how is our poor
scapegoat of a nineteenth century to blame? Why, for not being the
seventeenth, to be sure! It is always raining opportunity, but it
seems it was only the men two hundred years ago who were intelligent enough not to hold their cups bottom-up." He places the
blame for the prosaic and material quality of the nineteenth century
essentially upon science—science and technology: "What need of

---

a comparison of the texts of the two essays as they appeared in the *Century* and in
their original form as part of Lowell's Lowell Institute Lectures of 1855 (printed
from a reporter's notes of them as *Lectures on English Poets* [Cleveland, The Rowfant
Club, 1897]) suggests rather that Lowell viewed these two essays as major works
which demanded a kind of perfection that he was unable to give them.

Aladdin's lamp when a man can build a palace with a patent pill?
The office of the poet seems to be reversed, and he must give back
these miracles of the understanding to poetry again, and find out
what there is imaginative in steam and iron and telegraph wires."
One thinks of Whitman, and of Hart Crane. Poetry, he suggests, is
indestructible; "the soul of poetry survives in things prosaic." Perhaps he prophetically imagined the time when American imperialism
would become a cross for its citizens, when American inventiveness
and technology would turn upon their masters and attempt to
destroy them. That would be the moment when the latent seed of
poetry in the American character would burst forth:

> There is as much poetry as ever in the world if we only knew how
> to find it out; and as much imagination, perhaps, only that it takes a
> more prosaic direction. Every man who meets with misfortune, who is
> stripped of material prosperity, finds that he has a little outlying
> mountain-farm of imagination, which did not appear in the schedule
> of his effects, on which his spirit is able to keep itself alive, though he
> never thought of it while he was fortunate. Job turns out to be a great
> poet as soon as his flocks and herds are taken away from him.

If we consider Lowell's criticism in relation to the works of
modern critics, we find evidence besides his prophetic powers of his
contemporaneity. His most striking affinity, of course, is with the
New Humanists, particularly the followers of Irving Babbitt and
Paul E. More who struggled most directly with critics who favored
sensibility on the one hand and with sociologists who preached the
inevitability of history on the other. Like the New Humanists,
Lowell seems to accept the dualism of nature and culture, and finds
the artist's main concern to be that world of ethical values that
distinguishes man from the merely quantitative order of nature.
Like them also, he is self-consciously Hellenic, believing in reason
and grace and eschewing the wide-swinging alternatives of sensibility
on the one hand and materialism on the other. Yet, even among the
New Humanists who most closely felt the affinity of Lowell—those,
like Norman Foerster and Harry Hayden Clark, who specifically
defended him against the jibes of dialectical critics—one senses
almost as much Lowell's difference from their point of view as his

similarity. To begin with, he is not opposed to Romanticism as they are: his essay on Rousseau, for all its strictures on the man personally, ends in a confession of admiration for his genius; his many critiques of sentimentality are modified by admiration for sentiment, for emotion in art, and one concludes that it is only the *habitual* use of sentiment, as a substitute for honest emotion, to which he is opposed.[35] Perhaps more important, his consistent espousal of the need for roots in tradition and culture, particularly for archetypes and myth, caused his New Humanist defenders endless pain—indeed, led one of them to divide him, like Caesar's Gaul, *in partes tres*, so that his humanist self could be skimmed from his less pure nationalist and humanitarian self.[36] The fact is that Lowell was at least as much a Romantic critic as he was a neohumanist, his taste leading him in one direction, his erudition and academic status leading him in the other. Indeed, it is, by and large, the *least* part of Lowell's criticism that is closest to the New Humanists: his style, his conscious superiority, his belief that he was at the center.

The better part of his criticism, his feeling for myth, his organicism, his catholicity of taste, align him with other schools of modern criticism. Many of his remarks on myth, tradition, and the artist's need for roots generally precede T. S. Eliot's ideas on these subjects, as collected in *The Sacred Wood* and elsewhere. His organicism and particularly his emphasis on the need for total design in art ally him with R. S. Crane and the Chicago critics generally. Perhaps strangest of all, his insistence on the need to experience a work of art fully and his unwillingness to attempt to explicate any part at the expense of the total experience, his absolute certainty that manner and matter in art are inextricably combined, find curious echoes in the writings of Susan Sontag and other recent critics who have reacted against the New Criticism and the assumption by the academic world that criticism is their province only.

Thus we see that Lowell is not entirely dead as a critic. At first glance his affirmation seems too tentative. He seems, when compared to modern critics—even those who agree with large parts of his

35. See below, "The Imagination," p. 22.

36. Harry Hayden Clark, "Lowell—Humanitarian, Nationalist, or Humanist?" *Studies in Philology*, XXVII (1930), 411–441.

theoretical criticism—to be something of a fuddy-duddy, to be embarrassingly old-fashioned. But if we persist in our examination of him, if we break through the formality of his presentation, particularly in the longer essays, he comes to seem remarkably contemporary. We discover that what seemed to have only an antiquarian interest was really written under conditions which still prevail, and his voice, which seems at first merely quaint, is one to which the modern reader ought still to listen.

A Note on the Text

Bibliographical citations are given at the end of each selection in this volume. Although most of the selections first appeared in periodicals, I have used the Elmwood Edition of Lowell's collected works, edited by Charles Eliot Norton (16 vols.; Boston and New York: Houghton Mifflin and Co., 1904), cited simply as *Works*, wherever I could. This is both the most complete and the most accessible edition, and it was derived by Norton from the Riverside Edition of *The Writings of James Russell Lowell* (10 vols.; Boston and New York: Houghton Mifflin and Co., 1890–1892), revised by Lowell himself. The only exception to this procedure is *A Fable for Critics*; the text for that is the first edition (New York: G. P. Putnam, 1848). To that I have added the Preliminary Note to the Second Edition from the second edition of the same year, and I have noted a few significant variants in subsequent editions. Of all Lowell's writings, *A Fable for Critics* is the one in which reflection, second thoughts, and qualifications by the author seemed most unnecessary and perhaps even inhibiting. The selection given here is, I believe, the only modern reprinting of at least most of it in its uninhibited form.

For the works not collected by Lowell, I have regularized spelling and punctuation to the standards of the Elmwood Edition and corrected obvious typographical errors where necessary. I have collated each text with its first periodical appearance, first collected appearance, and Riverside text, where these were available. Although I have treated the Elmwood text as the preferred text, I have made some emendations from it where an earlier text was clearly superior. Where I have given a selection a title other than the one Lowell gave it, the original title is given in the headnote. Periodical selections reprinted in works other than the Elmwood Edition are cited in the bibliographical note. Where no reference to reprinting is given, the work has gone uncollected. Three asterisks (* * *) are used to indicate editorial deletions.

HERBERT F. SMITH

University of Wisconsin

I

DEFENSE OF POETRY

The Function of the Poet

This apology for poetry in a materialistic age is an expanded version of the concluding lecture read by Lowell before the Lowell Institute in the winter of 1855. Its defensive tone does not conceal Lowell's fundamental credo as a critic: man is dual—material and spiritual, temporal and infinite. Poetry (and he means here poesis, *creative writing in the broadest sense) calls upon the material, the temporal, but spiritualizes it and creates something eternal.*

The opening paragraph contrasts a romantic theory of history with the favored theory of the nineteenth century, placing the notion of decline from a golden age side by side with the notion of progress. One's choice of theory is unimportant, Lowell announces, as long as one realizes that the poet is necessary to the growth of culture. Science—primarily, for Lowell, technology —has assumed the existence only of the material, and has thus cast a shadow, which he is quick to assert is only temporary, over the power of the imagination and the capacity for mythic creation. The fault is not in science—it deserves its poetry, too, and better poetry than the rationalist verses of the eighteenth century, perhaps typified by Pope's lines to Newton:

> *Nature and nature's laws lay hid in night*
> *God said, "Let Newton be," and all was light.*

Curiously, the one nineteenth-century American poet who may be said to have written imaginatively on the subjects of science and technology, and who surely spiritualized them, published his major work the same year as this address and revised and added to it through his lifetime. Yet Lowell never recognized the genius of Walt Whitman.

Whether, as some philosophers assume, we possess only the fragments of a great cycle of knowledge in whose center stood the primeval man in friendly relation with the powers of the universe, and build our hovels out of the ruins of our ancestral palace; or

3

whether, according to the development theory of others, we are rising gradually, and have come up out of an atom instead of descending from an Adam, so that the proudest pedigree might run up to a barnacle or a zoöphyte at last, are questions that will keep for a good many centuries yet. Confining myself to what little we can learn from history, we find tribes rising slowly out of barbarism to a higher or lower point of culture and civility, and everywhere the poet also is found, under one name or other, changing in certain outward respects, but essentially the same.

And however far we go back, we shall find this also—that the poet and the priest were united originally in the same person; which means that the poet was he who was conscious of the world of spirit as well as that of sense, and was the ambassador of the gods to men. This was his highest function, and hence his name of "seer." He was the discoverer and declarer of the perennial beneath the deciduous. His were the *epea pteroenta*, the true "winged words" that could fly down the unexplored future and carry the names of ancestral heroes, of the brave and wise and good. It was thus that the poet could reward virtue and, by and by, as society grew more complex could burn in the brand of shame. This is Homer's character of Demodocus, in the eighth book of the *Odyssey*, "whom the Muse loved and gave the good and ill"—the gift of conferring good or evil immortality. The first histories were in verse; and sung as they were at feasts and gatherings of the people, they awoke in men the desire of fame, which is the first promoter of courage and self-trust, because it teaches men by degrees to appeal from the present to the future. We may fancy what the influence of the early epics was when they were recited to men who claimed the heroes celebrated in them for their ancestors, by what Bouchardon,[1] the sculptor, said, only two centuries ago: "When I read Homer, I feel as if I were twenty feet high." Nor have poets lost their power over the future in modern times. Dante lifts up by the hair the face of some petty traitor, the Smith or Brown of some provincial Italian town, lets the fire of his Inferno glare upon it for a moment, and it is printed forever on the memory of mankind. The historians may iron out the shoulders of Richard the Third as smooth as they

1. Edme Bouchardon (1698–1762), French sculptor.

can, they will never get over the wrench that Shakespeare gave them. The peculiarity of almost all early literature is that it seems to have a double meaning, that, underneath its natural, we find ourselves continually seeing or suspecting a supernatural meaning. In the older epics the characters seem to be half typical and only half historical. Thus did the early poets endeavor to make realities out of appearances; for, except a few typical men in whom certain ideas get embodied, the generations of mankind are mere apparitions who come out of the dark for a purposeless moment, and reënter the dark again after they have performed the nothing they came for.

Gradually, however, the poet as the "seer" became secondary to the "maker." His office became that of entertainer rather than teacher. But always something of the old tradition was kept alive. And if he has now come to be looked upon merely as the best expresser, the gift of seeing is implied as necessarily antecedent to that, and of seeing very deep, too. If any man would seem to have written without any conscious moral, that man is Shakespeare. But that must be a dull sense, indeed, which does not see through his tragic—yes, and his comic—masks awful eyes that flame with something intenser and deeper than a mere scenic meaning—a meaning out of the great deep that is behind and beyond all human and merely personal character. Nor was Shakespeare himself unconscious of his place as a teacher and profound moralist: witness that sonnet in which he bewails his having neglected sometimes the errand that was laid upon him:

> Alas, 't is true I have gone here and there,
> And made myself a motley to the view,
> Gored mine own thoughts, sold cheap what is most dear,
> Made old offences of affections new;
> Most true it is that I have look'd on truth
> Askance and strangely;[2]

the application of which is made clear by the next sonnet in which he distinctly alludes to his profession.

There is this unmistakable stamp on all the great poets—that, however in little things they may fall below themselves, whenever

2. Sonnet 110.

there comes a great and noble thing to say, they say it greatly and nobly, and bear themselves most easily in the royalties of thought and language. There is not a mature play of Shakespeare's in which great ideas do not jut up in mountainous permanence, marking forever the boundary of provinces of thought, and known afar to many hundreds of men.

And it is for this kind of sight, which we call insight, and not for any faculty of observation and description, that we value the poet. It is in proportion as he has this that he is an adequate expresser, and not a juggler with words. It is by means of this that for every generation of man he plays the part of "namer." Before him, as before Adam, the creation passes to be named anew: first the material world; then the world of passions and emotions; then the world of ideas. But whenever a great imagination comes, however it may delight itself with imaging the outward beauty of things, however it may seem to flow thoughtlessly away in music like a brook, yet the shadow of heaven lies also in its depth beneath the shadow of earth. Continually the visible universe suggests the invisible. We are forever feeling this in Shakespeare. His imagination went down to the very bases of things, and while his characters are the most natural that poet ever created, they are also perfectly ideal, and are more truly the personifications of abstract thoughts and passions than those of any allegorical writer whatever.

Even in what seems so purely a picturesque poem as the *Iliad*, we feel something of this. Beholding as Homer did, from the tower of contemplation, the eternal mutability and nothing permanent but change, he must look underneath the show for the reality. Great captains and conquerors came forth out of the eternal silence, entered it again with their trampling hosts, and shoutings, and trumpet-blasts, and were as utterly gone as those echoes of their deeds which he sang, and which faded with the last sound of his voice and the last tremble of his lyre. History relating outward events alone was an unmeaning gossip, with the world for a village. This life could only become other than phantasmagoric, could only become real, as it stood related to something that was higher and permanent. Hence the idea of Fate, of a higher power unseen— that shadow, as of an eagle circling to its swoop, which flits stealthily and swiftly across the windy plains of Troy. In the *Odyssey* we find pure allegory.

Now, under all these names—praiser, seer, soothsayer—we find the same idea lurking. The poet is he who can best see and best say what is ideal—what belongs to the world of soul and of beauty. Whether he celebrate the brave and good man, or the gods, or the beautiful as it appears in man or nature, something of a religious character still clings to him; he is the revealer of Deity. He may be unconscious of his mission; he may be false to it; but in proportion as he is a great poet, he rises to the level of it the more often. He does not always directly rebuke what is bad and base, but indirectly by making us feel what delight there is in the good and fair. If he besiege evil, it is with such beautiful engines of war (as Plutarch tells us of Demetrius) that the besieged themselves are charmed with them.[3] Whoever reads the great poets cannot but be made better by it, for they always introduce him to a higher society, to a greater style of manners and of thinking. Whoever learns to love what is beautiful is made incapable of the low and mean and bad. If Plato excludes the poets from his Republic, it is expressly on the ground that they speak unworthy things of the gods; that is, that they have lost the secret of their art, and use artificial types instead of speaking the true universal language of imagination. He who translates the divine into the vulgar, the spiritual into the sensual, is the reverse of a poet.

The poet, under whatever name, always stands for the same thing —imagination. And imagination in its highest form gives him the power, as it were, of assuming the consciousness of whatever he speaks about, whether man or beast, or rock or tree. It is the ring of Canace,[4] which whoso has on understands the language of all created things. And as regards expression, it seems to enable the poet to condense the whole of himself into a single word. Therefore, when a great poet has said a thing, it is finally and utterly expressed, and has as many meanings as there are men who read his verse. A

3. Demetrius Poliorcetes, son of Antigonus, took the city of Athens in 307 B.C., and was granted divine honors by its citizens as a result.
4. In Chaucer's *Squire's Tale*, Canace's ring allows her to understand the love song of a female hawk.

great poet is something more than an interpreter between man and nature; he is also an interpreter between man and his own nature. It is he who gives us those key-words, the possession of which makes us masters of all the unsuspected treasure-caverns of thought, and feeling, and beauty which open under the dusty path of our daily life.

And it is not merely a dry lexicon that he compiles,—a thing which enables us to translate from one dead dialect into another as dead, —but all his verse is instinct with music, and his words open windows on every side to pictures of scenery and life. The difference between the dry fact and the poem is as great as that between reading the shipping news and seeing the actual coming and going of the crowd of stately ships,—"the city on the inconstant billows dancing,"—as there is between ten minutes of happiness and ten minutes by the clock. Everybody remembers the story of the little Montague who was stolen and sold to the chimney-sweep: how he could dimly remember lying in a beautiful chamber; how he carried with him in all his drudgery the vision of a fair, sad mother's face that sought him everywhere in vain; how he threw himself one day, all sooty as he was from his toil, on a rich bed and fell asleep, and how a kind person woke him, questioned him, pieced together his broken recollections for him, and so at last made the visions of the beautiful chamber and the fair, sad countenance real to him again. It seems to me that the offices that the poet does for us are typified in this nursery-tale. We all of us have our vague reminiscences of the stately home of our childhood,—for we are all of us poets and geniuses in our youth, while earth is all new to us, and the chalice of every buttercup is brimming with the wine of poesy,—and we all remember the beautiful, motherly countenance which nature bent over us there. But somehow we all get stolen away thence; life becomes to us a sooty task-master, and we crawl through dark passages without end—till suddenly the word of some poet redeems us, makes us know who we are, and of helpless orphans makes us the heir to a great estate. It is to our true relations with the two great worlds of outward and inward nature that the poet reintroduces us.

But the imagination has a deeper use than merely to give poets a power of expression. It is the everlasting preserver of the world from blank materialism. It forever puts matter in the wrong, and compels it to show its title to existence. Wordsworth tells us that in his youth he was sometimes obliged to touch the walls to find if they were visionary or no, and such experiences are not uncommon with persons who converse much with their own thoughts. Dr. Johnson said that to kick one's foot against a stone was a sufficient confutation of Berkeley, and poor old Pyrrho[5] has passed into a proverb because, denying the objectivity of matter, he was run over by a cart and killed. But all that he affirmed was that to the soul the cart was no more real than its own imaginative reproduction of it, and perhaps the shade of the philosopher ran up to the first of his deriders who crossed the Styx with a triumphant "I told you so! The cart did not run over *me*, for here I am without a bone broken."

And, in another sense also, do those poets who deal with human character, as all the greater do, continually suggest to us the purely phantasmal nature of life except as it is related to the world of ideas. For are not their personages more real than most of those in history? Is not Lear more authentic and permanent than Lord Raglan?[6] Their realm is a purely spiritual one in which space and time and costume are nothing. What matters it that Shakespeare puts a seaport in Bohemia, and knew less geography than Tommy who goes to the district school? He understood eternal boundaries, such as are laid down on no chart, and are not defined by such transitory affairs as mountain chains, rivers, and seas.

No great movement of the human mind takes place without the concurrent beat of those two wings, the imagination and the understanding. It is by the understanding that we are enabled to make the most of this world, and to use the collected material of experience

5. Pyrrhon of Elis (*ca.* 365–275 B.C.) founded the skeptic school of philosophy. He inferred from the unreliability of the evidence of the senses that knowledge of the nature of things is unattainable. George Berkeley (1685–1753) traveled the same road and arrived at the same conclusions, that data of the senses were subjective and therefore untrue—which Johnson's kick refutes, though simplistically.

6. Fitzroy James Henry Somerset, Lord Raglan (1788–1855), is not a bad choice for a contemporary Lear. An unquestionable hero of British arms (he lost his sword arm at Waterloo), Raglan was victimized by politics in the pursuance of the Crimean War and died, if not tragically, at least sordidly. Lowell's point is that the imaginative *type* of Lear describes its hundreds of Raglans.

in its condensed form of practical wisdom; and it is the imagination which forever beckons toward that other world which is always future, and makes us discontented with this. The one rests upon experience; the other leans forward and listens after the *in*experienced, and shapes the features of that future with which it is forever in travail. The imagination might be defined as the common sense of the invisible world, as the understanding is of the visible; and as those are the finest individual characters in which the two moderate and rectify each other, so those are the finest eras where the same may be said of society. In the voyage of life, not only do we depend on the needle, true to its earthly instincts, but upon observation of the fixed stars, those beacons lighted upon the eternal promontories of heaven above the stirs and shiftings of our lower system.

But it seems to be thought that we have come upon the earth too late, that there has been a feast of imagination formerly, and all that is left for us is to steal the scraps. We hear that there is no poetry in railroads and steamboats and telegraphs, and especially none in Brother Jonathan.[7] If this be true, so much the worse for him. But because *he* is a materialist, shall there be no more poets? When we have said that we live in a materialistic age we have said something which meant more than we intended. If we say it in the way of blame, we have said a foolish thing, for probably one age is as good as another, and, at any rate, the worst is good enough company for us. The age of Shakespeare was richer than our own, only because it was lucky enough to have such a pair of eyes as his to see it, and such a gift of speech as his to report it. And so there is always room and occasion for the poet, who continues to be, just as he was in the early time, nothing more nor less than a "seer." He is always the man who is willing to take the age he lives in on trust, as the very best that ever was. Shakespeare did not sit down and cry for the water of Helicon to turn the wheels of his little private mill at the Bankside. He appears to have gone more quietly about his business than any other playwright in London, to have drawn off what water-power he needed from the great prosy current of affairs that flows alike for all and in spite of all, to have ground for the public what grist they wanted, coarse or fine, and it seems a mere piece of

7. Colloquial for "American," like "Yankee" or "Uncle Sam."

luck that the smooth stream of his activity reflected with such ravishing clearness every changing mood of heaven and earth, every stick and stone, every dog and clown and courtier that stood upon its brink. It is a curious illustration of the friendly manner in which Shakespeare received everything that came along,—of what a *present* man he was,—that in the very same year that the mulberry-tree was brought into England, he got one and planted it in his garden at Stratford.[8]

It is perfectly true that this is a materialistic age, and for that very reason we want our poets all the more. We find that every generation contrives to catch its singing larks without the sky's falling. When the poet comes, he always turns out to be the man who discovers that the passing moment is the inspired one, and that the secret of poetry is not to have lived in Homer's day, or Dante's, but to be alive now. To be alive now, that is the great art and mystery. They are dead men who live in the past, and men yet unborn that live in the future. We are like Hans in Luck, forever exchanging the burdensome good we have for something else, till at last we come home empty-handed.

That palefaced drudge of Time opposite me there, that weariless sexton whose callous hands bury our rosy hours in the irrevocable past, is even now reaching forward to a moment as rich in life, in character, and thought, as full of opportunity, as any since Adam. This little isthmus that we are now standing on is the point to which martyrs in their triumphant pain, prophets in their fervor, and poets in their ecstasy, looked forward as the golden future, as the land too good for them to behold with mortal eyes; it is the point toward which the faint-hearted and desponding hereafter will look back as the priceless past when there was still some good and virtue and opportunity left in the world.

The people who feel their own age prosaic are those who see only its costume. And that is what makes it prosaic—that we have not faith enough in ourselves to think our own clothes good enough to be

8. This view of Shakespeare as a man of affairs and a true contemporary man suits Lowell's essay, certainly, and is also something of a typical American poet's view of him. See Edwin Arlington Robinson's poem "Ben Jonson Entertains a Man from Stratford" for a similar statement.

presented to posterity in. The artists fancy that the court dress of posterity is that of Van Dyck's time, or Caesar's. I have seen the model of a statue of Sir Robert Peel,—a statesman whose merit consisted in yielding gracefully to the present,—in which the sculptor had done his best to travesty the real man into a make-believe Roman. At the period when England produced its greatest poets, we find exactly the reverse of this, and we are thankful that the man who made the monument of Lord Bacon had genius to copy every button of his dress, everything down to the rosettes on his shoes, and then to write under his statue, "Thus sat Francis Bacon"—not "Cneius Pompeius"—"Viscount Verulam." Those men had faith even in their own shoe-strings.

After all, how is our poor scapegoat of a nineteenth century to blame? Why, for not being the seventeenth, to be sure! It is always raining opportunity, but it seems it was only the men two hundred years ago who were intelligent enough not to hold their cups bottom-up. We are like beggars who think if a piece of gold drop into their palm it must be counterfeit, and would rather change it for the smooth-worn piece of familiar copper. And so, as we stand in our mendicancy by the wayside, Time tosses carefully the great golden to-day into our hats, and we turn it over grumblingly and suspiciously, and are pleasantly surprised at finding that we can exchange it for beef and potatoes. Till Dante's time the Italian poets thought no language good enough to put their nothings into but Latin,—and indeed a dead tongue was the best for dead thoughts,—but Dante found the common speech of Florence, in which men bargained and scolded and made love, good enough for him, and out of the world around him made a poem such as no Roman ever sang.

In our day, it is said despairingly, the understanding reigns triumphant: it is the age of common sense. If this be so, the wisest way would be to accept it manfully. But, after all, what is the meaning of it? Looking at the matter superficially, one would say that a striking difference between our science and that of the world's gray fathers is that there is every day less and less of the element of wonder in it. What they saw written in light upon the great arch of heaven, and, by a magnificent reach of sympathy, of which we are incapable, associated with the fall of monarchs and the fate of man, is for us only a professor, a piece of chalk, and a blackboard. The solemn and unapproachable skies we have vulgarized; we have peeped and botanized among the flowers of light, pulled off every petal, fumbled in every calyx, and reduced them to the bare stem of order and class. The stars can no longer maintain their divine reserves, but whenever there is a conjunction and congress of planets, every enterprising newspaper sends thither its special reporter with his telescope. Over those arcana of life where once a mysterious presence brooded, we behold scientific explorers skipping like so many incarnate notes of interrogation. We pry into the counsels of the great powers of nature, we keep our ears at the keyhole, and know everything that is going to happen. There is no longer any sacred inaccessibility, no longer any enchanting unexpectedness, and life turns to prose the moment there is nothing unattainable. It needs no more a voice out of the unknown proclaiming "Great Pan is dead!"[9] We have found his tombstone, deciphered the arrowheaded inscription upon it, know his age to a day, and that he died universally regretted.

Formerly science was poetry. A mythology which broods over us in our cradle, which mingles with the lullaby of the nurse, which peoples the day with the possibility of divine encounters, and night with intimation of demonic ambushes, is something quite other, as the material for thought and poetry, from one that we take down from our bookshelves, as sapless as the shelf it stood on, as remote from all present sympathy with man or nature as a town history with its genealogies of Mr. Nobody's great-grandparents.

We have utilized everything. The Egyptians found a hint of the solar system in the concentric circles of the onion, and revered it as a symbol, while we respect it as a condiment in cookery, and can pass through all Weathersfield without a thought of the stars. Our world is a museum of natural history; that of our forefathers was a museum of supernatural history. And the rapidity with which the change has been going on is almost startling, when we consider that so modern and historical a personage as Queen Elizabeth was reigning at the time of the death of Dr. John Faustus, out of whose story the Teutonic

9. Plutarch, "Why the Oracles Cease to Give Answers." Lowell may have had in mind Mrs. Browning's poem "The Dead Pan."

imagination built up a mythus that may be set beside that of Prometheus.

Science, looked at scientifically, is bare and bleak enough. On those sublime heights the air is too thin for the lungs, and blinds the eyes. It is much better living down in the valleys, where one cannot see farther than the next farm-house. Faith was never found in the bottom of a crucible, nor peace arrived at by analysis or synthesis. But all this is because science has become too grimly intellectual, has divorced itself from the moral and imaginative part of man. Our results are not arrived at in that spirit which led Kepler (who had his theory-traps set all along the tracks of the stars to catch a discovery) to say, "In my opinion the occasions of new discoveries have been no less wonderful than the discoveries themselves."

But we are led back continually to the fact that science cannot, if it would, disengage itself from human nature and from imagination. No two men have ever argued together without at least agreeing in this, that something more than proof is required to produce conviction, and that a logic which is capable of grinding the stubbornest facts to powder (as every man's *own* logic always is) is powerless against so delicate a structure as the brain. Do what we will, we cannot contrive to bring together the yawning edges of proof and belief, to weld them into one. When Thor strikes Skrymir with his terrible hammer, the giant asks if a leaf has fallen. I need not appeal to the Thors of argument in the pulpit, the senate, and the mass-meeting, if they have not sometimes found the popular giant as provokingly insensible. The $\sqrt{-x}$ is nothing in comparison with the chance-caught smell of a single flower which by the magic of association recreates for us the unquestioning day of childhood. Demonstration may lead to the very gate of heaven, but there she makes us a civil bow, and leaves us to make our way back again to Faith, who has the key.[10] That science which is of the intellect alone steps with indifferent foot upon the dead body of Belief, if only she may reach higher or see farther.

But we cannot get rid of our wonder—we who have brought

10. Lowell may be thinking here of Virgil's inability to lead Dante to Paradise, or of the morality play *Everyman*, in which Knowledge can accompany Everyman to the grave, but not beyond.

down the wild lightning, from writing fiery doom upon the walls of heaven, to be our errand-boy and penny-postman. Wonder is crude imagination; and it is necessary to us, for man shall not live by bread alone, and exact knowledge is not enough. Do we get nearer the truth or farther from it that we have got a gas or an imponderable fluid instead of a spirit? We go on exorcising one thing after another, but what boots it? The evasive genius flits into something else, and defies us. The powers of the outer and inner world form hand in hand a magnetic circle for whose connection man is necessary. It is the imagination that takes his hand and clasps it with that other stretched to him in the dark, and for which he was vainly groping. It is that which renews the mystery in nature, makes it wonderful and beautiful again, and out of the gases of the man of science remakes the old spirit. But we seem to have created too many wonders to be capable of wondering any longer; as Coleridge said, when asked if he believed in ghosts, that he had seen too many of them. But nature all the more imperatively demands it, and science can at best but scotch it, not kill it. In this day of newspapers and electric telegraphs, in which common sense and ridicule can magnetize a whole continent between dinner and tea, we say that such a phenomenon as Mahomet were impossible, and behold Joe Smith and the State of Deseret! Turning over the yellow leaves of the same copy of "Webster on Witchcraft" which Cotton Mather studied, I thought, "Well, that goblin is laid at last!" and while I mused the tables were turning, and the chairs beating the devil's tattoo all over Christendom.[11] I have a neighbor who dug down through tough strata of clay to a spring pointed out by a witch-hazel rod in the hands of a seventh son's seventh son, and the water is the sweeter to him for the wonder that is mixed with it. After all, it seems that our scientific gas, be it never so brilliant, is not equal to the dingy old Aladdin's lamp.

It is impossible for men to live in the world without poetry of some sort or other. If they cannot get the best they will get some substitute for it, and thus seem to verify Saint Augustine's slur that it

11. Joseph Smith was the founder of the Mormon Church; Deseret was his name for modern Utah. The "turning tables" refers to the contemporary fad of spiritualism.

is wine of devils. The mind bound down too closely to what is practical either becomes inert, or revenges itself by rushing into the savage wilderness of "isms." The insincerity of our civilization has disgusted some persons so much that they have sought refuge in Indian wigwams and found refreshment in taking a scalp now and then. Nature insists above all things upon balance. She contrives to maintain a harmony between the material and spiritual, nor allows the cerebrum an expansion at the cost of the cerebellum. If the character, for example, run on one side into religious enthusiasm, it is not unlikely to develop on the other a counterpoise of worldly prudence. Thus the Shaker and the Moravian are noted for thrift, and mystics are not always the worst managers. Through all changes of condition and experience man continues to be a citizen of the world of idea as well as the world of fact, and the tax-gatherers of both are punctual.

And these antitheses which we meet with in individual character we cannot help seeing on the larger stage of the world also, a moral accompanying a material development. History, the great satirist, brings together Alexander and the blower of peas to hint to us that the tube of the one and the sword of the other were equally transitory; but meanwhile Aristotle was conquering kingdoms out of the unknown, and establishing a dynasty of thought from whose hand the scepter has not yet passed. So there are Charles V. and Luther; the expansion of trade resulting from the Spanish and Portuguese discoveries, and the Elizabethan literature; the Puritans seeking spiritual El Dorados while so much valor and thought were spent in finding mineral ones. It seems to be the purpose of God that a certain amount of genius shall go to each generation, particular quantities being represented by individuals, and while no *one* is complete in himself, all collectively make up a whole ideal figure of a man. Nature is not like certain varieties of the apple that cannot bear two years in succession. It is only that her expansions are uniform in all directions, that in every age she completes her circle, and like a tree adds a ring to her growth be it thinner or thicker.

Every man is conscious that he leads two lives, the one trivial and ordinary, the other sacred and recluse; the one which he carries to the dinner-table and to his daily work, which grows old with his body and dies with it, the other that which is made up of the few inspiring moments of his higher aspiration and attainment, and in which his youth survives for him, his dreams, his unquenchable longings for something nobler than success. It is this life which the poets nourish for him, and sustain with their immortalizing nectar. Through them he feels once more the white innocence of his youth. His faith in something nobler than gold and iron and cotton comes back to him, not as an upbraiding ghost that wrings its pale hands and is gone, but beautiful and inspiring as a first love that recognizes nothing in him that is not high and noble. The poets are nature's perpetual pleaders, and protest with us against what is worldly. Out of their own undying youth they speak to ours. "Wretched is the man," says Goethe, "who has learned to despise the dreams of his youth!" It is from this misery that the imagination and the poets, who are its spokesmen, rescue us. The world goes to church, kneels to the eternal Purity, and then contrives to sneer at innocence and ignorance of evil by calling it green. Let every man thank God for what little there may be left in him of his vernal sweetness. Let him thank God if he have still the capacity for feeling an unmarketable enthusiasm, for that will make him worthy of the society of the noble dead, of the companionship of the poets. And let him love the poets for keeping youth young, woman womanly, and beauty beautiful.

There is as much poetry as ever in the world if we only knew how to find it out; and as much imagination, perhaps, only that it takes a more prosaic direction. Every man who meets with misfortune, who is stripped of material prosperity, finds that he has a little outlying 'mountain-farm of imagination, which did not appear in the schedule of his effects, on which his spirit is able to keep itself alive, though he never thought of it while he was fortunate. Job turns out to be a great poet as soon as his flocks and herds are taken away from him.

There is no reason why our continent should not sing as well as the rest. We have had the practical forced upon us by our position. We have had a whole hemisphere to clear up and put to rights. And we are descended from men who were hardened and stiffened by a downright wrestle with necessity. There was no chance for poetry among the Puritans. And yet if any people have a right to imagination, it should be the descendants of these very Puritans. They had enough of it, or they could never have conceived the great epic they did, whose books are States, and which is written on this continent from Maine to California.

But there seems to be another reason why we should not become a poetical people. Formerly the poet embodied the hopes and desires of men in visible types. He gave them the shoes of swiftness, the cap of invisibility, and the purse of Fortunatus. These were once stories for grown men, and not for the nursery as now. We are apt ignorantly to wonder how our forefathers could find satisfaction in fiction the absurdity of which any of our primary-school children could demonstrate. But we forget that the world's gray fathers were children themselves, and that in their little world, with its circle of the black unknown all about it, the imagination was as active as it is with people in the dark. Look at a child's toys, and we shall understand the matter well enough. Imagination is the fairy godmother (every child has one still), at the wave of whose wand sticks become heroes, the closet in which she has been shut fifty times for being naughty is turned into a palace, and a bit of lath acquires all the potency of Excalibur.

But nowadays it is the understanding itself that has turned poet. In her railroads she has given us the shoes of swiftness. Fine-ear herself could not hear so far as she, who in her magnetic telegraph can listen in Boston and hear what is going on in New Orleans. And what need of Aladdin's lamp when a man can build a palace with a patent pill? The office of the poet seems to be reversed, and he must give back these miracles of the understanding to poetry again, and find out what there is imaginative in steam and iron and telegraph-wires. After all, there is as much poetry in the iron horses that eat fire as in those of Diomed that fed on men. If you cut an apple across you may trace in it the lines of the blossom that the bee hummed around in May, and so the soul of poetry survives in things prosaic. Borrowing money on a bond does not seem the most promising subject in the world, but Shakespeare found the *Merchant of Venice* in it. Themes of song are waiting everywhere for the right man to sing them, like those enchanted swords which no one can pull out of the rock till the hero comes, and he finds no more trouble than in plucking a violet.

John Quincy Adams, making a speech at New Bedford, many years ago, reckoned the number of whaleships (if I remember rightly) that sailed out of that port, and, comparing it with some former period, took it as a type of American success. But, alas! it is with quite other oil that those far-shining lamps of a nation's true glory which burn forever must be filled. It is not by any amount of material splendor or prosperity, but only by moral greatness, by ideas, by works of imagination, that a race can conquer the future. No voice comes to us from the once mighty Assyria but the hoot of the owl that nests amid her crumbling palaces. Of Carthage, whose merchant-fleets once furled their sails in every port of the known world, nothing is left but the deeds of Hannibal. She lies dead on the shore of her once subject sea, and the wind of the desert only flings its handfuls of burial-sand upon her corpse. A fog can blot Holland or Switzerland out of existence. But how large is the space occupied in the maps of the soul by little Athens and powerless Italy! They were great by the soul, and their vital force is as indestructible as the soul.

Till America has learned to love art, not as an amusement, not as the mere ornament of her cities, not as a superstition of what is *comme il faut* for a great nation, but for its humanizing and ennobling energy, for its power of making men better by arousing in them a perception of their own instincts for what is beautiful, and therefore sacred and religious, and an eternal rebuke of the base and worldly, she will not have succeeded in that high sense which alone makes a nation out of a people, and raises it from a dead name to a living power. Were our little mother-island sunk beneath the sea, or, worse, were she conquered by Scythian barbarians, yet Shakespeare would be an immortal England, and would conquer countries, when the bones of her last sailor had kept their ghastly watch for ages in unhallowed ooze beside the quenched thunders of her navy.

Old Purchas in his "Pilgrims"[12] tells of a sacred caste in India who, when they go out into the street, cry out, "Poo! poo!" to warn all the world out of their way lest they should be defiled by something unclean. And it is just so that the understanding in its pride of success thinks to pooh-pooh all that it considers unpractical and visionary.

12. Samuel Purchas (1575?–1626) published *Purchas His Pilgrimes* in 1625.

But whatever of life there is in man, except what comes of beef and pudding, is in the visionary and unpractical, and if it be not encouraged to find its activity or its solace in the production or enjoyment of art and beauty, if it be bewildered or thwarted by an outward profession of faith covering up a practical unbelief in anything higher and holier than the world of sense, it will find vent in such wretched holes and corners as table-tippings and mediums who sell news from heaven at a quarter of a dollar the item. Imagination cannot be banished out of the world. She may be made a kitchen-drudge, a Cinderella, but there are powers that watch over her. When her two proud sisters, the intellect and understanding, think her crouching over her ashes, she startles and charms by her splendid apparition, and Prince Soul will put up with no other bride.

The practical is a very good thing in its way—if it only be not another name for the worldly. To be absorbed in it is to eat of that insane root which the soldiers of Antonius found in their retreat from Parthia—which whoso tasted kept gathering sticks and stones as if they were some great matter till he died.

One is forced to listen, now and then, to a kind of talk which makes him feel as if this were the after-dinner time of the world, and mankind were doomed hereafter forever to that kind of contented materialism which comes to good stomachs with the nuts and raisins. The dozy old world has nothing to do now but stretch its legs under the mahogany, talk about stocks, and get rid of the hours as well as it can till bedtime. The centuries before us have drained the goblet of wisdom and beauty, and all we have left is to cast horoscopes in the dregs. But divine beauty, and the love of it, will never be without apostles and messengers on earth, till Time flings his hour-glass into the abyss as having no need to turn it longer to number the indistinguishable ages of Annihilation. It was a favorite speculation with the learned men of the sixteenth century that they had come upon the old age and decrepit second childhood of creation, and while they maundered, the soul of Shakespeare was just coming out of the eternal freshness of Deity, "trailing" such "clouds of glory" as would beggar a Platonic year of sunsets.

No; morning and the dewy prime are born into the earth again with every child. It is our fault if drought and dust usurp the noon.

Every age says to her poets, like the mistress to her lover, "Tell me what I am like"; and, in proportion as it brings forth anything worth seeing, has need of seers and will have them. Our time is not an unpoetical one. We are in our heroic age, still face to face with the shaggy forces of unsubdued Nature, and we have our Theseuses and Perseuses, though they may be named Israel Putnam and Daniel Boone.[13] It is nothing against us that we are a commercial people. Athens was a trading community; Dante and Titian were the growth of great marts, and England was already commercial when she produced Shakespeare.

This lesson I learn from the past: that grace and goodness, the fair, the noble, and the true, will never cease out of the world till the God from whom they emanate ceases out of it; that they manifest themselves in an eternal continuity of change to every generation of men, as new duties and occasions arise; that the sacred duty and noble office of the poet is to reveal and justify them to men; that so long as the soul endures, endures also the theme of new and unexampled song; that while there is grace in grace, love in love, and beauty in beauty, God will still send poets to find them and bear witness of them, and to hang their ideal portraitures in the gallery of memory. God with us is forever the mystical name of the hour that is passing. The lives of the great poets teach us that they were the men of their generation who felt most deeply the meaning of the present.

Century, XLVII (January 1844), 432–439. Reprinted in Albert Mordell (ed.), *The Function of the Poet and Other Essays by James Russell Lowell* (Boston and New York: Houghton Mifflin, 1920), pp. 3–32.

13. The American backwoodsman as military man and Indian fighter had mythic proportions in Putnam (1718–1790) and Boone (1735?–1820).

The Imagination

Where "The Function of the Poet" rather defensively justified literature on pragmatic grounds, this essay takes the offensive against the Philistines. It remains unfinished. Its roots, are in Lowell's lectures of 1855, but one can trace elements of it through his works as late as the 1880's. It is, of course, not surprising that it should be unfinished, because in it Lowell is attempting the impossible—a definition of "the name and nature of poetry" in terms of the effect of the transforming imagination. And, as if that were not difficult enough, his technique is by comparative analysis of what were clearly intended to be parallel but unequal works.

His assumptions are, by and large, Platonic, but they have nevertheless much that is Lowell's own to recommend them. His distinctions between the subjective and objective in poetry, particularly in the light of the examples he gives, are concrete and meaningful. And when he denies the possibility of definition, as with the quote from Gongora, p. 32, we willingly take the leap he implies. His insistence on the organic and on quiditas—"thingness"—of poetry suggests that he is much more modern in his theories of criticism than has been supposed. His emphasis is clearly away from the emblem and the icon and toward the allusive.

Imagination is the wings of the mind; the understanding, its feet. With these it may climb high, but can never soar into that ampler ether and diviner air whence the eye dominates so uncontrolled a prospect on every hand. Through imagination alone is something like a creative power possible to man. It is the same in Aeschylus as in Shakespeare, though the form of its manifestation varies in some outward respects from age to age. Being the faculty of vision, it is the essential part of expression also, which is the office of all art.

But in comparing ancient with modern imaginative literature, certain changes especially strike us, and chief among them a stronger infusion of sentiment and what we call the picturesque. I shall endeavor to illustrate this by a few examples. But first let us discuss imagination itself, and give some instances of its working.

"Art," says Lord Verulam, "is man added to Nature" (*homo additus naturae*); and we may modernize his statement, and adapt it to the demands of esthetics, if we define art to be Nature infused with and shaped by the imaginative faculty of man; thus, as Bacon says elsewhere, "conforming the shows of things to the desires of the mind." Art always platonizes: it results from a certain finer instinct for form, order, proportion, a certain keener sense of the rhythm there is in the eternal flow of the world about us, and its products take shape around some idea preëxistent in the mind, are quickened into life by it, and strive always (cramped and hampered as they are by the limitations and conditions of human nature, of individual temperament, and outward circumstances) toward ideal perfection—toward what Michelangelo called

> Ideal form, the universal mold.

Shakespeare, whose careless generalizations have often the exactness of scientific definitions, tells us that

> The lunatic, the lover, and the poet
> Are of imagination all compact;

that

> as imagination bodies forth
> The forms of things unknown, the poet's pen
> Turns them to shapes, and gives to airy nothing
> A local habitation and a name.

And a little before he had told us that

> Lovers and madmen have such seething brains,
> Such shaping fantasies, that apprehend
> More than cool reason ever comprehends.[1]

Plato had said before him (in his "Ion") that the poet is possessed by a spirit not his own, and that he cannot poetize while he has a particle of understanding left. Again he says that the bacchantes, possessed by the god, drink milk and honey from the rivers, and

1. *Midsummer Night's Dream*, V. i. 7–8, 14–17, 4–6.

cannot believe, *till they recover their senses,* that they have been drinking mere water. Empedocles[2] said that "the mind could only conceive of fire by being fire."

All these definitions imply in the imaginative faculty the capabilities of ecstasy and possession, that is, of projecting itself into the very consciousness of its object, and again of being so wholly possessed by the emotion of its object that in expression it takes unconsciously the tone, the color, and the temperature thereof. Shakespeare is the highest example of this—for example, the parting of Romeo and Juliet. There the poet is so possessed by the situation, has so mingled his own consciousness with that of the lovers, that all nature is infected too, and is full of partings:

> Look, love, what envious streaks
> Do lace the *severing* clouds in yonder east.[3]

In Shelley's "Cenci," on the other hand, we have an instance of the poet's imagination giving away its own consciousness to the object contemplated, in this case an inanimate one.

> Two miles on this side of the fort, the road
> Crosses a deep ravine; 't is rough and narrow,
> And winds with short turns down the precipice;
> And in its depth there is a mighty rock
> Which has, from unimaginable years,
> Sustained itself with terror and with toil
> Over a gulf, and with the agony
> With which it clings seems slowly coming down;
> Even as a wretched soul hour after hour
> Clings to the mass of life; yet clinging, leans;
> And leaning, makes more dark the dread abyss
> In which it fears to fall: beneath this crag,
> Huge as despair, as if in weariness,
> The melancholy mountain yawns.[4]

The hint of this Shelley took from a passage in the second act of Calderón's "Purgatorio de San Patricio."

2. Greek philosopher, fifth century B.C.
3. *Romeo and Juliet*, III. v. 7–8.
4. III. i. 244–257.

No ves ese peñasco, que parece
Que se está sustentando con trabajo,
Y con el ansia misma que padece
Ha tantos siglos que se viene abajo? [5]

which, retaining the measure of the original, may be thus paraphrased:

Do you not see that rock there which appeareth
To hold itself up with a throe appalling,
And, through the very pang of what it feareth,
So many ages hath been falling, falling?

You will observe that in the last instance quoted the poet substitutes his own *impression* of the thing for the thing itself; he forces his own consciousness upon it, and herein is the very root of all sentimentalism. Herein lies the fault of that subjective tendency whose excess is so lamented by Goethe and Schiller, and which is one of the main distinctions between ancient and modern poetry. I say in its excess, for there are moods of mind of which it is the natural and healthy expression. Thus Shakespeare in his ninety-seventh sonnet:

How like a winter hath my absence been
From thee, the pleasure of the fleeting year!
What freezings have I felt, what dark days seen,
What old December's bareness everywhere!
And yet this time remov'd was summer's time.

It is only when it becomes a habit, instead of a mood of the mind, that it is a token of disease. Then it is properly dyspepsia, liver-complaint—what you will, but certainly not imagination as the handmaid of art. In that service she has two duties laid upon her: one as the *plastic* or *shaping* faculty, which gives form and proportion, and reduces the several parts of any work to an organic unity fore-ordained in that idea which is its germ of life; and the other as the *realizing* energy of thought which conceives clearly all the parts, not only in relation to the whole, but each in its several integrity and coherence.

We call the imagination the creative faculty. Assuming it to be so, in the one case it acts by deliberate forethought, in the other by

5. From Polonia's speech to Patricio, near the end of Act II.

intense sympathy—a sympathy which enables it to realize an Iago as happily as a Cordelia, a Caliban as a Prospero. There is a passage in Chaucer's "House of Fame" which very prettily illustrates this latter function:

> Whan any speche ycomen ys
> Up to the paleys, anon ryght
> Hyt wexeth lyke the same wight,
> Which that the worde in erthe spak,
> Be hyt clothed rede or blak;
> And so were hys lykenesse,
> And spake the word, that thou wilt gesse
> That it the same body be,
> Man or woman, he or she.[6]

We have the highest, and indeed an almost unique, example of this kind of sympathetic imagination in Shakespeare, who becomes so sensitive, sometimes, to the thought, the feeling, nay, the mere whim or habit of body of his characters, that we feel, to use his own words, as if "the dull substance of his flesh were thought." It is not in mere intensity of phrase, but in the fitness of it to the feeling, the character, or the situation, that this phase of the imaginative faculty gives witness of itself in expression. I know nothing more profoundly imaginative therefore in its bald simplicity than a line in Webster's *Duchess of Malfy.* Ferdinand has procured the murder of his sister the duchess. When her dead body is shown to him he stammers out:

> Cover her face; mine eyes dazzle; she died young.[7]

The difference between subjective and objective in poetry would seem to be that the aim of the former is to express a mood of the mind, often something in itself accidental and transitory, while that of the latter is to convey the impression made upon the mind by something outside of it, but taken up into the mind and idealized (that is, stripped of all unessential particulars) by it. The one would fain set forth your view of the thing (modified, perhaps, by your breakfast), the other would set forth the very thing itself in its most concise individuality. Subjective poetry may be profound and

6. Book II, 1074–1082.
7. IV. ii. 281.

imaginative if it deal with the primary emotions of our nature, with the soul's inquiries into its own being and doing, as was true of Wordsworth; but in the very proportion that it is profound, its range is limited. Great poetry should have breadth as well as height and depth; it should meet men everywhere on the open levels of their common humanity, and not merely on their occasional excursions to the heights of speculation or their exploring expeditions among the crypts of metaphysics.

But however we divide poetry, the office of imagination is to disengage what is essential from the crowd of accessories which is apt to confuse the vision of ordinary minds. For our perceptions of things are gregarious, and are wont to huddle together and jostle one another. It is only those who have been long trained to shepherd their thoughts that can at once single out each member of the flock by something peculiar to itself. That the power of abstraction has something to do with the imagination is clear, I think, from the fact that everybody is a dramatic poet (so far as the conception of character goes) in his sleep. His acquaintances walk and talk before him on the stage of dream precisely as in life. When he wakes, his genius has flown away with his sleep. It was indeed nothing more than that his mind was not distracted by the multiplicity of details which the senses force upon it by day. He thinks of Smith, and it is no longer a mere name on a door-plate or in a directory; but Smith himself is there, with those marvelous commonplaces of his which, could you only hit them off when you were awake, you would have created Justice Shallow. Nay, is not there, too, that offensively supercilious creak of the boots with which he enforced his remarks on the war in Europe, when he last caught you at the corner of the street and decanted into your ears the stale settlings of a week of newspapers? Now, did not Shakespeare tell us that the imagination *bodies forth*? It is indeed the *verbum caro factum*—the word made flesh and blood.

I said that the imagination always idealizes, that in its highest exercise, for example, as in the representation of character, it goes behind the species to the genus, presenting us with everlasting types of human nature, as in Don Quixote and Hamlet, Antigone and Cordelia, Alcestis and Amelia. By this I mean that those features are most constantly insisted upon, not in which they differ from other men, but from other kinds of men. For example, Don Quixote is never set before us as a mere madman, but as the victim of a monomania, and that, when you analyze it, of a very noble kind— nothing less, indeed, than devotion to an unattainable ideal, to an anachronism, as the ideals of imaginative men for the most part are. Amid all his ludicrous defeats and disillusions, this poetical side of him is brought to our notice at intervals, just as a certain theme recurs again and again in one of Beethoven's symphonies, a kind of clue to guide us through those intricacies of harmony. So in Lear, one of Shakespeare's profoundest psychological studies, the weakness of the man is emphasized, as it were, and forced upon our attention by his outbreaks of impotent violence; so in Macbeth, that imaginative bias which lays him open to the temptation of the weird sisters is suggested from time to time through the whole tragedy, and at last unmans him, and brings about his catastrophe in his combat with Macduff. This is what I call ideal and imaginative representation, which marks the outlines and boundaries of character, not by arbitrary lines drawn at this angle or that, according to the whim of the tracer, but by those mountain-ranges of human nature which divide man from man and temperament from temperament. And as the imagination of the reader must reinforce that of the poet, reducing the generic again to the specific, and defining it into sharper individuality by a comparison with the experiences of actual life, so, on the other hand, the popular imagination is always poetic, investing each new figure that comes before it with all the qualities that belong to the genus. Thus Hamlet, in some one or other of his characteristics has been the familiar of us all, and so from an ideal and remote figure is reduced to the standard of real and contemporary existence; while Bismarck, who, if we knew him, would probably turn out to be a comparatively simple character, is invested with all the qualities which have ever been attributed to the typical statesman, and is clearly as imaginative a personage as the Marquis of Posa, in Schiller's *Don Carlos*. We are ready to accept any *coup de théâtre* of him. Now, this prepossession is precisely that for which the imagination of the poet makes us ready by working on our own.

But there are also lower levels on which this idealization plays its tricks upon our fancy. The Greeks, who had studied profoundly what may be called the machinery of art, made use even of mechanical contrivances to delude the imagination of the spectator, and to entice him away from the associations of every-day life. The cothurnus lifted the actor to heroic stature, the mask prevented the ludicrous recognition of a familiar face in "Oedipus" and "Agamemnon"; it precluded grimace, and left the countenance as passionless as that of a god; it gave a more awful reverberation to the voice, and it was by the voice, that most penetrating and sympathetic, one might almost say incorporeal, organ of expression, that the great effects of the poet and tragic actor were wrought. Everything, you will observe, was, if not lifted above, at any rate removed, however much or little, from the plane of the actual and trivial. Their stage showed nothing that could be met in the streets. We barbarians, on the other hand, take delight precisely in that. We admire the novels of Trollope and the groups of Rogers [8] because, as we say, they are so *real*, while it is only because they are so matter-of-fact, so exactly on the level with our own trivial and prosaic apprehensions. When Dante lingers to hear the dispute between Sinon and Master Adam, Virgil, type of the higher reason and the ideal poet, rebukes him, and even angrily.

> E fa ragion ch'io ti sia sempre allato
> Si più avvien che fortuna t'accoglia
> Ove sien genti in simigliante piato;
> Chè voler ciò udire è bassa voglia. [9]

> Remember, *I* am always at thy side,
> If ever fortune bring thee once again
> Where there are people in dispute like this,
> For wishing to hear that is vulgar wish.

Verse is another of these expedients for producing that frame of mind, that prepossession, on the part of hearer or reader which is

8. John Rogers (1829–1904), American sculptor famous for his small groups of figures in domestic situations. The point of this observation, so often echoed in nineteenth-century statements of esthetics—see Chapter 37 of Hawthorne's *The Marble Faun*, for example—depends upon the major question raised in the previous essay, "The Function of the Poet." "Prosaic apprehensions," or realism, or even naturalism are the greatest expression that can be expected in an art which is bounded by the material.

9. *Inferno*, XXX, 145–148.

essential to the purpose of the poet, who has lost much of his advantage by the invention of printing, which obliges him to appeal to the eye rather than the ear. The rhythm is no arbitrary and artificial contrivance. It was suggested by an instinct natural to man. It is taught him by the beating of his heart, by his breathing, hastened or retarded by the emotion of the moment. Nay, it may be detected by what seems the most monotonous of motions, the flow of water, in which, if you listen intently, you will discover a beat as regular as that of the metronome. With the natural presumption of all self-taught men, I thought I had made a discovery in this secret confided to me by Beaver Brook, till Professor Pierce told me it was always allowed for in the building of dams.[10] Nay, for my own part, I would venture to affirm that not only meter but even rhyme itself was not without suggestion in outward nature. Look at the pine, how its branches, balancing each other, ray out from the tapering stem in stanza after stanza, how spray answers to spray in order, strophe, and antistrophe, till the perfect tree stands an embodied ode, Nature's triumphant vindication of proportion, number, and harmony. Who can doubt the innate charm of rhyme who has seen the blue river repeat the blue o'erhead; who has been ravished by the visible consonance of the tree growing at once toward an upward and downward heaven on the edge of the twilight cove; or who has watched how, as the kingfisher flitted from shore to shore, his visible echo flies under him, and completes the fleeting couplet in the visionary vault below? At least there can be no doubt that meter, by its systematic and regular occurrence, gradually subjugates and tunes the senses of the hearer, as the wood of the violin arranges itself in sympathy with the vibration of the strings, and thus that predisposition to the proper emotion is accomplished which is essential to the purpose of the poet. You must not only expect, but you must expect in the right way; you must be magnetized beforehand in every fiber by your own sensibility in order that you may feel what and how you ought. The right reception of whatever is ideally represented demands as a preliminary condition an exalted, or, if not that, then

10. Not all of Lowell's metaphors were reserved for his poetry. Compare this with Thoreau's statement in "Spring" that "the Maker of this earth but patented a leaf," and see my notes on Lowell's concept of organicism in art in the Introduction.

an excited, frame of mind both in poet and hearer. The imagination must be sensitized ere it will take the impression of those airy nothings whose image is traced and fixed by appliances as delicate as the golden pencils of the sun. Then that becomes a visible reality which before was but a phantom of the brain. Your own passion must penetrate and mingle with that of the artist that you may interpret him aright. You must, I say, be prepossessed, for it is the mind which shapes and colors the reports of the senses. Suppose you were expecting the bell to toll for the burial of some beloved person and the church-clock should begin to strike. The first lingering blow of the hammer would beat upon your very heart, and thence the shock would run to all the senses at once; but after a few strokes you would be undeceived, and the sound would become commonplace again. On the other hand, suppose that at a certain hour you knew that a criminal was to be executed; then the ordinary striking of the clock would have the sullen clang of a funeral bell. So in Shakespeare's instance of the lover, does he not suddenly find himself sensible of a beauty in the world about him before undreamed of, because his passion has somehow got into whatever he sees and hears? Will not the rustle of silk across a counter stop his pulse because it brings back to his sense the odorous whisper of Parthenissa's robe? Is not the beat of the horse's hoofs as rapid to Angelica pursued as the throbs of her own heart huddling upon one another in terror, while it is slow to Sister Anne, as the pulse that pauses between hope and fear, as she listens on the tower for rescue, and would have the rider "spur, though mounted on the wind"?

Doctor Johnson tells us that that only is good poetry which may be translated into sensible prose. I greatly doubt whether any very profound emotion can be so rendered. Man is a metrical animal, and it is not in prose but in nonsense verses that the young mother croons her joy over the new center of hope and terror that is sucking life from her breast. Translate passion into sensible prose and it becomes absurd, because subdued to workaday associations, to that level of common sense and convention where to betray intense feeling is ridiculous and unmannerly. Shall I ask Shakespeare to translate me his love "still climbing trees in the Hesperides"? Shall I ask Marlowe how Helen could "make him immortal with a kiss," or how, in the name of all the Monsieur Jourdains,[11] at once her face could "launch a thousand ships and burn the topless towers of Ilion"? Could Aeschylus, if put upon the stand, defend his making Prometheus cry out,

> O divine ether and swift-winged winds,
> Ye springs of rivers, and of ocean waves
> The innumerable smile, all-mother Earth,
> And Helios' all-beholding round, I call:
> Behold what I, a god, from gods endure![12]

Or could Lear justify his

> I tax not you, you elements, with unkindness;
> I never gave you kingdoms, call'd you children![13]

No; precisely what makes the charm of poetry is what we cannot explain any more than we can describe a perfume. There is a little quatrain of Gongora's quoted by Calderón in his *Alcalde of Zalamea* which has an inexplicable charm for me:

> Las flores del romero,
> Niña Isabel,
> Hoy son flores azules,
> Y mañana serán miel.[14]

If I translate it, 't is nonsense, yet I understand it perfectly, and it will, I dare say, outlive much wiser things in my memory. It is the very function of poetry to free us from that witch's circle of common sense which holds us fast in its narrow enchantment. In this dis-

11. The title character of Molière's *Le Bourgeois Gentilhomme* who was surprised to discover that he had been speaking prose all his life.

12. *Prometheus Bound*, 89–93.

13. *King Lear*, III. ii. 16–17.

14. Luis de Gongora y Argote (1561–1627), Spanish poet. Literally translated, the quatrain reads: "The rosemary blossoms, / Baby Isabel, / Are blue flowers today, / And tomorrow will be honey." Although Lowell finds the charm of the quatrain inexplicable, the reader might compare it with his other statements concerning the wonder of nature to the poetic sensibility, like his comment from "The Function of the Poet": "The $\sqrt{-x}$ is nothing in comparison with the chance-caught smell of a single flower which . . . recreates for us the unquestioning day of childhood." The contrast between the natural state—the blossom—and the "manufactured state"—the honey—is directly to Lowell's purpose here.

enthralment, language and verse have their share, and we may say that language also is capable of a certain idealization. Here is a passage from the XXXth song of Drayton's *Poly-Olbion*:

Which Copland scarce had spoke, but quickly every Hill
Upon her verge that stands, the neighbouring valleys fill;
Helvillon from his height, it through the mountains threw,
From whom as soon again, the sound Dunbalrase drew,
From whose stone-trophied head, it on to Wendrosse went,
Which tow'rds the sea again, resounded it to Dent,
That Broadwater therewith within her banks astound,
In sailing to the sea, told it in Egremound.

This gave a hint to Wordsworth, who, in one of his "Poems on the Naming of Places," thus prolongs the echo of it:

Joanna, looking in my eyes, beheld
That ravishment of mine, and laughed aloud.
The Rock, like something starting from a sleep,
Took up the Lady's voice, and laughed again;
The ancient Woman seated on Helm-crag
Was ready with her cavern; Hammar-scar,
And the tall steep of Silver-how, sent forth
A noise of laughter; southern Loughrigg heard,
And Fairfield answered with a mountain tone;
Helvellyn far into the clear blue sky
Carried the Lady's voice,—old Skiddaw blew
His speaking-trumpet;—back out of the clouds
Of Glaramara southward came the voice;
And Kirkstone tossed it from his misty head.

Now, this passage of Wordsworth I should call the idealization of that of Drayton, who becomes poetical only in the "stone-trophied head of Dunbalrase"; and yet the thought of both poets is the same.

Even what is essentially vulgar may be idealized by seizing and dwelling on the generic characteristics. In *Antony and Cleopatra* Shakespeare makes Lepidus tipsy, and nothing can be droller than the drunken gravity with which he persists in proving himself capable of bearing his part in the conversation. We seem to feel the whirl in his head when we find his mind revolving round a certain fixed point to which he clings as to a post. Antony is telling stories of Egypt to Octavius, and Lepidus, drawn into an eddy of the talk, interrupts him:

Lepidus: You've strange serpents there.
Antony [*trying to shake him off*]: Aye, Lepidus.
Lepidus: Your serpent of Egypt is bred now of your mud by the operation of your sun; so is your crocodile.
Antony [*thinking to get rid of him*]: They are so.

Presently Lepidus has revolved again, and continues, as if he had been contradicted:

Nay, certainly, I have heard the Ptolemies' pyramises are very goodly things; without contradiction, I have heard that.

And then, after another pause, still intent on proving himself sober, he asks, coming round to the crocodile again:

What manner o' thing is your crocodile?

Antony answers gravely:

It is shaped, sir, like itself, and it is as broad as it hath breadth; it is just so high as it is, and moves with its own organs: it lives by that which nourisheth it; and the elements once out of it, it transmigrates.
Lepidus: What color is it of?
Antony: Of its own color, too.
Lepidus [*meditatively*]: 'T is a strange serpent.[15]

The ideal in expression, then, deals also with the generic, and evades embarrassing particulars in a generalization. We say Tragedy with the dagger and bowl, and it means something very different to the esthetic sense from Tragedy with the case-knife and the phial of laudanum, though these would be as effectual for murder. It was a misconception of this that led poetry into that slough of poetic diction where everything was supposed to be made poetical by being called something else, and something longer. A boot became "the shining leather that the leg encased"; coffee, "the fragrant juice of Mocha's berry brown," whereas the imaginative way is the most condensed and shortest, conveying to the mind a feeling of the thing, and not a paraphrase of it. Akin to this was a

15. II. vii. 27–32, 39–41, 46–54.

confounding of the pictorial with the imaginative, and personification with that typical expression which is the true function of poetry. Compare, for example, Collins's Revenge with Chaucer's.

> Revenge impatient rose;
> He threw his blood-stained sword in thunder down,
> And, with a withering look,
> The war-denouncing trumpet took,
> And blew a blast so loud and dread,
> Were ne'er prophetic sound so full of woe!
> And ever and anon he beat
> The doubling drum with furious heat.[16]

"Words, words, Horatio!" Now let us hear Chaucer with his single stealthy line that makes us glance over our shoulder as if we heard the murderous tread behind us:

> The smiler with the knife hid under the cloak.[17]

Which is the more terrible? Which has more danger in it—Collins's noise or Chaucer's silence? Here is not the mere difference, you will perceive, between ornament and simplicity, but between a diffuseness which distracts, and a condensation which concenters the attention. Chaucer has chosen out of all the rest the treachery and the secrecy as the two points most apt to impress the imagination.

The imagination, as concerns expression, condenses; the fancy, on the other hand, adorns, illustrates, and commonly amplifies. The one is suggestive, the other picturesque. In Chapman's *Hero and Leander*, I read

> Her fresh-heat blood cast figures in her eyes,
> And she supposed she saw in Neptune's skies
> How her star wander'd, wash'd in smarting brine,
> For her love's sake, that with immortal wine
> Should be embathed, and swim in more heart's-ease
> Than there was water in the Sestian seas.[18]

In the epithet "star," Hero's thought implies the beauty and brightness of her lover and his being the lord of her destiny, while in

16. From "The Passions, An Ode for Music," ll. 40–47.
17. *The Knight's Tale*, I, 1998.
18. Third Sestiad, 335–340.

"Neptune's skies" we have not only the simple fact that the waters are the atmosphere of the sea-god's realm, but are reminded of that reflected heaven which Hero must have so often watched as it deepened below her tower in the smooth Hellespont. I call this as high an example of fancy as could well be found; it is picture and sentiment combined—the very essence of the picturesque. But when Keats calls Mercury "the star of Lethe," the word "star" makes us see him as the poor ghosts do who are awaiting his convoy, while the word "Lethe" intensifies our sympathy by making us feel his coming as they do who are longing to drink of forgetfulness. And this again reacts upon the word "star," which, as it before expressed only the shining of the god, acquires a metaphysical significance from our habitual association of star with the notions of hope and promise. Again nothing can be more fanciful than this bit of Henry More the Platonist:

> What doth move
> The nightingale to sing so fresh and clear?
> The thrush or lark that, mounting high above,
> Chants her shrill notes to heedless ears of corn
> Heavily hanging in the dewy morn?

But compare this with Keats again:

> The voice I hear this passing night was heard
> In ancient days by emperor and clown;
> Perhaps the self-same song that found a path
> Through the sad heart of Ruth when, sick for home,
> She stood in tears amid the alien corn.[19]

The imagination has touched that word "alien," and we see the field through Ruth's eyes, as she looked round on the hostile spikes, not merely through those of the poet.

Century, XLVII (March 1894), 716–721. Reprinted in Albert Mordell (ed.), *The Function of the Poet and Other Essays by James Russell Lowell* (Boston and New York: Houghton Mifflin, 1920), pp. 68–88.

19. Stanza seven of "Ode to a Nightingale."

Criticism and Culture

This fragment also grew from the Lowell Institute lectures of 1855, although little except the reference to Langland's Piers Plowman *may be dated to that year. It is one of Lowell's best statements about his compromise position of "selective catholicity" in literature, as well as his most concise appraisal of the critic's job of work.*

The same laws apply to all literature looked at simply as literature, and in honestly studying that of any country you will find yourself gradually becoming competent to understand that of all others. You would say, for example, that there was no point of analogy between the *Prometheus Bound* and *Piers the Plowman*, and yet I think we may find one that is neither fanciful nor far-fetched, namely, that the primary object of both is not literature but dogma, and that both in this way illustrate what we may fairly call a certain natural order of succession. Looked at esthetically, Aeschylus stands related to Sophocles very much as Langland does to Chaucer. I do not mean that the analogy is perfect—no analogies are—but enough so for the purpose of criticism, and to make our view at once broader and clearer. Again, the three great tragic dramatists of Greece illustrate this order in another way: Aeschylus being more purely imaginative, Sophocles dealing with character and reflection, and Euripides with passion and sentiment. All criticism is comparative. The tumor of Lucan helps us to appreciate the elegance of Virgil, while that very elegance which we have just learned to value seems a little thin if compared with the grave splendor of Lucretius.[1] The different arts, also, throw light upon each other. There is something of Lucan in Michelangelo. In both there is a struggle after originality,

1. M. Annaeus Lucan (A.D. 39–65), P. Virgilius Maro (70–19 B.C.), and T. Lucretius Carus (95–52? B.C.), Roman poets.

a tendency to confound the big with the great. And yet the real grandeur, in certain respects, of both is not to be overlooked. Again, I can never think of Dryden without recalling Rubens, and the association, involuntary as it was at first, led me to discover the singular merit of Dryden as a rapid colorist in words. It is curious, also, but as natural as it is curious, that Pope, who was the disciple of Dryden, should have a certain analogy with Vandyke, the pupil of Rubens. Both reacted, to a certain degree, from the faults of their masters. As in them force had sometimes degenerated into exaggeration, so these carried their love of elegance to the verge of becoming conventional. The verse in which Pope characterized that most gentlemanlike of artists,

> The clear precision of the soft Vandyke,

is also the happiest definition of what is best in his own style. In the same way, I make Mendelssohn help me to criticize Tennyson, and I see that the same causes which produced Euripides in Greece produced Verdi in Italy. The object of all criticism is not to criticize, but to understand. More than this. As you will find it more wholesome in life, and more salutary to your own character to study the virtues than the defects of your friends, so in literature it seems to me wiser to look for an author's strong points than his weak ones, and to consider that every man, as the French say, is liable to have the defects of his qualities. Above all, criticism is useful in inducing a judicial habit of mind, and teaching us to keep our intellectual tempers. When Mr. Matthew Arnold charges Shakespeare with exaggeration, it shall not set me in a passion, but put me upon honest inquiry rather to find out whether the fault is in the greatest of poets or in one of the subtlest of critics. My duty is to discover exactly what he means, and this again helps me to a knowledge of his own limitations as a critic. I think I see that his love of French neatness has carried him too far, and that he applies a too exclusively intellectual test. I mean by this that we must, as Shakespeare himself says,

> Play with our fancies and believe we *see*.[2]

2. This is slightly misquoted from *Henry V*, III, Prologue, 7: "Play with your fancies; and in them behold."

* * *

I would not advocate a critical habit at the expense of an unquestioning and hearty enjoyment of literature in and for itself. Nay, as I think the great advantage to be gained by it is that it compels us to see two sides to every question, it should, when rightly understood and fairly applied, tend to liberality of mind and hospitality of thought. A true scholar should be able to value Wordsworth for his depth of sympathy with nature, without therefore losing all power to enjoy the sparkling shallowness of Pope; he should be able to feel the beauty of Herbert's puritanism, the naked picturesqueness of his style, and yet not refuse to be delighted with the sensuous paganism of Herrick. The gracious naturalness and intense flavor of the elder dramatists should not put him out of conceit with the splendid artificiality and the sonorous ecstasy of Gray. "In my father's house are many mansions" conveys a lesson of criticism no less than of charity. But while insisting on the excellence of openmindedness, let us not confound liberality with indifference, nor be willing to be easily *satisfied* because we are content to be easily entertained. Let us have a high standard, whether in life or literature, and, however charitable we may be and should be to those who fall below it (unless it be our own case), let us not stupidly deny that they have fallen below it. Let us never condescend to that vulgarity too common in this country, where half-culture is apt to be defiant rather than modest, which affirms that one thing is as good as another if only a man *think* it as good.

Century, XLVII (February 1894), 515–516.

II

PRINCIPLES OF CRITICISM

Ancients and Moderns

This discussion, taken from Lowell's essay "Swinburne's Tragedies,"
first published in the North American Review *in 1866, defines his position*
on the question of mimesis. For Lowell, imitation must be organic, and a
proper reading of the classical writers ought only to strengthen that assump-
tion. Lowell's analysis here is far from outdated. As recently as 1966,
Harvey D. Goldstein's "Mimesis and Catharsis Reëxamined" (Journal of
Aesthetics and Art Criticism, *XXIV, 567–577) reaffirmed the central*
principle.

* * * I do not mean to renew the old quarrel of Fontenelle's day as
to the comparative merits of ancients and moderns.[1] That is an affair
of taste, which does not admit of any authoritative settlement. My
concern is about a principle which certainly demands a fuller
discussion, and which is important enough to deserve it. Do we show
our appreciation of the Greeks most wisely in attempting the mechanical reproduction of their forms, or by endeavoring to comprehend
the thoughtful spirit of full-grown manhood in which they wrought,
to kindle ourselves by the emulation of it, and to bring it to bear with
all its plastic force upon our wholly new conditions of life and
thought? It seems to me that the question is answered by the fact,
patent in the history of all the fine arts, that every attempt at
reproducing a bygone excellence by external imitation of it, or even
by applying the rules which analytic criticism has formulated from
the study of it, has resulted in producing the artificial, and not the

1. Bernard le Bovier de Fontenelle (1657–1757), French poet and critic, may be
said to have begun the battle between the ancients and the moderns with his
Digression sur les Anciens et les Modernes (1688). Swift's "The Battle of the Books"
(1697) is the most important English work resulting from the controversy.

artistic. That most subtile of all essences in physical organization, which eludes chemist, anatomist, and microscopist, the life, is in aesthetics not less shy of the critic, and will not come forth in obedience to his most learned spells, for the very good reason that it cannot, because in all works of art it is the joint product of the artist and of the time. Faust may believe he is gazing on "the face that launched a thousand ships," but Mephistopheles knows very well that it is only shadows that he has the skill to conjure. He is not merely the spirit that ever denies, but the spirit also of discontent with the present, that material in which every man shall work who will achieve realities and not their hollow semblance. The true anachronism, in my opinion, is not in Shakespeare's making Ulysses talk as Lord Bacon might, but in attempting to make him speak in a dialect of thought utterly dead to all present comprehension. Ulysses was the type of long-headedness; and the statecraft of an Ithacan cateran would have seemed as childish to the age of Elizabeth and Burleigh as it was naturally sufficing to the first hearers of Homer. Ulysses, living in Florence during the fifteenth century, might have been Machiavelli; in France, during the seventeenth, Cardinal Richelieu; in America, during the nineteenth, Abraham Lincoln, but not Ulysses. Truth to nature can be reached ideally, never historically; it must be a study from the life, and not from the scholiasts. Theocritus[2] lets us into the secret of his good poetry, when he makes Daphnis tell us that he preferred his rock with a view of the Siculian Sea to the kingdom of Pelops.

It is one of the marvels of the human mind, this sorcery which the fiend of technical imitation weaves about his victims, giving a phantasmal Helen to their arms, and making an image of the brain seem substance. Men still pain themselves to write Latin verses, matching their wooden bits of phrase together as children do dissected maps, and measuring the value of what they have done, not by any standard of intrinsic merit, but by the difficulty of doing it. Petrarch expected to be known to posterity by his "Africa." Gray hoped to make a Latin poem his monument. Goethe, who was classic in the only way it is now possible to be classic, in his "Hermann and

2. One of the first and greatest pastoral poets, flourished around the beginning of the third century B.C. He originated most of the conventions of pastoral poetry.

Dorothea," and at least Propertian in his "Roman Idyls," wasted his time and thwarted his creative energy on the mechanical mock-antique of an unreadable "Achilleïs." Landor prized his waxen "Gebirus Rex" above all the natural fruits of his mind; and we have no doubt that, if some philosopher should succeed in accomplishing Paracelsus's problem of an artificial *homunculus*, he would dote on this misbegotten babe of his science, and think him the only genius of the family. We cannot overestimate the value of some of the ancient classics, but a certain amount of superstition about Greek and Latin has come down to us from the revival of learning, and seems to hold in mortmain the intellects of whoever has, at some time, got a smattering of them. Men quote a platitude in either of those tongues with a relish of conviction as droll to the uninitiated as the knight-hood of freemasonry. Horace Walpole's nephew, the Earl of Orford, when he was in his cups, used to have Statius read aloud to him every night for two hours by a tipsy tradesman, whose hiccupings threw in here and there a kind of caesural pause, and found some strange mystery of sweetness in the disquantitied syllables. So powerful is this hallucination that we can conceive of *festina lente* as the favorite maxim of a Mississippi steamboat captain, and ἄριστον μὲν ὕδωρ[3] cited as conclusive by a gentleman for whom the bottle before him reversed the wonder of the stereoscope, and substituted the Gascon *v* for *b* in binocular.

Something of this singular superstition has infected the minds of those who confound the laws of conventional limitation which governed the practice of Greek authors in dramatic composition, laws adapted to the habits and traditions and preconceptions of their audience, with that sense of ideal form which made the Greeks masters in art to all succeeding generations. Aristophanes is beyond question the highest type of pure comedy, etheralizing his humor by the infusion, or intensifying it by the contrast of poetry, and deodorizing the personality of his sarcasm by a sprinkle from the clearest springs of fancy. His satire, aimed as it was at typical characteristics, is as fresh as ever; but we doubt whether an Aristo-phanic drama, retaining its exact form, but adapted to present

3. "The more haste, the less speed," and "water is most excellent." Both are proverbial, and both comically inappropriate to this context.

events and personages, would keep the stage as it is kept by *The Rivals*, for example, immeasurably inferior as that is in every element of genius except the prime one of liveliness. Something similar in purpose to the parabasis[4] was essayed in one, at least, of the comedies of Beaumont and Fletcher, and in our time by Tieck; but it took, of necessity, a different form of expression, and does not seem to have been successful. Indeed, the fact that what is called the legitimate drama of modern times in England, Spain, and France has been strictly a growth, and not a manufacture, that in each country it took a different form, and that, in all, the period of its culminating and beginning to decline might be measured by a generation, seems to point us toward some natural and inevitable law of human nature, and to show that, while the principles of art are immutable, their application must accommodate itself to the material supplied to them by the time and by the national character and traditions. The Spanish tragedy inclines more toward the lyrical, the French toward the epical, the English toward the historical, in the representation of real life; the Spanish and English agree in the Teutonic peculiarity of admitting the humorous antithesis of the clown, though in the one case he parodies the leading motive of the drama, and represents the self-consciousness of the dramatist, while in the other he heightens the tragic effect by contrast (as in the grave-digging scene of *Hamlet*), and suggests that stolid but wholesome indifference of the general life, of what, for want of a better term, we call Nature, to the sin and suffering, the weakness and misfortune of the individual man. All these nations had the same ancient examples before them, had the same reverence for antiquity, yet they involuntarily deviated, more or less happily, into originality, success, and the freedom of a living creativeness. The higher kinds of literature, the only kinds that live on because they had life at the start, are not, then, it should seem, the fabric of scholarship, of criticism, diligently studying and as diligently copying the best models, but are much

4. In Greek drama, a "stepping forward" of the chorus to address the audience directly and usually in the name of the author. Beaumont and Fletcher's *The Knight of the Burning Pestle* uses parabasis rather successfully, at least to twentieth-century tastes. What play of Johann Ludwig Tieck (1773–1853) Lowell had in mind I have been unable to determine.

rather born of some genetic principle in the character of the people and the age which produce them. One drop of ruddy human blood puts more life into the veins of a poem than all the delusive *aurum potabile*[5] that can be distilled out of the choicest library.

The opera is the closest approach we have to the ancient drama in the essentials of structure and presentation; and could we have a *libretto* founded on a national legend and written by one man of genius to be filled out and accompanied by the music of another, we might hope for something of the same effect upon the stage. But themes of universal familiarity and interest are rare,—Don Giovanni and Faust, perhaps, most nearly, though not entirely, fulfilling the required conditions,—and men of genius rarer. The oratorio seeks to evade the difficulty by choosing Scriptural subjects, and it may certainly be questioned whether the day of popular mythology, in the sense in which it subserves the purposes of epic or dramatic poetry, be not gone by forever. Longfellow is driven to take refuge among the red men, and Tennyson in the Cambro-Breton cyclus of Arthur; but it is impossible that such themes should come so intimately home to us as the semi-fabulous stories of their own ancestors did to the Greeks. The most successful attempt at reproducing the Greek tragedy, both in theme and treatment, is the *Samson Agonistes,* as it is also the most masterly piece of English versification. Goethe admits that it alone, among modern works, has caught life from the breath of the antique spirit. But he failed to see, or at least to give, the reason of it; probably failed to see it, or he would never have attempted the *Iphigenie.* Milton not only subjected himself to the structural requirements of the Attic tragedy, but with a true poetic instinct availed himself of the striking advantage it had in the choice of a subject. No popular tradition lay near enough to him for his purpose; none united in itself the essential requisites of human interest and universal belief. He accordingly chose a Jewish mythus, very near to his own heart as a blind prisoner, betrayed by his wife, among the Philistines of the Restoration, and familiar to the earliest associations of his readers. This subject, and this alone, met all the demands both of living poetic production and of antique form,—the action grandly simple, the personages few, the protagonist at once a victim

5. "Drinkable gold."

of divine judgment and an executor of divine retribution, an intense personal sympathy in the poet himself, and no strangeness to the habitual prepossessions of those he addressed to be overcome before he could touch their hearts or be sure of aid from their imaginations. To compose such a drama on such a theme was to *be* Greek, and not to counterfeit it; for Samson was to Milton traditionally just what Herakles was to Sophocles, and personally far more. The *Agonistes* is still fresh and strong as morning, but where are *Caractacus* and *Elfrida*? Nay, where is the far better work of a far abler man, where is *Merope*?[6] If the frame of mind which performs a deliberate experiment were the same as that which produces poetry vitalized through and through by the conspiring ardors of every nobler passion and power of the soul, then *Merope* might have had some little space of life. But without color, without harmonious rhythm of movement, with less passion than survived in an average Grecian ghost, and all this from the very theory of her creation, she has gone back, a shadow, to join her shadowy Italian and French namesakes in that limbo of things that would be and cannot be. Mr. Arnold but retraces, in his preface to *Merope*, the arguments of Mason in the letters prefixed to his classical experiments. What finds defenders, but not readers, may be correct, classic, right in principle, but it is not poetry of that absolute kind which may and does help men, but needs no help of theirs; and such surely we have a right to demand in tragedy, if nowhere else. I should not speak so unreservedly if I did not set a high value on Mr. Arnold and his poetic gift. But *Merope* has that one fault against which the very gods, we are told, strive in vain. It is dull, and the seed of this dulness lay in the system on which it was written.

Pseudo-classicism takes two forms. Sometimes, as Mr. Landor has done, it attempts truth of detail to ancient scenery and manners, which may be attained either by hard reading and good memory, or at a cheaper rate from such authors as Becker.[7] The *Moretum*,

---

6. *Elfrida* (1752) and *Caractacus* (1759) were both plays based upon Anglo-Saxon legend by William Mason (1725–1797), a minor English poet. *Merope, A Tragedy* (1858) was by Matthew Arnold.

7. Lowell is alluding here to a kind of false verisimilitude produced by acquaintance with superficial detail of, for example, the classical past as it was exhumed by

once attributed to Virgil, and the idyll of Theocritus lately chosen as a text by Mr. Arnold, are interesting, because they describe real things; but the mock-antique, if not true, is nothing, and how true such poems are likely to be we can judge by *Punch's* success at Yankee-isms, by all England's accurate appreciation of the manners and minds of a contemporary people one with herself in language, laws, religion, and literature. The eye is the only note-book of the true poet; but a patchwork of second-hand memories is a laborious futility, hard to write and harder to read, with about as much nature in it as a dialogue of the Deipnosophists. Alexander's bushel of peas was a criticism worthy of Aristotle's pupil. We should reward such writing with the gift of a classical dictionary. In this idyllic kind of poetry also we have a classic, because Goldsmith went to Nature for his "Deserted Village," and borrowed of tradition nothing but the poetic diction in which he described it. This is the only method by which a poet may surely reckon on ever becoming an ancient himself. When I heard it said once that a certain poem might have been written by Simonides, I could not help thinking that, if it were so, then it was precisely what Simonides could never have written, since he looked at the world through his own eyes, not through those of Linus or Hesiod, and thought his own thoughts, not theirs, or we should never have had him to imitate.[8]

Objections of the same nature, but even stronger, lie against a servile copying of the form and style of the Greek tragic drama, and yet more against the selection of a Greek theme. As I said before, the life we lead and the views we take of it are more complex than those of men who lived five centuries before Christ. They may be better or worse, but, at any rate, they are different, and irremediably so. The idea and the form in which it naturally embodies itself,

---

Wilhelm Adolf Becker (1796–1846), the German classical archaeologist. Landor was guilty of providing a background for his *Imaginary Conversations* which would suggest that all Greeks were shaped and habitually posed liked the statues of Praxiteles. These comments should be compared to Lowell's statements about domestic realism in "The Imagination," p. 29.

8. Simonides of Amorgos flourished about 660 B.C.; Hesiod, one of the earliest Greek poets, about 735 B.C.; and Linus was a mythical poet, supposed to have been a son of Apollo.

mutually sustaining and invigorating each other, cannot be divided without endangering the lives of both. For in all real poetry the form is not a garment, but a body. Our very passion has become metaphysical, and speculates upon itself. Their simple and downright way of thinking loses all its savor when we assume it to ourselves by an effort of thought. Human nature, it is true, remains always the same, but the displays of it change; the habits which are a second nature modify it inwardly as well as outwardly, and what moves it to passionate action in one age may leave it indifferent in the next. Between us and the Greeks lies the grave of their murdered paganism, making our minds and theirs irreconcilable. Christianity as steadily intensifies the self-consciousness of man as the religion of the Greeks must have turned their thoughts away from themselves to the events of this life and the phenomena of nature. We cannot even conceive of their conception of Phoibos[9] with any plausible assurance of coming near the truth. To take lesser matters, since the invention of printing and the cheapening of books have made the thought of all ages and nations the common property of educated men, we cannot so dis-saturate our minds of it as to be keenly thrilled in the modern imitation by those commonplaces of proverbial lore in which the chorus and secondary characters are apt to indulge, though in the original they may interest us as being natural and characteristic. In the German-silver of the modern we get something of this kind, which does not please us the more by being cut up into single lines that recall the outward semblance of some pages in Sophocles. We find it cheaper to make a specimen than to borrow one.

CHORUS: Foolish who bites off nose, his face to spite.
OUTIS: Who fears his fate, him Fate shall one day spurn.
CHORUS: The gods themselves are pliable to Fate.
OUTIS: The strong self-ruler owns no other sway.
CHORUS: Sometimes the shortest way goes most about.
OUTIS: Why fetch a compass, having stars within?
CHORUS: A shepherd once, I know that stars may set.
OUTIS: That thou led'st sheep fits not for leading men.
CHORUS: To sleep-sealed eyes the wolf-dog barks in vain.

9. Phoebus, that is, Apollo; hence, the prophetic or inspired as seen by the Greeks.

We protest that we have read something very like this, we will not say where, and we might call it the battledoor and shuttlecock style of dialogue, except that the players do not seem to have any manifest relation to each other, but each is intent on keeping his own bit of feathered cork continually in the air.

The first sincerely popular yearning toward antiquity, the first germ of Schiller's "Götter Griechenland's" is to be found in the old poem of "Tannhäuser," very nearly coincident with the beginnings of the Reformation.[10] And if we might allegorize it, we should say that it typified precisely that longing after Venus, under her other name of Charis, which represents the relation in which modern should stand to ancient art. It is the virile grace of the Greeks, their sense of proportion, their distaste for the exaggerated, their exquisite propriety of phrase, which steadies imagination without cramping it,—it is these that we should endeavor to assimilate without the loss of our own individuality. We should quicken our sense of form by intelligent sympathy with theirs, and not stiffen it into formalism by a servile surrender of what is genuine in us to what *was* genuine in them. "A pure form," says Schiller, "helps and sustains, an impure one hinders and shatters." But we should remember that the spirit of the age must enter as a modifying principle, not only into ideas, but into the best manner of their expression. The old bottles will not always serve for the new wine. A principle of life is the first requirement of all art, and it can only be communicated by the touch of the time and a simple faith in it; all else is circumstantial and secondary. The Greek tragedy passed through the three natural stages of poetry,—the imaginative in Aeschylus, the thoughtfully artistic in Sophocles, the sentimental in Euripides,—and then

10. Lowell is here identifying racial or national roots, as typified by "Tannhäuser," a national poem, with cultural roots, Schiller's need to comprehend the allegories of the specific Greek deities, and placing the beginnings of both phenomena at the moment of religious, cultural, and national enlightenment. He is anticipating Jung and much of modern anthropological criticism by doing so. This is made even clearer by the following reference to the "longing after Venus under her other name of Charis." Charis, the name of the chief of the Graces was indeed identified with Venus. In the *Iliad*, the wife of Hephaestus is identified as Charis, in the *Odyssey*, Aphrodite, or Venus. Thus Lowell clearly hints that the classical and the Romantic spring from one root.

died. If people could only learn the general applicability to periods and schools of what young Mozart says of Gellert,[11] that "he had written no poetry since his death"! No effort to raise a defunct past has ever led to anything but just enough galvanic twitching of the limbs to remind us unpleasantly of life. The romantic movement of the school of German poets which succeeded Goethe and Schiller ended in extravagant unreality, and Goethe himself, with his unerring common sense, has given us, in the second part of *Faust*, the result of his own and Schiller's common striving after a Grecian ideal. Euphorion, the child of Faust and Helen, falls dead at their feet; and Helen herself soon follows him to the shades, leaving only her mantle in the hands of her lover. This, he is told, shall lift him above the earth. We fancy we can interpret the symbol. Whether we can or not, it is certainly suggestive of thought that the only immortal production of the greatest of recent poets was conceived and carried out in that Gothic spirit and form from which he was all his life struggling to break loose.

Works, II, 165–179.

11. Christian Fürchtegott Gellert (1715–1769), German poet.

Originality

This brief extract is from a much longer essay "Chaucer," first published in the North American Review *in 1870. The context is an examination of Chaucer's sources, particularly in Provençal poetry, but the remarks might stand for Lowell's most mature thoughts on the subject for any poet.*

* * * The first question we put to any poet, nay, to any so-called national literature, is that which Farinata addressed to Dante, *Chi fur li maggior tui?*[1] Here is no question of plagiarism, for poems are not made of words and thoughts and images, but of that something in the poet himself which can compel them to obey him and move to the rhythm of his nature. Thus it is that the new poet, however late he come, can never be forestalled, and the ship-builder who built the pinnace of Columbus has as much claim to the discovery of America as he who suggests a thought by which some other man opens new worlds to us has to a share in that achievement by him unconceived and inconceivable. Chaucer undoubtedly began as an imitator, perhaps as mere translator, serving the needful apprenticeship in the use of his tools. Children learn to speak by watching the lips and catching the words of those who know how already, and poets learn in the same way from their elders. They import their raw material from any and everywhere, and the question at last comes down to this,—whether an author have original force enough to assimilate all he has acquired, or that he be so overmastering as to assimilate *him*. If the poet turn out the stronger, we allow him to help himself from other people with wonderful equanimity. Should a man discover the art of transmuting metals and present us with a lump of

---

1. "Who were thy forebears?" (*Inferno*, X, 42). Farinata was Manenete degli Uberti (d. 1264), Chief of the Ghibellines of Florence.

gold as large as an ostrich-egg, would it be in human nature to inquire too nicely whether he had stolen the lead?

Nothing is more certain than that great poets are not sudden prodigies, but slow results. As an oak profits by the foregone lives of immemorial vegetable races that have worked-over the juices of earth and air into organic life out of whose dissolution a soil might gather fit to maintain that nobler birth of Nature, so we may be sure that the genius of every remembered poet drew the forces that built it up out of the decay of a long succession of forgotten ones. Nay, in proportion as the genius is vigorous and original will its indebtedness be greater, will its roots strike deeper into the past and grope in remoter fields for the virtue that must sustain it. Indeed, if the works of the great poets teach anything, it is to hold mere invention somewhat cheap. It is not the finding of a thing, but the making something out of it after it is found, that is of consequence. Accordingly, Chaucer, like Shakespeare, invented almost nothing. Wherever he found anything directed to Geoffrey Chaucer, he took it and made the most of it. It was not the subject treated, but himself, that was the new thing. *Cela m'appartient de droit*,[2] Molière is reported to have said when accused of plagiarism. Chaucer pays that "usurious interest which genius," as Coleridge says, "always pays in borrowing." The characteristic touch is his own. In the famous passage about the caged bird, copied from the "Romaunt of the Rose," the "gon eten wormes" was added by him.[3] We must let him, if he will, eat the heart out of the literature that had preceded him, as we sacrifice the mulberry-leaves to the silkworm, because he knows how to convert them into something richer and more lasting. The question of originality is not one of form, but of substance, not of cleverness, but of imaginative power. Given your material, in other words the life in which you live, how much can you see in it? For on that depends how much you can make of it. Is it merely

2. "That belongs to me by right."

3. Chaucer translated 7,700 lines from a much longer thirteenth-century French poem, *La Roman de la Rose*, by Guillaume de Lorris and Jean de Meun. In the earlier poem, in a part not translated by Chaucer, there is a simile about a bird who, though caged, will escape if he can. Chaucer adopted the simile for *The Manciple's Tale*, lines 163 ff., and added the detail that the bird will "gon ete worms" if he can flee the cage.

an arrangement of man's contrivance, a patchwork of expediencies for temporary comfort and convenience, good enough if it last your time, or is it so much of the surface of that ever-flowing deity which we call Time, wherein we catch such fleeting reflection as is possible for us, of our relation to perdurable things? This is what makes the difference between Aeschylus and Euripides, between Shakespeare and Fletcher, between Goethe and Heine, between literature and rhetoric. Something of this depth of insight, if not in the fullest, yet in no inconsiderable measure, characterizes Chaucer. We must not let his playfulness, his delight in the world as mere spectacle, mislead us into thinking that he was incapable of serious purpose or insensible to the deeper meanings of life.

Works, II, 193–195.

Sentimentalism

Always an eclectic, Lowell drew from neoclassical and Romantic esthetic theory for his ideas on sentimentalism. As we have seen in his essay on the imagination, Lowell found sentimentalism to be "a token of disease" only "when it becomes a habit, instead of a mood of the mind." The excerpts which follow are taken from his quite formal essay "Rousseau and the Sentimentalists" (first published in the North American Review, *1867,) a study of both the man and the healthy and diseased forms of sentiment. It is likely that these ideas are the basis from which the comments in "The Imagination" are distilled.*

* * * It is when the sentimentalist turns preacher of morals that we investigate his character, and are justified in so doing. He may express as many and as delicate shades of feeling as he likes,—for this the sensibility of his organization perfectly fits him and no other person could do it so well,—but the moment he undertakes to establish his feeling as a rule of conduct, we ask at once how far are his own life and deed in accordance with what he preaches? For every man feels instinctively that all the beautiful sentiments in the world weigh less than a single lovely action; and that while tenderness of feeling and susceptibility to generous emotions are accidents of temperament, goodness is an achievement of the will and a quality of the life. Fine words, says our homely old proverb, butter no parsnips; and if the question be how to render those vegetables palatable, an ounce of butter would be worth more than all the orations of Cicero. The only conclusive evidence of a man's sincerity is that he give *himself* for a principle. Words, money, all things else, are comparatively easy to give away; but when a man makes a gift of his daily life and practice, it is plain that the truth, whatever it may be, has taken possession of him. From that sincerity his words gain the force and pertinency of deeds, and his money is no longer the pale drudge 'twixt man and man, but, by a beautiful magic, what erewhile bore the image and superscription of Caesar seems now to bear the image and superscription of God. It is thus that there is a genius for goodness, for magnanimity, for self-sacrifice, as well as for creative art; and it is thus that by a more refined sort of Platonism the Infinite Beauty dwells in and shapes to its own likeness the soul which gives it body and individuality. But when Moore[1] charges genius with being an impostor, the confusion of his ideas is pitiable. There is nothing so true, so sincere, so downright and forthright, as genius. It is always truer than the man himself is, greater than he. If Shakespeare the man had been as marvellous a creature as the genius that wrote his plays, that genius so comprehensive in its intelligence, so wise even in its play that its clowns are moralists and philosophers, so penetrative that a single one of its phrases reveals to us the secret of our own character, would his contemporaries have left us so wholly without record of him as they have done, distinguishing him in no wise from his fellow players?

* * *

The sentimentalist is the spiritual hypochondriac, with whom fancies become facts, while facts are a discomfort because they will not be evaporated into fancy. In his eyes, Theory is too fine a dame to confess even a country-cousinship with coarse-handed Practice, whose homely ways would disconcert her artificial world. The very susceptiblity that makes him quick to feel, makes him also incapable of deep and durable feeling. He loves to think he suffers, and keeps a pet sorrow, a blue-devil familiar, that goes with him everywhere, like Paracelsus's black dog. He takes good care, however, that it shall not be the true sulphurous article that sometimes takes a fancy to fly away with his conjurer.

* * *

Among the ancients we find little or no trace of sentimentalism, though Euripides and still more Ovid give hints of it. Their masculine mood both of body and mind left no room for it, and hence the bracing quality of their literature compared with that of recent

1. Thomas Moore (1779–1852), Irish poet.

times, its tonic property, that seems almost too astringent to palates relaxed by a daintier diet. The first great example of the degenerate modern tendency was Petrarch, who may be said to have given it impulse and direction. A more perfect specimen of the type has not since appeared. An intellectual voluptuary, a moral *dilettante*, the first instance of that character, since too common, the gentleman in search of a sensation, seeking a solitude at Vaucluse because it made him more likely to be in demand at Avignon, praising philosophic poverty with a sharp eye to the next rich benefice in the gift of his patron, commending a good life but careful first of a good living, happy only in seclusion but making a dangerous journey to enjoy the theatrical show of a coronation in the Capitol, cherishing a fruit-less passion which broke his heart three or four times a year and yet could not make an end of him till he had reached the ripe age of seventy and survived his mistress a quarter of a century,—surely a more exquisite perfection of inconsistency would be hard to find.

* * *

Certainly I do not mean to say that a work of art should be looked at by the light of the artist's biography, or measured by our standard of his character. Nor do I reckon what was genuine in Petrarch— his love of letters, his refinement, his skill in the superficial graces of language, that rhetorical art by which the music of words supplants their meaning, and the verse moulds the thought instead of being plastic to it—after any such fashion. I have no ambition for that character of *valet de chambre* which is said to disenchant the most heroic figures into mere every-day personages, for it implies a mean soul no less than a servile condition. But we have a right to demand a certain amount of reality, however small, in the emotion of a man who makes it his business to endeavor at exciting our own. We have a privilege of nature to shiver before a painted flame, how cunningly soever the colors be laid on. Yet our love of minute biographical detail, our desire to make ourselves spies upon the men of the past, seems so much of an instinct in us, that we must look for the spring of it in human nature, and that somewhat deeper than mere curiosity or love of gossip. It should seem to arise from what must be con-sidered on the whole a creditable feeling, namely, that we value character more than any amount of talent,—the skill to *be* something, above that of doing anything but the best of its kind. The highest creative genius, and that only, is privileged from arrest by this personality, for there the thing produced is altogether disengaged from the producer. But in natures incapable of this escape from themselves, the author is inevitably mixed with his work, and we have a feeling that the amount of his sterling character is the security for the notes he issues. Especially we feel so when truth to self, which is always self-forgetful, and not truth to nature, makes an essential part of the value of what is offered us; as where a man undertakes to narrate personal experience or to enforce a dogma. This is particularly true as respects sentimentalists, because of their intrusive self-consciousness; for there is no more universal characteristic of human nature than the instinct of men to apologize to themselves for themselves, and to justify personal failings by generalizing them into universal laws. A man would be the keenest devil's advocate against himself, were it not that he has always taken a retaining-fee for the defence; for I think that the indirect and mostly unconscious pleas in abatement which we read between the lines in the works of many authors are oftener written to set themselves right in their own eyes than in those of the world. And in the real life of the sentimentalist it is the same. He is under the wretched necessity of keeping up, at least in public, the character he has assumed, till he at last reaches that last shift of bankrupt self-respect, to play the hypocrite with himself.

Works, IV, 185–187, 193–194, 196–197, 200–202.

Style

Lowell's essay "Carlyle," from which the following extracts have been taken, was first published in the North American Review *in 1866. The comments on style include a good deal of Lowell's thought about organic creation as well as more specifically rhetorical matter. The estimate of Carlyle's work here suggested was typical of Lowell through his life-time: real admiration for his facility with language, but a persistent distrust of ideas that sprang from a less ample "ether and divine air" than the thought in which "Emerson dwelt"* (Works, XVI, 104).

* * * The first element of contemporary popularity is undoubtedly the power of entertaining. If a man have anything to tell, the world cannot be expected to listen to him unless he have perfected himself in the best way of telling it. People are not to be argued into a pleasurable sensation, nor is taste to be compelled by any syllogism, however stringent. An author may make himself very popular, however, and even justly so, by appealing to the passion of the moment, without having anything in him that shall outlast the public whim which he satisfies. Churchill[1] is a remarkable example of this. He had a surprising extempory vigor of mind; his phrase carries great weight of blow; he undoubtedly surpassed all contemporaries, as Cowper says of him, in a certain rude and earth-born vigor; but his verse is dust and ashes now, solemnly inurned, of course, in the Chalmers columbarium,[2] and without danger of violation. His brawn and muscle are fading traditions, while the fragile, shivering genius of Cowper is still a good life on the

1. Charles Churchill (1731–1764), English satiric poet.
2. Alexander Chalmers (1759–1834) published *A General Biographical Dictionary* in thirty-two volumes (1812–1817).

books of the Critical Insurance Office. "Is it not, then, loftiness of mind that puts one by the side of Virgil?" cries poor old Cavalcanti[3] at his wits' end. Certainly not altogether that. There must be also the great Mantuan's art; his power, not only of being strong in parts, but of making those parts coherent in an harmonious whole, and tributary to it. Gray, if we may believe the commentators, has not an idea, scarcely an epithet, that he can call his own; and yet he is, in the best sense, one of the classics of English literature. He had exquisite felicity of choice; his dictionary had no vulgar word in it, no harsh one, but all culled from the luckiest moods of poets, and with a faint but delicious aroma of association; he had a perfect sense of sound, and one idea without which all the poetic outfit (*si absit prudentia*)[4] is of little avail,—that of combination and arrangement, in short, of art. The poets from whom he helped himself have no more claim to any of his poems as wholes, than the various beauties of Greece (if the old story were true) to the Venus of the artist.

Imagination, as we have said, has more virtue to keep a book alive than any other single faculty. Burke is rescued from the usual doom of orators, because his learning, his experience, his sagacity are rimmed with a halo by this bewitching light behind the intellectual eye from the highest heaven of the brain. Shakespeare has impregnated his common sense with the steady glow of it, and answers the mood of youth and age, of high and low, immortal as that dateless substance of the soul he wrought in. To have any chance of lasting, a book must satisfy, not merely some fleeting fancy of the day, but a constant longing and hunger of human nature; and it needs only a superficial study of literature to be convinced that real fame depends rather on the sum of an author's powers than on any brilliancy of

3. Although the modern reader is likely to grant Lowell his point about Churchill and Cowper, he may come up short over this judgment of Guido Cavalcanti (*ca.* 1250–1300). Since Ezra Pound focused modern attention on Cavalcanti, both by virtue of his criticism and through his exquisite translations of poems like "Donna me prega" ("A Lady Asks Me"), critical estimates of Cavalcanti have been much higher. One might say that in these comments generally, Lowell is expressing his century's distaste for the kind of intellectual poetry written by the metaphysical poets, for example.

4. "If prudence be missing."

special parts. There must be wisdom as well as wit, sense no less than imagination, judgment in equal measure with fancy, and the fiery rocket must be bound fast to the poor wooden stick that gives it guidance if it would mount and draw all eyes. There are some who think that the brooding patience which a great work calls for belonged exclusively to an earlier period than ours. Others lay the blame on our fashion of periodical publication, which necessitates a sensation and a crisis in every number, and forces the writer to strive for startling effects, instead of that general lowness of tone which is the last achievement of the artist.[5] The simplicity of antique passion, the homeliness of antique pathos, seem not merely to be gone out of fashion, but out of being as well. Modern poets appear rather to tease their words into a fury, than to infuse them with the deliberate heats of their matured conception, and strive to replace the rapture of the mind with a fervid intensity of phrase. Our reaction from the decorous platitudes of the last century has no doubt led us to excuse this, and to be thankful for something like real fire, though of stubble; but our prevailing style of criticism, which regards parts rather than wholes, which dwells on the beauty of passages, and, above all, must have its languid nerves pricked with the expected sensation at whatever cost, has done all it could to confirm us in our evil way. Passages are good when they lead to something, when they are necessary parts of the building, but they are not good to dwell in. This taste for the startling reminds us of something which happened once at the burning of a country meeting-house. The building stood on a hill, and, apart from any other considerations, the fire was as picturesque as could be desired. When all was a black heap, licking itself here and there with tongues of fire, there rushed up a farmer gasping anxiously, "Hez the bell fell yit?" An ordinary fire was no more to him than that on his hearthstone; even the burning of a meeting-house, in itself a vulcanic rarity (so long as he was of another parish), could not tickle his outworn palate; but he had hoped for a certain *tang* in the downcome of the bell that might recall the boyish flavor of conflagration. There was something

---

5. The most popular (and lucrative) method of publication in Lowell's day was in serial, or "parts," monthly numbers which required the writer to move from one climax to another to ensure interest.

dramatic, no doubt, in this surprise of the brazen sentinel at his post, but the breathless rustic has always seemed to us a type of the prevailing delusion in aesthetics. Alas! if the bell must fall in every stanza or every monthly number, how shall an author contrive to stir us at last, unless with whole Moscows, crowned with the tintinnabulary crash of the Kremlin? For ourselves, we are glad to feel that we are still able to find contentment in the more conversational and domestic tone of our old-fashioned wood-fire. No doubt a great part of our pleasure in reading is unexpectedness, whether in turn of thought or of phrase; but an emphasis out of place, an intensity of expression not founded on sincerity of moral or intellectual conviction, reminds one of the underscorings in young ladies' letters, a wonder even to themselves under the colder north-light of matronage. It is the part of the critic, however, to keep cool under whatever circumstances, and to reckon that the excesses of an author will be at first more attractive to the many than that average power which shall win him attention with a new generation of men. It is seldom found out by the majority, till after a considerable interval, that he was the original man who contrived to be simply natural,—the hardest lesson in the school of art and the latest learned, if, indeed, it be a thing capable of acquisition at all. The most winsome and wayward of brooks draws now and then some lover's foot to its intimate reserve, while the spirt of a bursting water-pipe gathers a gaping crowd forthwith.

Mr. Carlyle is an author who has now been so long before the world, that we may feel toward him something of the unprejudice of posterity. It has long been evident that he had no more ideas to bestow upon us, and that no new turn of his kaleidoscope would give us anything but some variation of arrangement in the brilliant colors of his style. It is perhaps possible, then, to arrive at some not wholly inadequate estimate of his place as a writer, and especially of the value of the ideas whose advocate he makes himself, with a bitterness and violence that increase, as it seems to us, in proportion as his inward conviction of their truth diminishes.

* * *

Everything that Mr. Carlyle wrote during this first period thrills with the purest appreciation of whatever is brave and beautiful in human nature, with the most vehement scorn of cowardly compromise with things base; and yet, immitigable as his demand for the highest in us seems to be, there is always something reassuring in the humorous sympathy with mortal frailty which softens condemnation and consoles for shortcoming. The remarkable feature of Mr. Carlyle's criticism (see, for example, his analysis and exposition of Goethe's "Helena") is the sleuth-hound instinct with which he presses on to the *matter* of his theme,—never turned aside by a false scent, regardless of the outward beauty of form, sometimes almost contemptuous of it, in his hunger after the intellectual nourishment which it may hide. The delicate skeleton of admirably articulated and related parts which underlies and sustains every true work of art, and keeps it from sinking on itself a shapeless heap, he would crush remorselessly to come at the marrow of meaning. With him the ideal sense is secondary to the ethical and metaphysical, and he has but a faint conception of their possible unity.[6]

By degrees the humorous element in his nature gains ground, till it overmasters all the rest. Becoming always more boisterous and obtrusive, it ends at last, as such humor must, in cynicism. In *Sartor Resartus* it is still kindly, still infused with sentiment; and the book, with its mixture of indignation and farce, strikes one as might the prophecies of Jeremiah, if the marginal comments of the Rev. Mr. Sterne in his wildest mood had by some accident been incorporated with the text. In *Sartor* the marked influence of Jean Paul[7] is undeniable, both in matter and manner. It is curious for one who studies the action and reaction of national literatures on each other, to see the humor of Swift and Sterne and Fielding, after filtering through Richter, reappear in Carlyle with a tinge of Germanism that makes it novel, alien, or even displeasing, as the case may be, to the English mind. Unhappily the bit of *mother* from Swift's vinegar-barrel has had strength enough to sour all the rest.

6. Lowell here means that Carlyle's concern is primarily with content, ethical and metaphysical, and not with organic relatedness of idea and form.

7. Sterne is of course Laurence Sterne (1713–1768), the author of *Tristram Shandy*; Jean Paul is Jean Paul Friedrich Richter (1763–1825), a German writer, who, like Sterne, used an eccentric style, but combined it with highly romantic flights of ideas.

The whimsicality of *Tristram Shandy*, which, even in the original, has too often the effect of forethought, becomes a deliberate artifice in Richter, and at last a mere mannerism in Carlyle.

Mr. Carlyle in his critical essays had the advantage of a well-defined theme, and of limits both in the subject and in the space allowed for its treatment, which kept his natural extravagance within bounds, and compelled some sort of discretion and compactness. The great merit of these essays lay in a criticism based on wide and various study, which, careless of tradition, applied its standard to the real and not the contemporary worth of the literary or other performance to be judged, and in an unerring eye for that fleeting expression of the moral features of character, a perception of which alone makes the drawing of a coherent likeness possible. Their defect was a tendency, gaining strength with years, to confound the moral with the aesthetic standard, and to make the value of an author's work dependent on the general force of his nature rather than on its special fitness for a given task. In proportion as his humor gradually overbalanced the other qualities of his mind, his taste for the eccentric, amorphous, and violent in men became excessive, disturbing more and more his perception of the more commonplace attributes which give consistency to portraiture. His *French Revolution* is a series of lurid pictures, unmatched for vehement power, in which the figures of such sons of earth as Mirabeau and Danton loom gigantic and terrible as in the glare of an eruption, their shadows swaying far and wide grotesquely awful. But all is painted by eruption-flashes in violent light and shade. There are no half-tints, no gradations, and we find it impossible to account for the continuance in power of less Titanic actors in the tragedy like Robespierre, on any theory whether of human nature or of individual character supplied by Mr. Carlyle. Of his success, however, in accomplishing what he aimed at, which was to haunt the mind with memories of a horrible political nightmare, there can be no doubt.

Goethe says, apparently thinking of Richter, "The worthy Germans have persuaded themselves that the essence of true humor is formlessness." Heine had not yet shown that a German might combine the most airy humor with a sense of form as delicate as Goethe's own, and that there was no need to borrow the bow of

Philoctetes [8] for all kinds of game. Mr. Carlyle's own tendency was toward the lawless, and the attraction of Jean Paul made it an over-mastering one. Goethe, we think, might have gone farther, and affirmed that nothing but the highest artistic sense can prevent humor from degenerating into the grotesque, and thence downwards to utter anarchy. Rabelais is a striking example of it. The moral purpose of his book cannot give it that unity which the instinct and forethought of art only can bring forth. Perhaps we owe the masterpiece of humorous literature to the fact that Cervantes had been trained to authorship in a school where form predominated over substance, and the most convincing proof of the supremacy of art at the highest period of Greek literature is to be found in Aristophanes. Mr. Carlyle has no artistic sense of form or rhythm, scarcely of proportion. Accordingly he looks on verse with contempt as something barbarous,—a savage ornament which a higher refinement will abolish, as it has tattooing and nose-rings. With a conceptive imagination vigorous beyond any in his generation, with a mastery of language equalled only by the greatest poets, he wants altogether the plastic imagination, the shaping faculty, which would have made him a poet in the highest sense. He is a preacher and a prophet,—anything you will,—but an artist he is not, and never can be. It is always the knots and gnarls of the oak that he admires, never the perfect and balanced tree.

It is certainly more agreeable to be grateful for what we owe an author, than to blame him for what he cannot give us. But it is sometimes the business of a critic to trace faults of style and of thought to their root in character and temperament,—to show their necessary relation to, and dependence on, each other,—and to find some more trustworthy explanation than mere wantonness of will for the moral obliquities of a man so largely moulded and gifted as Mr. Carlyle. So long as he was merely an exhorter or dehorter, we were thankful for such eloquence, such humor, such vivid or grotesque images, and such splendor of illustration as only he could give; but when he assumes to be a teacher of moral and political philosophy, when he himself takes to compounding the social panaceas he has

8. Philoctetes inherited his bow from Hercules; hence it was very powerful and suited only to hunting large game.

made us laugh at so often, and advertises none as genuine but his own, we begin to inquire into his qualifications and his defects, and to ask ourselves whether his patent pill differs from others except in the larger amount of aloes, or has any better recommendation than the superior advertising powers of a mountebank of genius. Comparative criticism teaches us that moral and aesthetic defects are more nearly related than is commonly supposed. Had Mr. Carlyle been fitted out completely by nature as an artist, he would have had an ideal in his work which would have lifted his mind away from the muddier part of him, and trained him to the habit of seeking and seeing the harmony rather than the discord and contradiction of things. His innate love of the picturesque (which is only another form of the sentimentalism he so scoffs at, perhaps as feeling it a weakness in himself), once turned in the direction of character, and finding its chief satisfaction there, led him to look for that ideal of human nature in individual men which is but fragmentarily represented in the entire race, and is rather divined from the aspiration, forever disenchanted to be forever renewed, of the immortal part in us, than found in any example of actual achievement. A wiser temper would have found something more consoling than disheartening in the continual failure of men eminently endowed to reach the standard of this spiritual requirement, would perhaps have found in it an inspiring hint that it is mankind, and not special men, that are to be shaped at last into the image of God, and that the endless life of the generations may hope to come nearer that goal of which the short-breathed threescore years and ten fall too unhappily short.

* * *

The very qualities, it seems to us, which came so near making a great poet of Mr. Carlyle, disqualify him for the office of historian. The poet's concern is with the appearances of things, with their harmony in that whole which the imagination demands for its satisfaction, and their truth to that ideal nature which is the proper object of poetry. History, unfortunately, is very far from being ideal, still farther from an exclusive interest in those heroic or typical figures which answer all the wants of the epic and the drama and fill their utmost artistic limits. Mr. Carlyle has an unequalled power and vividness in painting detached scenes, in bringing out in their full relief the oddities or peculiarities of character; but he has a far feebler sense of those gradual changes of opinion, that strange communication of sympathy from mind to mind, that subtile influence of very subordinate actors in giving a direction to policy or action, which we are wont somewhat vaguely to call the progress of events. His scheme of history is purely an epical one, where only leading figures appear by name and are in any strict sense operative. He has no conception of the people as anything else than an element of mere brute force in political problems, and would sniff scornfully at that unpicturesque common-sense of the many, which comes slowly to its conclusions, no doubt, but compels obedience even from rulers the most despotic when once its mind is made up. His history of Frederick is, of course, a Fritziad; but next to his hero, the cane of the drill-sergeant and iron ramrods appear to be the conditions which to his mind satisfactorily account for the result of the Seven Years War. It is our opinion, which subsequent events seem to justify, that, had there not been in the Prussian people a strong instinct of nationality, Protestant nationality too, and an intimate conviction of its advantages, the war might have ended quite otherwise. Frederick II. left the machine of war which he received from his father even more perfect than he found it, yet within a few years of his death it went to pieces before the shock of French armies animated by an idea. Again a few years, and the Prussian soldiery, inspired once more by the old national fervor, were victorious. After all, is it not moral forces that make the heaviest battalions, other things being tolerably equal? Were it not for the purely picturesque bias of Mr. Carlyle's genius, for the necessity which his epical treatment lays upon him of always having a protagonist, we should be astonished that an idealist like him should have so little faith in ideas and so much in matter.

Mr. Carlyle's manner is not so well suited to the historian as to the essayist. He is always great in single figures and striking episodes, but there is neither gradation nor continuity. He has extraordinary patience and conscientiousness in the gathering and sifting of his material, but is scornful of commonplace facts and characters, impatient of whatever will not serve for one of his clever sketches, or group well in a more elaborate figurepiece. He sees history, as it were, by flashes of lightning. A single scene, whether a landscape or an interior, a single figure or a wild mob of men, whatever may be snatched by the eye in that instant of intense illumination, is minutely photographed upon the memory. Every tree and stone, almost every blade of grass; every article of furniture in a room; the attitude or expression, nay, the very buttons and shoe-ties of a principal figure; the gestures of momentary passion in a wild throng, —everything leaps into vision under that sudden glare with a painful distinctness that leaves the retina quivering. The intervals are absolute darkness. Mr. Carlyle makes us acquainted with the isolated spot where we happen to be when the flash comes, as if by actual eyesight, but there is no possibility of a comprehensive view. No other writer compares with him for vividness.

Works, II, 56–61, 64–80.

Neoclassical and Romantic

On this question as on so many others, Lowell represents the via media. *A distaste for Pope's poetic diction is almost perfectly balanced by a distrust of a poetry which "seems to have deserted the strong and palpable motions of the common heart, and to have devoted itself to the ecstatic exploration of solitary nerves." The selection is from Lowell's review of Bulwer-Lytton's* The New Timon *for the* North American Review *in April, 1867. Another excerpt from the same review is given below, pages 107–115.*

* * * But the book, which we have made the text of our somewhat erratic discourse, is not only worthy of notice, inasmuch as it may serve as a model, but still more from its own intrinsic merits, and because it is a strong protest against the form and spirit of the poetry now in vogue. It once more unburies the hatchet of the ancient feud between what are called the "natural" and "artificial" schools.

The dispute in this case, as in most others, has concerned itself chiefly about words. An exact definition of the terms used by the contending parties would have been the best flag of truce. Grant the claims of the disciples of Pope, and you blot out at once the writings of the greatest poets that ever lived. Grant those of the opposite party, and you deny to Pope any merit whatever. The cardinal point of the whole quarrel lies in the meaning attached to the single word *poet*. The most potent champion of *Popery* in our day[1] gave by his practice the direct lie to his assumed theory. "The Age of Bronze," the only poem which he wrote professedly upon this model, is unreadable from sheer dulness. His prose letters in the Bowles controversy were far more in Pope's vein and spirit.

1. That is, Byron.

The author of *The New Timon* avows himself a follower of Pope. We shall by-and-by have occasion to try him by his own standard. In the mean time, we shall barely remark, that his allusions to Wordsworth, Tennyson, and Keats are presumptuous and in bad taste. The fact that he misspells the name of one of these poets argues either a very petty affectation, or a shameful unfamiliarity with what he pretends to criticize.

The truth is, that Pope's merit lies in the concinnity and transparency of his style. It is this, rather than the sentiment, which charms. Thousands of readers find no want of orthodoxy in *The Essay on Man*, who would recoil in horror from the rough draught of Bolingbroke,[2] on which it was based. Fancy, purity of diction, conciseness, unfailing wit, all these are Pope's, and they have given him immortality. But these are not essentially the attributes of a poet. In imagination, the crowning faculty of the poet, nay, the one quality which emphatically distinguishes him as such, Pope is wanting. A single example of the pure exercise of this faculty is not to be found in his works.

A profusion of ignorance and bad temper have been lavished on this topic. Had the controversy been understandingly carried on, there would have been no occasion for ill-feeling. One chief blunder has been the defining of authors as belonging to a certain school because they happened to be addicted to the use of a measure consisting of a certain number of feet, yet not the less variable on that account. Dryden, Pope, and Goldsmith are commonly named together,— authors as dissimilar as Chaucer and Racine. Crabbe, Campbell, and Rogers[3] have all three used the same measure, yet are wholly unlike each other and unlike their three predecessors above named. Byron, who also used the "English Heroic" (as it is commonly called) in *The Corsair* and some other poems, presents still another totally distinct variety.

2. Henry St. John, Lord Bolingbroke (1678–1751), English deist, whose ideas, as Lowell wrote, are the source of Pope's poem, but are far less orthodox.

3. George Crabbe (1754–1832), Thomas Campbell (1777–1844), and Samuel Rogers (1763–1855), English poets who also wrote in heroic couplets.

What, then, is the secret of that predilection in the minds of many to that kind of writing which is rather vaguely defined to be "of the Pope school"? Many, no doubt, adhere to it on the ground of its age and respectability,—a prejudice which Pope himself has admirably satirized. Others commend it on the score of its being easily comprehensible. Others again are charmed with what they esteem the grace, precision, and finish of its metre.

It is unquestionably the prime merit of style, that it conveys the author's ideas exactly and clearly. But after all, the ideas to be conveyed are of more importance than the vehicle, and it is one thing to see distinctly what they are, and another to comprehend them. Undoubtedly the first requisite is that they be worth comprehending. Once establish the principle, that easiness of comprehension is the chief merit in literature, and the lowest order of minds will legislate for the exercise of that faculty which should give law to the highest. Every new book would come to us with the ambiguous compliment, that it was adapted to the meanest capacity. We have never been able to appreciate with any tolerable distinctness the grounds of that complacent superiority implied in the confession of not being able to understand an author, though we have frequently seen airs assumed on the strength of that acknowledged incapacity. One has a vision of the lame, halt, and blind dropping compassionate fourpences into the hats of their unmutilated fellow-citizens. Apelles[4] judged rightly in pronouncing Alexander's horse a better critic than his master. The equine was more liberal than the imperial appreciation.

The merit of Pope is wholly of the intellect. There is nothing in him of that finer instinct which characterizes all those who, by universal consent, have been allowed as great poets, and have received the laurel from posterity. His instinct is rather that of a man of taste than of genius. In reading Shakespeare, we do not concern ourselves as to the particular shape which his thoughts assume. That is wholly a secondary affair. We should as soon think of criticizing the peculiar form of a tree or a fern. Though we may not be able to codify the law which governs them, we cannot escape a feeling of the harmony and fitness resulting from an obedience to that law.

4. The most celebrated of the Greek painters, fourth century B.C.

There is a necessity for their being of that precise mould, and no other, which peremptorily overrules all cavil. With Pope, on the contrary, the form is what first demands notice. It is here that the poet has put forth his power and displayed his skill. He makes verses by a voluntary exercise of the intellect, rather than from the overflow of the creative power. We feel that he had his choice between several forms of expression, and was not necessarily constrained to the one he has selected. His verses please us, as any display of mental skill and vigor never fails to do. The pleasure he gives us is precisely similar to that we derive from reading *The Spectator*, and is in both cases the result of identical causes. His apothegms are wholly of the intellect, and that, too, of the intellect applied to the analysis of artificial life. He does not, according to Bacon's definition of poetry, "conform the shows of things to the desires of the soul." Yet he dwells in the shows of things rather than in the substances, and conforms them, sometimes despotically, to the necessities of his satire. He jeers and flouts the artificial life which he sees. He mocks at it, as Lucian[5] derided Zeus,—an atheist to the gods of the day, with no settled belief in any higher gods. He does not confute the artificial by comparison with any abiding real. He impales all contemporary littlenesses upon the sharp needles of his wit, and in his poems, as in an entomological cabinet, we see preserved all the ugly insects of his day. He does not tacitly rebuke meanness by looking over it to the image of a perennial magnanimity. He does not say sternly, "Get thee behind me, Satan!" but mischievously affixes a stinging epigram to horns, hoof, and tail, and sends Beelzebub away ridiculous. His inkstand was his arsenal, but it was not his to use it in Luther's hearty catapultic fashion.

We do not so much commend *The New Timon*, then, as being a return to purer models, but as a protest against the excesses into which the prevailing school had degenerated. Latterly, poetry seems to have deserted the strong and palpable motions of the common heart, and to have devoted itself to the ecstatic exploration of solitary nerves,—the less tangible, the better. The broad view attainable from those two peaks of Parnassus, which Sir John Denham sensibly

5. Sophist writer, second century B.C.

defined to be "Nature and Skill," seems to be wellnigh neglected.[6] Our young poets, instead of that healthy glow of cheek earned only by conversation with the robust air of the summit, and the labor incident to the rugged ascent, seem to value themselves upon their paleness, and to think him the better man who has spent most time in peering dizzily down the dark rifts and chasms round the base of the mountain, or in gazing into the potential millstones of its solid rock. The frailer the tissue of the feeling, the greater the merit in tracing it to its extremes,—a spiderlike accomplishment at best. Their philosophy (if we call that so which they esteem as such, and which is certainly nothing else) stands in grave need of Philotas's leaden soles.[7] One might almost expect to see them blown out of existence by the incautious puffs of their own publisher or clique. The farther the poet can put himself out of the common, the more admirable is he. The reflections of Perillus in his bull, of Regulus in his hogshead, or of Clarence in his malmsey-butt,[8] would furnish an ample stock in trade to any young poet. Or a nearer approach to nature and the interests of every-day life might be found in the situation of Terence McHugh, buried alive at the bottom of a well, and so finding it to be the residence of at least one unquestionable verity.

Mystery, too, has become a great staple with our poets. Every thing must be accounted for by something more unaccountable. Grandgousier's simple and pious theory to explain the goodliness of

6. Sir John Denham (1615–1659), "On Mr. John Fletcher's *Works*," lines 39–40 (last two lines of the poem):

'Twas this the ancients meant: Nature and Skill
Are the two tops of their Parnassus Hill.

7. Philotas was a friend of Alexander the Great, executed in 330 B.C. for plotting against Alexander's life; what his "leaden soles" were, I have been unable to determine. The style of poetry that Lowell is attacking here would seem to be very like that of Edgar Allan Poe, who was surely the major American exponent of the "exposed ganglia" school of poetry. Lowell was sympathetic to Poe himself, but could and did scourge writers like Percival who lacked Poe's genius but had a full measure of his sensibility.

8. Perillus, inventor of the brazen bull in which Phalaris roasted his victims, was the first to be so roasted; M. Attilius Regulus was martyred in Carthage in 250 B.C.; Clarence was drowned in a butt of Malmsey by Richard III. Again, the criticism would seem to be directed at Poe, but see Percival's "The Suicide."

Friar John's nose would hardly pass muster now. The "mystery of our being" has become a favorite object of contemplation. Egoism has been erected into a system of theology. Self has been deified like the Egyptian onion,—

> Nascuntur in hortis
> Numina.[9]

Poets used to look before and after. Now, their eyes are turned wholly inward, and ordinarily with as useful result as was attained by the Brahmin who spent five years in the beatific inspection of his own navel. Instead of poems, we have lectures on the morbid anatomy of self. Nature herself must subscribe their platform of doctrine, and that not "for substance, scope, and aim," but without qualification. If they turn their eyes outward for a moment, they behold in the landscape only a smaller image of themselves. The mountain becomes a granite Mr. Smith, and the ocean (leaving out the salt) a watery Mr. Brown,—in other words a Mr. Brown with the milky particles of his composition deducted. A new *systema mundi*[10] is constructed, with the individual idiosyncrasy of the poet for its base. And, to prolong the delight of swallowing all this sublime mystification, enraptured simplicity prays fervently, with the old epicure, for the neck of a crane. Fortunately, that of a goose will suffice.

Nor has our mother tongue been safe from the experimental incursions of these philosophers. They have plunged so deeply into the well of English undefiled as to bring up the mud from the bottom. This they call "Saxon," and infuse portions of it into their productions, deepening the turbid obscurity. Strange virtues have been discovered in compound words, and the greater the incongruity of the mixture, the more potent the conjuration. Phrases, simple or unmeaning enough in themselves, acquire force and become mystical by repetition, like the three *Iods* of the Cabalists, or the Κόξγ "Ομπαξ[11] of the Eleusinian mysteries. Straightforwardness has become a prose

9. "Deity is born in a garden."   10. "World system."

11. Although these words are associated with the Eleusinian mysteries, chiefly by Hesychius, they are ritual phrases, meaningless in themselves. Κόγξ, for example, is thought to be an onomatopoeic word derived from the sound a pebble makes when dropped in a voting urn.

virtue. The poet wanders about his subject, looks for it where he knows it is not, and avoids looking where he knows it is, like a child playing at hide-and-seek, who, to lengthen the pleasure of the hunt, peeps cautiously into keyholes and every other impossible place, leaving to the last the table, under which lurks, with ostrich-like obviousness, the object of his search. It had been fortunate for Columbus, could he have recruited his crews with such minstrels, whose only mutiny would have been at the finding of the expected continent. We have seen the translation of a Hindoo deed which affords an exact parallel to such poetry. It begins with a general history of India, diverges into a system of theology, exhausts all the grantor's knowledge of natural history and astronomy, relates a few fables on different subjects, throws in a confused mass of compound words (one of them containing one hundred and fifty-two syllables), and finally reveals the object of this ponderous legal machine in a postscript of six lines conveying an acre or two of land.

The New Timon, if not the exact reverse of all this, is at least a resolute attempt in the opposite direction. We do not believe it possible to revive the style of Pope. It was a true mirror of its own age, but it would imperfectly reflect ours. Its very truth then would make it false now. The *petere fontes*[12] points to other springs than these. Much less do we believe in confining literature to the strait channel of any one period. That is surely a very jejune kind of conservatism, which, with the Athenian Ephorus,[13] would cut every new string added to the lyre. The critics have too often assumed the office of Ephorus in our commonwealth of letters, and have unfortunately become impressed with the notion, that this chordisection is the chief part of their official duty. As Selden[14] said that equity was measured by the length of my Lord Chancellor's foot for the time being, so has judgment in these cases been too often meted, if not by the length, at least by the susceptibility, of my Lord Ephorus's ear. If every Phrynio[15] had been thus dealt with, the lyre would

12. "Search for the source."

13. Lowell is slightly in error here; the Ephors was the sovereign board of overseers in Sparta.

14. John Selden (1584–1654), English prose writer.

15. Perhaps Phrynis, a dithyrambic musician satirized by Aristophanes in *The Frogs*.

never have lost that pristine simplicity and compactness, and that facility at making itself understood, which characterized it when it was a plain tortoise-shell, ere idle Hermes had embarrassed and perplexed it with a single string.

North American Review, LXIV (April 1847), 467–473; reprinted in *The Round Table* (Boston: Richard G. Badger, The Gorham Press, 1913), 134–143.

Humor, Wit, Fun, and Satire

The psychology of humor was one of the provinces of criticism in which Lowell was almost completely at home. This essay, one of his Lowell Institute lectures of 1855, is an attempt at a definition and a theoretical justification of humor. As we might expect, Lowell's center of interest is with zeugma and syllepsis, particularly with the examples he gives from Hood and Marvell. These were his own delights. But the essay ranges concisely yet incisively through the entire history of comedy and is filled with both theoretical and practical criticism.

Hippel,[1] the German satirist, divides the life of man into five periods, according to the ruling desires which successively displace each other in the human soul. Our first longing, he says, is for trousers, the second for a watch, the third for an angel in pink muslin, the fourth for money, and the fifth for a "place" in the country. I think he has overlooked one, which I should be inclined to place second in point of time—the ambition to escape the gregarious nursery, and to be master of a chamber to one's self.

How charming is the memory of that cloistered freedom, of that independence, wide as desire, though, perhaps, only ten feet by twelve! How much of future tastes and powers lay in embryo there in that small chamber! It is the egg of the coming life. There the young sailor pores over the *Narratives of Remarkable Shipwrecks*, his longing heightened as the storm roars on the roof, or blows its trumpet in the chimney. There the unfledged naturalist gathers his

1. Theodore Gottlieb von Hippel (1741–1796). It is perhaps worth noting that although Lowell decries eccentricity in style (see above, pp. 60–69), he is remarkably well read in such writers as Hippel, Jean Paul, Sterne, etc. Clearly, this essay suggests that his own tastes run in that direction, but that he felt he must repress such ideas in favor of "high seriousness."

menagerie, and empties his pockets of bugs and turtles that awaken the ignorant animosity of the housemaid. There the commencing chemist rehearses the experiment of Schwarz,[2] and singes off those eyebrows which shall some day feel the cool shadow of the discoverer's laurel. There the antiquary begins his collections with a bullet from Bunker Hill, as genuine as the epistles of Phalaris,[3] or a button from the coat-tail of Columbus, late the property of a neighboring scarecrow, and sold to him by a schoolmate, who thus lays the foundation of that colossal fortune which is to make his children the ornaments of society. There the potential Dibdin or Dowse[4] gathers his library on a single pendulous shelf—more fair to him than the hanging gardens of Babylon. There stand *Robinson Crusoe*, and *Gulliver*, perhaps *Gil Blas*, Goldsmith's Histories of Greece and Rome, *Original Poems for Infant Minds*, the *Parent's Assistant*, and (for Sundays) the *Shepherd of Salisbury Plain*, with other narratives of the excellent Mrs. Hannah More[5] too much neglected in maturer life. With these are admitted also *Viri Romae*, Nepos, Florus, Phaedrus, and even the Latin grammar,[6] because they *count*, playing here upon these mimic boards the silent but awful part of second and third conspirators, a rôle in after years assumed by statelier and more celebrated volumes—the "books without which no gentleman's library can be complete."

I remember (for I must call my memory back from this garrulous rookery of the past to some perch nearer the matter in hand) that when I was first installed lord of such a manor, and found myself the Crusoe of that remote attic-island, which for near thirty years was to be my unmolested hermitage, I cast about for works of art with which to adorn it. The garret, that El Dorado of boys, supplied me with some prints which had once been the chief ornament of my

2. Berthold Schwarz (*fl.* 1320) brought gunpowder into practical use.

3. Phalaris, the tyrant of Agrigentum in Sicily; his supposed epistles were shown to be forgeries in 1699.

4. Thomas F. Dibdin (1776–1807) and Thomas Dowse (1772–1856), English and American bibliophiles.

5. Mrs. More (1745–1833), was the author of innumerable tracts aimed at the moral reformation of the poor.

6. All of these are common grammar school texts of Lowell's day, with no more bibliographic value than the fact that they "count," as he says.

great-grandfather's study, but which the growth of taste or luxury had banished from story to story till they had arrived where malice could pursue them no farther. These were heads of ancient worthies —Plato, Pythagoras, Socrates, Seneca, and Cicero, whom, from a prejudice acquired at school, I shortly banished again with a *quousque tandem!*[7] Besides those I have mentioned, there were Democritus and Heraclitus,[8] which last, in those days less the slave of tradition, I called Heraclìtus—an error which my excellent schoolmaster (I thank him for it) would have expelled from my head by the judicious application of a counter-irritant; for he regarded the birch as a kind of usher to the laurel, as indeed the true tree of knowledge, whose advantages could Adam have enjoyed during early life, he had known better than to have yielded to the temptation of any other.

Well, over my chimney hung those two antithetical philosophers —the one showing his teeth in an eternal laugh, while the tears on the cheek of the other forever ran, and yet, like the leaves on Keats's Grecian urn, could never be shed. I used to wonder at them sometimes, believing, as I did firmly, that to weep and laugh had been respectively the sole business of their lives. I was puzzled to think which had the harder time of it, and whether it were more painful to be under contract for the delivery of so many tears *per diem*, or to compel that ἀνήριθμον γέλασμα.[9] I confess, I pitied them both; for if it be difficult to produce on demand what Laura Matilda would call the "tender dew of sympathy," he is also deserving of compassion who is expected to be funny whether he will or no. As I grew older, and learned to look on the two heads as types, they gave rise to many reflections, raising a question perhaps impossible to solve: whether the vices and follies of men were to be washed away, or exploded by a broadside of honest laughter. I believe it is Southwell[10] who says that Mary Magdalene went to Heaven by water, and it is certain

7. "*. . . abatere, Catilina, patientia nostra.*" "How long, Catilina, do you intend to abuse our patience?" (Cicero, *Against Catiline*, I. i).

8. Called, respectively, the "laughing" and the "weeping" philosophers.

9. "Many-twinkling smile" (Aeschylus, *Prometheus Bound*, 90).

10. Robert Southwell, S. J. (1561–1591), English Catholic poet, wrote a poem to Magdalene, but did not use that particular image. Perhaps Lowell is thinking of Crashaw here; both his "The Weeper" and "The Tear" present this conceit.

that the tears that people shed for themselves are apt to be sincere; but I doubt whether we are to be saved by any amount of vicarious salt water, and, though the philosophers should weep us into another Noah's flood, yet commonly men have lumber enough of self-conceit to build a raft of, and can subsist a good while on that beautiful charity of their own weaknesses in which the nerves of conscience are embedded and cushioned, as in similar physical straits they can upon their fat.

On the other hand, man has a wholesome dread of laughter, as he is the only animal capable of that phenomenon—for the laugh of the hyena is pronounced by those who have heard it to be no joke, and to be classed with those γέλασματα ἀγέλαστα[11] which are said to come from the other side of the mouth. Whether, as Shaftesbury will have it, ridicule be absolutely the test of truth or no, we may admit it to be relatively so, inasmuch as by the *reductio ad absurdum* it often shows that abstract truth may become falsehood, if applied to the practical affairs of life, because its relation to other truths equally important, or to human nature, has been overlooked. For men approach truth from the circumference, and, acquiring a knowledge at most of one or two points of that circle of which God is the center, are apt to assume that the fixed point from which it is described is that where they stand. Moreover, "Ridentem dicere verum, quid vetat?"[12]

I side rather with your merry fellow than with Dr. Young[13] when he says:

> Laughter, though never censured yet as sin,
>
> . . . .
>
> Is half immoral, be it much indulged;
> By venting spleen, or dissipating thought,
> It shows a scorner, or it makes a fool;
> And sins, as hurting others or ourselves.
>
> . . . .
>
> Yet would'st thou laugh (but at thine own expense),
> This counsel strange should I presume to give—
> "Retire, and read thy Bible, to be gay."

11. "Laughs which are not laughs."
12. "Why not smile when you tell the truth?" (Horace, *Satire I.* i. 24).
13. Edward Young (1683–1769), lugubrious English poet.

With shame I confess it, Dr. Young's *Night Thoughts* have given me as many hearty laughs as any humorous book I ever read.

Men of one idea,—that is, who have one idea at a time,—men who accomplish great results, men of action, reformers, saints, martyrs, are inevitably destitute of humor; and if the idea that inspires them be great and noble, they are impervious to it. But through the perversity of human affairs it not infrequently happens that men are possessed by a single idea, and that a small and rickety one—some seven months' child of thought—that maintains a querulous struggle for life, sometimes to the disquieting of a whole neighborhood. These last commonly need no satirist, but, to use a common phrase, make themselves absurd, as if Nature intended them for parodies on some of her graver productions. For example, how could the attempt to make application of mystical prophecy to current events be rendered more ridiculous than when we read that two hundred years ago it was a leading point in the teaching of Lodowick Muggleton, a noted heresiarch, "that one John Robins was the last great antichrist and son of perdition spoken of by the Apostle in Thessalonians"? I remember also an eloquent and distinguished person who, beginning with the axiom that all the disorders of this microcosm, the body, had their origin in diseases of the soul, carried his doctrine to the extent of affirming that all derangements of the macrocosm likewise were due to the same cause. Hearing him discourse, you would have been well nigh persuaded that you had a kind of complicity in the spots upon the sun, had he not one day condensed his doctrine into an epigram which made it instantly ludicrous. "I consider myself," exclaimed he, "personally responsible for the obliquity of the earth's axis." A prominent Come-outer once told me, with a look of indescribable satisfaction, that he had just been kicked out of a Quaker meeting. "I have had," he said, "Calvinistic kicks and Unitarian kicks, Congregational, Presbyterian, and Episcopalian kicks, but I never succeeded in getting a Quaker kick before." Could the fanaticism of the collectors of worthless rarities be more admirably caricatured than thus unconsciously by our passive enthusiast?

I think no one can go through a museum of natural curiosities, or see certain animals, without a feeling that Nature herself has a sense of the comic. There are some donkeys that one can scarce look at without laughing (perhaps on Cicero's principle of the *haruspex haruspicem*) 14 and feeling inclined to say, "My good fellow, if you will keep my secret I will keep yours." In human nature, the sense of the comic seems to be implanted to keep man sane, and preserve a healthy balance between body and soul. But for this, the sorcerer Imagination or the witch Enthusiasm would lead us an endless dance.

The advantage of the humorist is that he cannot be a man of one idea—for the essence of humor lies in the contrast of two. He is the universal disenchanter. He makes himself quite as much the subject of ironical study as his neighbor. Is he inclined to fancy himself a great poet, or an original thinker, he remembers the man who dared not sit down because a certain part of him was made of glass, and muses smilingly, "There are many forms of hypochondria." This duality in his mind which constitutes his intellectual advantage is the defect of his character. He is futile in action because in every path he is confronted by the horns of an eternal dilemma, and is apt to come to the conclusion that nothing is very much worth the while. If he be independent of exertion his life commonly runs to waste. If he turn author, it is commonly from necessity; Fielding wrote for money, and *Don Quixote* was the fruit of a debtors' prison.

It seems to be an instinct of human nature to analyze, to define, and to classify. We like to have things conveniently labeled and laid away in the mind, and feel as if we knew them better when we have named them. And so to a certain extent we do. The mere naming of things by their appearance is science; the knowing them by their qualities is wisdom; and the being able to express them by some intense phrase which combines appearance and quality as they affect the imagination through the senses by impression, is poetry. A great part of criticism is scientific, but as the laws of art are only echoes of the laws of nature, it is possible in this direction also to arrive at real knowledge, or, if not so far as that, at some kind of classification that may help us toward that excellent property—compactness of mind.

Addison has given the pedigree of humor: the union of truth and

14. "The soothsayer on soothsayers" (Cicero, *De Divinatione*).

goodness produces wit; that of wit with wrath produces humor. We should say that this was rather a pedigree of satire. For what trace of wrath is there in the humor of Chaucer, Shakespeare, Rabelais, Cervantes, Sterne, Fielding, or Thackeray? The absence of wrath is the characteristic of all of them. Ben Jonson says that

> . . . when some one peculiar quality
> Doth so possess a man that it doth draw
> All his affects, his spirits, and his powers
> In their confluctions all to run one way,
> This may be truly said to be a humor.[15]

But this, again, is the definition of a humorous character,—of a good subject for the humorist—such as Don Quixote, for example.

Humor—taken in the sense of the faculty to perceive what is humorous, and to give it expression—seems to be greatly a matter of temperament. Hence, probably, its name. It is something quite indefinable, diffused through the whole nature of the man; so that it is related of the great comic actors that the audience begin to laugh as soon as they show their faces, or before they have spoken a word.

The sense of the humorous is certainly closely allied with the understanding, and no race has shown so much of it on the whole as the English, and next to them the Spanish—both inclined to gravity. Let us not be ashamed to confess that, if we find the tragedy a bore, we take the profoundest satisfaction in the farce. It is a mark of sanity. Humor, in its highest level, is the sense of comic contradiction which arises from the perpetual comment which the understanding makes upon the impressions received through the imagination. Richter, himself a great humorist, defines it thus:

> Humor is the sublime reversed; it brings down the great in order to set the little beside it, and elevates the little in order to set it beside the great—that it may annihilate both, because in the presence of the infinite all are alike nothing. Only the universal, only totality, moves its deepest spring, and from this universality, the leading component of Humor, arise the mildness and forbearance of the humorist toward the individual, who is lost in the mass of little consequence; this also distinguishes the Humorist from the Scoffer.

15. *Every Man Out of His Humor*, Induction, 105–109.

We find it very natural accordingly to speak of the breadth of humor, while wit is, by the necessity of its being, as narrow as a flash of lightning, and as sudden. Humor may pervade a whole page without our being able to put our finger on any passage, and say, "It is here." Wit must sparkle and snap in every line, or it is nothing. When the wise deacon shook his head, and said that "there was a good deal of human natur' in man," he might have added that there was a good deal more in some men than in others. Those who have the largest share of it may be humorists, but wit demands only a clear and nimble intellect, presence of mind, and a happy faculty of expression. This perfection of phrase, this neatness, is an essential of wit, because its effect must be instantaneous; whereas humor is often diffuse and roundabout, and its impression cumulative, like the poison of arsenic. As Galiani[16] said of Nature that her dice were always loaded, so the wit must throw sixes every time. And what the same Galiani gave as a definition of sublime oratory may be applied to its dexterity of phrase: "It is the art of saying everything without being clapt in the Bastile, in a country where it is forbidden to say anything." Wit must also have the quality of unexpectedness. "Sometimes," says Barrow,[17] "an affected simplicity, sometimes a presumptuous bluntness, gives it being. Sometimes it rises only from a lucky hitting upon what is strange, sometimes from a crafty wresting of obvious matter to the purpose. Often it consisteth in one knows not what, and springeth up one can hardly tell how. Its ways are unaccountable and inexplicable, being answerable to the numberless rovings of fancy and windings of language."

That wit does not consist in the discovery of a merely unexpected likeness or even contrast in word or thought, is plain if we look at what is called a *conceit*, which has all the qualities of wit—except wit. For example, Warner,[18] a contemporary of Shakespeare, wrote a long poem called "Albion's England," which had an immense contemporary popularity, and is not without a certain value still to the student of language. In this I find a perfect specimen of what is

16. Ferdinando Galiani (1728–1787), Italian economist.
17. Sir John Barrow (1764–1848), English explorer and writer.
18. William Warner (1558?–1609), English writer.

called a conceit. Queen Eleanor strikes Fair Rosamond, and Warner says,

> Hard was the heart that gave the blow,
> Soft were those lips that bled.

This is bad as fancy for precisely the same reason that it would be good as a pun. The comparison is unintentionally wanting in logic, just as a pun is intentionally so. To make the contrast what it should have been,—to make it coherent, if I may use that term of a contrast, —it should read:

> Hard was the *hand* that gave the blow,
> Soft were those lips that bled,

for otherwise there is no identity of meaning in the word "hard" as applied to the two nouns it qualifies, and accordingly the proper logical copula is wanting. Of the same kind is the conceit which belongs, I believe, to our countryman General Morris:[19]

> Her heart and morning broke together
> In tears,

which is so preposterous that had it been intended for fun we might almost have laughed at it. Here again the logic is unintentionally violated in the word *broke*, and the sentence becomes absurd, though not funny. Had it been applied to a merchant ruined by the failure of the United States Bank, we should at once see the ludicrousness of it, though here, again, there would be no true wit:

> His heart and Biddle[20] broke together
> On 'change.

Now let me give an instance of true fancy from Butler, the author of *Hudibras*, certainly the greatest wit who ever wrote English, and whose wit is so profound, so purely the wit of thought, that we might almost rank him with the humorists, but that his genius was cramped with a contemporary, and therefore transitory, subject. Butler says of loyalty that it is

19. George Pope Morris (1802–1864), American journalist and versifier.
20. Nicholas Biddle (1786–1844), president of the Second Bank of the United States, 1823–1839.

> True as the dial to the sun
> Although it be not shined upon.

Now what is the difference between this and the examples from Warner and Morris which I have just quoted? Simply that the comparison turning upon the word *true*, the mind is satisfied, because the analogy between the word as used morally and as used physically is so perfect as to leave no gap for the reasoning faculty to jolt over. But it is precisely this jolt, not so violent as to be displeasing, violent enough to discompose our thoughts with an agreeable sense of surprise, which it is the object of a pun to give us. Wit of this kind treats logic with every possible outward demonstration of respect—"keeps the word of promise to the ear, and breaks it to the sense." Dean Swift's famous question to the man carrying the hare, "Pray, sir, is that your own hare or a wig?" is perfect in its way. Here there is an absolute identity of sound with an equally absolute and therefore ludicrous disparity of meaning. Hood[21] abounds in examples of this sort of fun—only that his analogies are of a more subtle and perplexing kind. In his elegy on the old sailor he says,

> His head was turned, and so he chewed
> His pigtail till he died.

This is inimitable, like all the best of Hood's puns. To the ear it is perfect, but so soon as you attempt to realize it to yourself, the mind is involved in an inextricable confusion of comical *non sequiturs*. And yet observe the gravity which which the forms of reason are kept up in the "and so." Like this is the peddler's recommendation of his ear-trumpet:

> I don't pretend with horns of mine,
> Like some in the advertising line,
> To magnify sounds on such marvelous scales
> That the sounds of a cod seem as large as a whale's.
>
> There was Mrs. F. so very deaf
> That she might have worn a percussion cap
> And been knocked on the head without hearing it snap.
> Well, I sold her a horn, and the very next day
> She heard from her husband in Botany Bay.

21. Thomas Hood (1799–1845), English poet and humorist.

Again, his definition of deafness:

> Deaf as the dog's ears in Enfield's "Speaker."

So, in his description of the hardships of the wild beasts in the menagerie,

> Who could not even prey
> In their own way,

and the monkey-reformer 'who resolved to set them all free, beginning with the lion; but

> Pug had only half unbolted Nero,
> When Nero bolted him.

In Hood there is almost always a combination of wit and fun, the wit always suggesting the remote association of ideas, and the fun jostling together the most obvious concords of sound and discords of sense. Hood's use of words reminds one of the kaleidoscope. Throw them down in a heap, and they are the most confused jumble of unrelated bits; but once in the magical tube of his fancy, and, with a shake and a turn, they assume figures that have the absolute perfection of geometry. In the droll complaint of the lover,

> Perhaps it was right to dissemble your love,
> But why did you kick me down-stairs?

the self-sparing charity of phrase that could stretch the meaning of the word "dissemble" so as to make it cover so violent a process as kicking down-stairs has the true zest, the tang, of contradiction and surprise. Hood, not content with such a play upon ideas, would bewitch the whole sentence with plays upon words also. His fancy has the enchantment of Huon's horn,[22] and sets the gravest conceptions a-capering in a way that makes us laugh in spite of ourselves.

Andrew Marvell's satire upon the Dutch is a capital instance of wit as distinguished from fun. It rather exercises than tickles the mind, so full is it of quaint fancy:

22. *Huon of Bordeau*, a late metrical romance, was translated into English about 1540 by Sir John Bourchier, Lord Berners. Huon's horn sounded by itself.

Holland, that scarce deserves the name of land,
As but the offscouring of the British sand,
And so much earth as was contributed
By English pilots when they heaved the lead,
Or what by ocean's slow alluvium fell
Of shipwrecked cockle and the muscle-shell;
This indigestful vomit of the sea
Fell to the Dutch by just propriety.

Glad, then, as miners who have found the ore
They, with mad labor, fished their land to shore,
And dived as desperately for each piece
Of earth as if't had been of ambergreese,
Collecting anxiously small loads of clay,
Less than what building swallows bear away,
Or than those pills which sordid beetles roll,
Transfusing into them their dunghill soul.

How did they rivet with gigantic piles
Thorough the centre their new-catchèd miles,
And to the stake a struggling country bound,
Where barking waves still bait the forcèd ground!

* * *

Yet still his claim the injured ocean laid,
And oft at leap-frog o'er their steeples played,
As if on purpose it on land had come
To show them what's their *mare liberum;*

* * *

The fish ofttimes the burgher dispossessed,
And sate, not as a meat, but as a guest;
And oft the Tritons and the sea-nymphs saw
Whole shoals of Dutch served up for *cabillau,*[23]
And, as they over the new level ranged,
For pickled herring pickled Heeren changed.

* * *

Therefore necessity, that first made kings,
Something like government among them brings;

* * *

23. French for "codfish."

> And as among the blind the blinkard reigns
> So rules among the drownèd he that drains;
>
> * * *
>
> Who best could know to pump on earth a leak,
> Him they their lord and Country's Father speak.
> To make a bank was a great plot of state,
> Invent a shovel and be a magistrate;
> Hence some small dykegrave, unperceived, invades
> The power, and grows, as 't were, a king of spades.[24]

I have cited this long passage not only because Marvell (both in his serious and comic verse) is a great favorite of mine, but because it is as good an illustration as I know how to find of that fancy flying off into extravagance, and that nice compactness of expression, that constitute genuine wit. On the other hand, Smollett is only funny, hardly witty, where he condenses all his wrath against the Dutch into an epigram of two lines:

> Amphibious creatures, sudden be your fall,
> May man undam you and God damn you all.

Of satirists I have hitherto said nothing, because some, perhaps the most eminent of them, do not come under the head either of wit or humor. With them, as Juvenal said of himself, "facit indignatio versus,"[25] and wrath is the element, as a general rule, neither of wit nor humor. Swift, in the epitaph he wrote for himself, speaks of the grave as a place "ubi saeva indignatio cor ulterius lacerare nequeat,"[26] and this hints at the sadness which makes the ground of all humor. There is certainly humor in *Gulliver*, especially in the chapters about the Yahoos, where the horses are represented as the superior beings, and disgusted at the filthiness of the creatures in human shape. But commonly Swift, too, must be ranked with the wits, if we measure him rather by what he wrote than by what he was. Take this for an example from the "Day of Judgment":

> With a whirl of thought oppressed
> I sank from reverie to rest,
> A horrid vision seized my head,

24. From Marvell's "The Character of Holland," lines 1–50.
25. "Indignation is the cause of my verses" (Juvenal, *Satire I*, 79).
26. "Where savage indignation cannot further rend his heart."

I saw the graves give up their dead!
Jove, armed with terrors, burst the skies,
And thunder roars, and lightning flies!
Amazed, confused, its fate unknown,
The world stands trembling at his throne!
While each pale sinner hung his head,
Jove, nodding, shook the heavens, and said:
"Offending race of human kind;
By nature, reason, learning, blind,
You who through frailty stepped aside,
And you who never fell through pride,
You who in different sects were shammed,
And come to see each other damned
(So some folks told you—but they knew
No more of Jove's designs than you)—
The world's mad business now is o'er,
And I resent these pranks no more—
I to such blockheads set my wit!
I damn such fools! Go, go! you're bit!"

The unexpectedness of the conclusion here, after the somewhat solemn preface, is entirely of the essence of wit. So, too, is the sudden flirt of the scorpion's tail to sting you. It is almost the opposite of humor in one respect—namely, that it would make us think the solemnest things in life were sham, whereas it is the sham-solemn ones which humor delights in exposing. This further difference is also true: that wit makes you laugh once, and loses some of its comicality (though none of its point) with every new reading, while humor grows droller and droller the oftener we read it. If we cannot safely deny that Swift was a humorist, we may at least say that he was one in whom humor had gone through the stage of acetous fermentation and become rancid. We should never forget that he died mad.[27] Satirists of this kind, while they have this quality of true humor, that they contrast a higher with a lower, differ from their nobler brethren inasmuch as their comparison is always to the disadvantage of the

27. Lowell is of course mistaken here—the common mistake of nineteenth-century writers about Swift. Modern research has indicated clearly that Swift was not insane while he was actively writing.

higher. They purposely disenchant us—while the others rather show us how sad a thing it is to be disenchanted at all.

Ben Jonson, who had in respect of sturdy good sense very much the same sort of mind as his namesake Samuel, and whose "Discoveries," as he calls them, are well worth reading for the sound criticism they contain, says:

> The parts of a comedy are the same with [those of] a tragedy, and the end is partly the same; for they both delight and teach: the comics are called *didaskaloi*[28] of the Greeks, no less than the tragics. Nor is the moving of laughter always the end of comedy; that is rather a fowling for the people's delight, or their fooling. For, as Aristotle says rightly, the moving of laughter is a fault in comedy; a kind of turpitude that depraves some part of a man's nature without a disease. As a wry face moves laughter, or a deformed vizard, or a rude clown dressed in a lady's habit and using her actions; we dislike and scorn such representations, which made the ancient philosophers ever think laughter unfitting in a wise man. So that what either in the words or sense of an author, or in the language and actions of men, is awry or depraved, does strongly stir mean affections, and provoke for the most part to laughter. And therefore it was clear that all insolent and obscene speeches, jests upon the best men, injuries to particular persons, perverse and sinister sayings (and the rather, unexpected) in the old comedy did move laughter, especially where it did imitate any dishonesty, and scurrility came forth in the place of wit; which, who understands the nature and genius of laughter cannot but perfectly know.

He then goes on to say of Aristophanes that

> he expressed all the moods and figures of what was ridiculous, oddly. In short, as vinegar is not accounted good till the wine be corrupted, so jests that are true and natural seldom raise laughter with that beast the multitude. They love nothing that is right and proper. The farther it runs from reason or possibility, with them the better it is.

In the latter part of this it is evident that Ben is speaking with a little bitterness. His own comedies are too rigidly constructed according to Aristotle's dictum, that the moving of laughter was a fault in comedy. I like the passage as an illustration of a fact undeniably true, that Shakespeare's humor was altogether a new thing

28. "Teachers."

upon the stage, and also as showing that satirists (for such were also
the writers of comedy) were looked upon rather as censors and
moralists than as movers of laughter. Dante, accordingly, himself in
this sense the greatest of satirists, in putting Horace among the five
great poets in limbo, qualifies him with the title of *satiro*.

But if we exclude the satirists, what are we to do with Aristophanes? Was he not a satirist, and in some sort also a censor? Yes;
but, as it appears to me, of a different kind, as well as in a different
degree, from any other ancient. I think it is plain that he wrote his
comedies not only to produce certain political, moral, and even
literary ends, but for the fun of the thing. I am so poor a Grecian that
I have no doubt I miss three quarters of what is most characteristic
of him. But even through the fog of the Latin on the opposite page
I can make out more or less of the true lineaments of the man. I can
see that he was a master of language, for it becomes alive under his
hands—puts forth buds and blossoms like the staff of Joseph, as it
does always when it feels the hand and recognizes the touch of its
legitimate sovereigns. Those prodigious combinations of his are like
some of the strange polyps we hear of that seem a single organism;
but cut them into as many parts as you please, each has a life of its
own and stirs with independent being. There is nothing that words
will not do for him; no service seems too mean or too high. And then
his abundance! He puts one in mind of the definition of a compe-
tence by the only man I ever saw who had the true flavor of Falstaff
in him—"a million a minute and your expenses paid." As Burns
said of himself, "The rhymes come skelpin, rank and file." Now they
are as graceful and sinuous as water-nymphs, and now they come
tumbling head over heels, throwing somersaults, like clowns in the
circus, with a "Here we are!" I can think of nothing like it but
Rabelais, who had the same extraordinary gift of getting all the *go*
out of words. They do not merely play with words; they romp with
them, tickle them, tease them, and somehow the words seem to like
it.

I dare say there may be as much fancy and fun in *The Clouds* or
The Birds, but neither of them seems so rich to me as *The Frogs*, nor
does the fun anywhere else climb so high or dwell so long in the
region of humor as here. Lucian makes Greek mythology comic, to be

sure, but he has nothing like the scene in "The Frogs" where Bacchus is terrified with the strange outcries of a procession celebrating his own mysteries, and of whose dithyrambic songs it is plain he can make neither head nor tail. Here is humor of the truest metal, and, so far as we can guess, the first example of it. Here is the true humorous contrast between the ideal god and the god with human weaknesses and follies as he had been degraded in the popular conception. And is it too absurd to be within the limits even of comic probability? Is it even so absurd as those hand-mills for grinding out so many prayers a minute which Huc and Gabet saw in Tartary? [29]

Century, XLVII (November 1893), 125–131; reprinted in Albert Mordell (ed.), *The Function of the Poet and Other Essays by James Russell Lowell* (Boston and New York: Houghton Mifflin, 1920), pp. 33–60.

29. Evariste Régis Huc and Joseph Gabet were among the first Westerners to travel through Tartary, between 1844 and 1846. Huc's account, *Souvenirs d'un voyage dans la Tartarie* (Paris, 1850), is one of the most delightful of travel books.

Didacticism and Literature

Although Lowell in these verses, first published in the Atlantic Monthly *in 1857, makes very clear his attitude toward didactic verse, he only very rarely practiced what he here preached. Yet he was perfectly aware of his inconsistency, as his (anonymous) comment on himself in* A Fable for Critics *proves:*

> *There is Lowell, who's striving Parnassus to climb*
> *With a whole bale of* isms *tied together with rhyme,*
> *He might get on alone, spite of brambles and boulders,*
> *But he can't with that bundle he has on his shoulders,*
> *The top of the hill he will ne'er come nigh reaching*
> *Till he learns the distinction 'twixt singing and preaching.*

THE ORIGIN OF DIDACTIC POETRY

When wise Minerva still was young
    And just the least romantic,
Soon after from Jove's head she flung
    That preternatural antic,
'T is said, to keep from idleness
    Or flirting, those twin curses,
She spent her leisure, more or less,
    In writing po——, no, verses.

How nice they were! to rhyme with *far*
    A kind *star* did not tarry;
The mètre, too, was regular
    As schoolboy's dot and carry;
And full they were of pious plums,
    So extra-super-moral,—
For sucking Virtue's tender gums
    Most tooth-enticing coral.

A clean, fair copy she prepares,
  Makes sure of moods and tenses,
With her own hand,—for prudence spares
  A man-(or woman)-uensis;
Complete, and tied with ribbons proud,
  She hinted soon how cosy a
Treat it would be to read them loud
  After next day's Ambrosia.

The Gods thought not it would amuse
  So much as Homer's Odyssees,
But could not very well refuse
  The properest of Goddesses;
So all sat round in attitudes
  Of various dejection,
As with a *hem*! the queen of prudes
  Began her grave prelection.

At the first pause Zeus said, "Well sung!—
  I mean—ask Phoebus,—*he* knows."
Says Phoebus, "Zounds! a wolf's among
  Admetus's merinos!
Fine! very fine! but I must go;
  They stand in need of me there;
Excuse me!" snatched his stick, and so
  Plunged down the gladdened ether.

With the next gap, Mars said, "For me
  Don't wait,—naught could be finer,
But I'm engaged at half past three,—
  A fight in Asia Minor!"
Then Venus lisped, "I'm sorely tried,
  These duty-calls are vip'rous;
But I *must* go; I have a bride
  To see about in Cyprus."

Then Bacchus,—"I must say good-bye,
  Although my peace it jeopards;
I meet a man at four, to try
  A well-broke pair of leopards."
His words woke Hermes. "Ah!" he said,
"I *so* love moral theses!"

Then winked at Hebe, who turned red,
  And smoothed her apron's creases.

Just then Zeus snored,—the Eagle drew
  His head the wing from under;
Zeus snored,—o'er startled Greece there flew
  The many-volumed thunder.
Some augurs counted nine, some, ten;
  Some said 't was war, some, famine,
And all, that other-minded men
  Would get a precious ——.

Proud Pallas sighed, "It will not do;
  Against the Muse I've sinned, oh!"
And her torn rhymes sent flying through
  Olympus's back window.
Then, packing up a peplus clean,
  She took the shortest path thence,
And opened, with a mind serene,
  A Sunday-school in Athens.

The verses? Some in ocean swilled,
  Killed every fish that bit to 'em;
Some Galen caught, and, when distilled,
  Found morphine the residuum;
But some that rotted on the earth
  Sprang up again in copies,
And gave two strong narcotics birth,
  Didactic verse and poppies.

Years after, when a poet asked
  The Goddess's opinion,
As one whose soul its wings had tasked
  In Art's clear-aired dominion,
"Discriminate," she said, "betimes;
  The Muse is unforgiving;
Put all your beauty in your rhymes,
  Your morals in your living."

Works, XIII, 238–241.

Poetic Diction

To berate Augustan poetic diction was already by Lowell's time to beat a dead horse; still, his comments on the subject in his essay, "Dryden" (North American Review, 1868), help to round out this summary of Lowell's principles of criticism.

* * * Has [Dryden's] influence on our literature, but especially on our poetry, been on the whole for good or evil? If he could have been read with the liberal understanding which he brought to the works of others, I should answer at once that it had been beneficial. But his translations and paraphrases, in some ways the best things he did, were done, like his plays, under contract to deliver a certain number of verses for a specified sum. The versification, of which he had learned the art by long practice, is excellent, but his haste has led him to fill out the measure of lines with phrases that add only to dilute, and thus the clearest, the most direct, the most manly versifier of his time became, without meaning it, the source (*fons et origo malorum*) [1] of that poetic diction from which our poetry has not even yet recovered. I do not like to say it, but he has sometimes smothered the child-like simplicity of Chaucer under feather-beds of verbiage. What this kind of thing came to in the next century, when everybody ceremoniously took a bushel-basket to bring a wren's egg to market in, is only too sadly familiar. It is clear that his natural taste led Dryden to prefer directness and simplicity of style. If he was too often tempted astray by Artifice, his love of Nature betrays itself in many an almost passionate outbreak of angry remorse. Addison tells us that he took particular delight in the reading of our old English ballads. What he valued above all things was Force, though in his haste he is willing to make a shift with its counterfeit, Effect.

1. "Source and spring of evil."

As usual, he had a good reason to urge for what he did: "I will not excuse, but justify myself for one pretended crime for which I am liable to be charged by false critics, not only in this translation, but in many of my original poems,—that I Latinize too much. It is true that when I find an English word significant and sounding, I neither borrow from the Latin or any other language; but when I want at home I must seek abroad. If sounding words are not of our growth and manufacture, who shall hinder me to import them from a foreign country? I carry not out the treasure of the nation which is never to return; but what I bring from Italy I spend in England: here it remains, and here it circulates; for if the coin be good, it will pass from one hand to another. I trade both with the living and the dead for the enrichment of our native language. We have enough in England to supply our necessity; but if we will have things of magnificence and splendor, we must get them by commerce. . . . Therefore, if I find a word in a classic author, I propose it to be naturalized by using it myself, and if the public approve of it the bill passes. But every man cannot distinguish betwixt pedantry and poetry; every man, therefore, is not fit to innovate."[2] This is admirably said, and with Dryden's accustomed penetration to the root of the matter. The Latin has given us most of our canorous words, only they must not be confounded with merely sonorous ones, still less with phrases that, instead of supplementing the sense, encumber it. It was of Latinizing in this sense that Dryden was guilty. Instead of stabbing, he "with steel invades the life." The consequence was that by and by we have Dr. Johnson's poet, Savage,[3] telling us,—

> "In front, a parlor meets my entering view,
> Opposed a room to sweet refection due";—

2. *A Discourse of Epick Poetry.* "If the *public* approve." "On ne peut pas admettre dans le développement des langues aucune revolution artificielle et sciemment exécutée; il n'y a pour elles ni conciles, ni assemblées délibérantes; on ne les réforme pas comme une constitution vicieuse." (Renan, *De l'Origine du Langage*, p. 95.) [Lowell's note.]

"No artificial and scientifically executed revolution may be admitted as part of the development of language; languages need no councils or deliberative assemblies; they are not reformed like an evil constitution."

3. Richard Savage (d. 1743), English poet. Johnson's biography of Savage was published in 1744.

Dr. Blacklock[4] making a forlorn maiden say of her "dear," who is out late,—

> "Or by some apoplectic fit deprest
> Perhaps, alas! he seeks eternal rest";—

and Mr. Bruce, in a Danish war-song, calling on the Vikings to "assume their oars." But it must be admitted of Dryden that he seldom makes the second verse of a couplet the mere trainbearer to the first, as Pope was continually doing. In Dryden the rhyme waits upon the thought; in Pope and his school the thought curtsys to the tune for which it is written.

Works, III, 101–104.

4. Dr. Thomas Blacklock (1721–1791), Scottish poet.

III

AMERICAN PROVINCIAL

Review of Halleck's *Alnwick Castle*

This excerpt and the succeeding selections illustrate one of the most common themes in Lowell's criticism—the various forms of provincialism in American letters and the absolute necessity not to lower critical standards in the judgment of American writings. From 1845, when this review appeared, until after the Civil War—in other words, during the most fruitful period of Lowell's writing of criticism—he constantly referred to this theme. The statements range from the vigorous denunciation of mediocrity in this essay to his bemused backward glance at the phenomenon in his essay on Percival. Of all Lowell's contributions to American criticism, perhaps this treatment of American provincialism is, finally, his most significant. By holding up high standards for American writers and insisting upon universal literary values, he performed the highest function of a traditionalist in criticism. The need for just such a discerning voice and discriminating taste in American criticism was greatest then, and Lowell's performance of his necessary function was constant and unremitting. Many other of the essays in this collection, notably A Fable for Critics, *touch upon the same matter, but it is such a significant part of Lowell's criticism that this section exhibits chronologically his development as a guardian of literary standards.*

The subject of this essay, Fitz-Greene Halleck (1790–1867), was a banker and a poet—in that order. He might very well stand today for the "Tompkins" Lowell cites as his mythic representative of the man on the street as poetaster.

The system of criticism which obtains among us, and which tries the productions of one American mind by those of another, instead of comparing them with some immutable standard, or with the best examples in the same kind with which other countries have supplied us, has done great injury to the cause of true Art in our Republic. It was our misfortune to be in too great a hurry to have a literature

103

of our own. We had built up an army and navy: we must build up a literature. It was further unanimously resolved that we had a national literature; and a score or two of terrified Tompkinses, who might otherwise have remained life-long the contented anchorites of the poet's corner in a village newspaper, were suddenly snatched up and set to bear the pitiless storm of foreign fun and criticism on the bald top of our American Parnassus. Henceforth every new work was measured by the Tompkins yardstick; and the "precision and elegance," "the refined dignity," "the exuberant humor" of Tompkins became proverbial. Under these favorable circumstances, the gentlemen thus ostracised from among their fellow citizens for their country's fame, plucked up courage, and by dint of well-directed energy succeeded in founding what we may call the Tompkins dynasty of American literature. A court dress of a certain innocuous drab-color was established, and any author who was detected without this Tompkins uniform was forthwith arrested and thrown into a review, or set in the pillory of the newspapers. The heresy of originality was everywhere industriously hunted out and crushed; and independence of judgment in criticism was declared to be immoral, or, what was far worse, anti-Tompkinsian. If man, woman, or child, was unwilling to receive the opinion of a Tompkins, how great an insensibility did it display to the numerous privileges we enjoy!

The truth is that we shall never have a literature until we become thoroughly persuaded that we have not yet done all that is needful to that end, and that it requires at least as much previous study and preparation to criticise a work of art as a steam engine. We must get over our cant of always speaking of certain of our authors and artists as if they filled up the majestic round of that circle which even Shakespeare did not touch at all points. We must no longer endeavor to measure anything really great by the rushlight criticism of the Tompkinses, but must look on it in the broad frank sunshine of honest desire after Truth. We must get rid also of this unhealthy hankering after a National Literature. The best and most enduring literature is that which has no nationality except of the heart,— that which is the same under all languages and under all skies. A poet's inspiration has no more intimate connection with the country in which he chances to be born, than with the village or the garret in which he may dwell. While yet a sojourner among our mists and shadows, he is made citizen of a higher country, whose language is an interpreter throughout the universe, and which has no words mean enough to express our paltry nationalities, nor indeed any thoughts but such as are primitive and universal.

The office of poet, then, is the highest to which any man, in these latter times, may aspire. The poet has taken the place of the prophet, and, without laying any claim to immediate inspiration, he yet, by force of seeing the heart of those mysteries whose shell only is visible to others, instructs and prophesies with an authority felt if not acknowledged. If his words inculcate no truth directly, yet, by their innate harmony with universal laws, and by the sweet domestic privilege with which they enter the heart without knocking, they clarify the conscience, and inspire us with an eagerness after truth, as would a tender or majestic landscape in outward nature. Let no man then take up the lyre hastily or irreverently, still less let him make its chords answerable for a gross and vulgar music.

In America we have been accustomed to confer the title of poet as if it were of no more value or import than a trumpery "Honorable" or "Excellency." We have something like a thousand individuals in the country to whom the critics of the newspapers and magazines concede the name. But there are half a dozen who form a kind of inner circle, who already, though in the prime of life, enjoy all the advantages of a posthumous fame, and whose portraits smile with an embarrassed air opposite all the title-pages of selections from American poets. It is to these that our critics periodically challenge England to produce a parallel. It is these who are led out and exhibited when the intelligent foreigner inquires after our poets— honest, matter-of-fact-looking men, as the poets of a business people ought to be.

Mr. Halleck has had the ill fortune to be one of these frontis- piecial exemplars. We call it ill fortune, for it is as unhappy a thing for a man to receive more as to receive less than his deserts. But in speaking of Mr. Halleck we shall treat him as if he were a young author now for the first time making his appearance before the world. What his reputation *has been* is nothing to us: what it *ought* to be is the only question. To have been always considered and treated as one of Fame's joint-heirs, and then to find that Fame has cut one off with a shilling, is worse than to have known the truth from the beginning.

If the volume before us, then, were the work of a young author, (and we should remember that in this case the real age of Mr. H. renders all faults less inexcusable) is there anything in it that would lead us to prophesy great things of his future career? To this question we must frankly and readily answer, no. There is none of that exuberance here, that seeming waste of energy, which characterises the springtide of a great poet's heart, of whose innumerable blossoms few will ever become anything more useful than an ornament and token of immortal plenty. Here is none of that felicitous sympathy of ear and eye which gives every word and image and harmonic invention of his as good a right to be in the world, as any blossom or bird or sigh of the wind can have. Here is none of that fine reverence which overhangs his heart like the broad free sky, now bare, simple, sustaining, now sprinkled thick with starry hopes and aspirations, and always the bestower of dignity, courage, and the calm majesty of entire humbleness. Here is none of that enthusiasm for his art which makes success but an argument for less self-glory, and which turns a whole unbelieving world's scorn into a stepping-stone to a higher peak of inspiration.

Broadway Journal, I (May 3, 1845), 281–282.

Review of Bulwer-Lytton's
The New Timon

Although this is a review and is therefore quite occasional criticism, it carries the question raised in the review of Halleck concerning the materialism of the American reading public to its larger significance: the identification of American themes, and the steps necessary to convert the raw material of the American experience into literature. This essay was written twenty years after the Halleck review and only two years after the American Civil War. It is therefore not surprising that it has a completely different tone, but the magnitude of the change is surprising: "There is no fear but we shall have a national literature soon enough." Essentially, Lowell identifies one American trait as the major impediment to great literature—the desire to hurry things up, to fabricate from the instant, to reject tradition instead of cultivating it. Clearly, Lowell believes that a national tradition and myth will grow up in America regardless, and that the tradition will be one with other traditions. When the American writer can use these true archetypes unselfconsciously, he will be mature. Lowell is stating positively what Henry James was to state negatively twelve years later in his essay Hawthorne. *Apparently the roots did not mature quite as quickly as Lowell would have had them.*

Another part of this review, on Augustan and Romantic manner, was excerpted earlier (pp. 70–77).

Fletcher of Saltoun's[1] apothegm would hardly answer for our latitude; song has no super-legislative force among us. The walls of one of our great political parties were thought to have risen from their ruins a few years ago, like those of Thebes, to the sound of singing; but this Amphionic masonwork was found not to resist

1. Andrew Fletcher (1655–1716), Scottish patriot. I have not been able to locate his apothegm.

our changeful climate. Our national melodies are of African descent.[2] If our brains be stolen, it will never be through our ears; the Sirens had sung in vain to a Nantucket Ulysses. We remember a nomadic minstrel, a dweller in tents, who picked up a scanty subsistence by singing "Proud Dacre sailed the sea," and "The Hunters of Kentucky," on election days, and at Commencements and musters. But he was merely the satellite to a dwarf, and the want of the aspirate betrayed a Transatlantic origin. Moreover, only slender-witted persons were betrayed into the extravagance of the initiatory ninepence, the shrewder citizens contenting themselves with what gratuitous music leaked through the rents in the canvas.

Mr. Barlow,[3] we believe, had a beatific vision of the nine immigrant Muses, somewhere on the top of the Alleghany mountains. A judicious selection of place;—for only in some such inaccessible spot would they be safe from the constable. Without question, a ship's captain importing nine ladies with so scanty a wardrobe would be compelled to give bonds. With us the bard has no chartered sacredness; cotton and the stocks refuse to budge at his vaticinations. The newspapers are our Westminster Abbey, in whose Poets' Corner the fugitive remains of our verse-makers slumber inviolate,—a sacred privacy, uninvaded save by the factory-girl or the seamstress. The price-current is our *Paradise of Daintie Devyces*;[4] and that necromancer, who might fill his pockets by contracting to bring back Captain Kidd to tell us where he buried treasure, would starve, were he to promise merely

> To call up him who left half told
> The story of Cambuscan bold.

2. A wonderfully prophetic comment, but it would be giving Lowell too much credit to believe he offers it straightforwardly.

3. Joel Barlow (1754–1812), American poet. His "The Vision of Columbus" (1787) locates the Muses in that unlikely spot, and the whole notion was expanded into the epic *Columbiad* (1807).

4. Published in 1576, the *Paradise of Daintie Devyces* was one of the works that were largely responsible for the flowering of poetry in sixteenth-century England; Lowell's comparison with the "price-current," a book used in many manufacturers to establish values, suggests that American poetry of his day is mercantile: the poetry is for hire, and business is closer to true poetry.

It is not that we are an antipoetical people. Our surveyors might fix that stigma upon us, by whose means Graylock becomes Saddle-mountain on the maps, and Tahconic is converted from his paganism, and undergoes baptism as Mount Everett. All the world over, the poet is not what he was in ruder times. If he ever unite, as formerly, the bardic and sacerdotal offices, that conjunction forebodes nothing graver than the publication of a new hymn-book. The sanctity of the character is gone; the garret is no safer than the first-floor. Every dun and tipstaff sets at naught the precedent of the great Emathian conqueror.[5] Poetry once concerned itself with the very staple of existence. Now it is a thing apart. The only time we were ever conscious that the Muse did still sometimes cast a halo round every-day life was when we heard the "Village Blacksmith" congratulating himself, that Longfellow had had his smithy "drawed as nateral as a picter."

Many respectable persons are greatly exercised in spirit at the slow growth of what they are pleased to call a national literature. They conjecture of the forms of our art from the shape of our continent, reversing the Platonic method. They deduce a literary from a geographical originality; a new country, therefore new thoughts. A *reductio ad absurdum* would carry this principle to the extent of conforming an author's mind to the house he lived in. These enthusiasts wonder, that our mountains have not yet brought forth a poet, forgetting that a mouse was the result of the only authentic mountainous parturition on record.[6] Others, more hopeful, believe the continent to be at least seven months gone with a portentous minstrel, who, according to the most definite augury we have seen, shall "string" our woods, mountains, lakes, and rivers, and then "wring" from them (no milder term, or less suggestive of the laundry, will serve) notes of "autochthonic significance." We have heard of one author, who thinks it quite needless to be at the pains of a jury of matrons on the subject, as he makes no doubt that the child of Destiny is already born, and that he has discovered in himself the genuine *Terrae Filius*.

Never was there so much debate of a national literature as during

5. That is, Alexander the Great.
6. An echo of Horace, *Ars Poetica*, line 184.

the period immediately succeeding our Revolution, and never did the Titan of native song make such efforts to get himself born as then. Hopkinson, Freneau, Paine,[7] and Barlow were the result of that travail. It was not the fault of the country; it was even newer then than now, and its shape (if that was to be effectual in the matter) was identical. Nor was zeal or pains wanting. It is believed that the "Conquest of Canaan"[8] and the "Vision of Columbus" were read by authentic men and women. The same pariotism which refused the tea swallowed the poetry. The same hardy spirit, the same patient endurance, which brought the Pilgrims to Plymouth rock, was not yet gone out of the stock. A nation which had just gone through a seven years' war could undergo a great deal.

But we must come sooner or later to the conclusion, that literature knows no climatic distinctions of that external kind which are presupposed in this clamor for a national literature. The climate in which the mind of an author habitually dwells—whether it be that of Greece, Asia, Italy, Germany, or England—moulds the thought and the expression. But that which makes poetry poetry, and not prose, is the same everywhere. The curse of Babel fell not upon the Muse. Climate gives inexorable laws to architecture, and all importations from abroad are contraband of nature, sure to be satirized by whatever is native to the soil. There is but one sky of song, and the growth of the tropics will bear the open air of the pole. For man is the archetype of poetry. Its measure and proportion, as Vitruvius[9] reports of the Doric pillar, are borrowed of him. Natural scenery has little hand in it, national peculiarities none at all. Not Simoïs or Scamander,[10] but Helen, Priam, Andromache, give divinity to the tale of Troy. Dante's Italicism is his lame foot. Shakespeare would fare ill, were we to put him upon proof of his Englishry. So homo-

7. Francis Hopkinson (1707–1785), Philip Freneau (1752–1832), and Thomas Paine (1737–1809) were all pamphleteers of the American Revolution; all but Paine turned their hands to poetry during and after the war, along with Barlow and Dwight.

8. A heroic poem published in 1785 by Timothy Dwight (1752–1817).

9. Vitruvius Pollio (*fl.* 40 B.C.), author of a ten-book treatise on architecture. His remark on the proportions of the Doric column may be found in Bk. IV, Chapter I, section 6.

10. Rivers on the plain of Troy.

geneous is the structure of the mind, that Sir William Jones[11] conceived Odin and Fo to be identical.

There is no fear but we shall have a national literature soon enough. Meanwhile, we may be sure that all attempts at the forcible manufacture of such a product (especially out of physical elements) will be as fruitless as the *opus magnum* of the alchemists. The cunning of man can only adroitly combine the materials lying ready to his hand. It has never yet compassed the creation of any seed, be it never so small. As a nation, we are yet too full of hurry and bustle. The perfectly balanced tree can grow only in the wind-bound shelter of the valley. Our national eagerness for immediate results infests our literature. We wish to taste the fruit of our culture, and as yet plant not that slower growth which ripens for posterity. The mental characteristic of the pioneer has become engrained in us, outliving the necessity which begot it. Everywhere the blackened stumps of the clearing jut out like rocks amid the yellow waves of our harvest. We have not learned to wait; our chief aim is to produce, and we are more careful of quantity than quality. We cannot bring ourselves to pinch off a part of the green fruit, that the ripe may be more perfect. To be left behind is the opprobrium; we desire an immediate effect. Hence, a large part of that mental energy, which would else find its natural bent in literary labor, turns to the lecture-room or the caucus, or mounts that ready-made rostrum of demagogues, the stump. If any man think he has an errand for the general ear, he runs at full speed with it, and delivers such fragments as he has breath left to utter. If we adopt a Coptic emblem, and paste it on the front of our pine-granite propylaea, it must have wings, implying speed. That symbol of wiser meaning, with finger upon lip, is not for us. We break our eggs, rather than await the antiquated process of incubation. We pull up what we have planted, to see if it have taken root. We fell the primeval forest, and thrust into the ground a row of bean-poles for shade. We cannot spare the time to sleep upon anything; we must be through by daylight. Our boys debate the tariff and the war. Scarce yet beyond the lacteal age, they leave hoop, and ball, and taw, to discuss the tea and coffee tax.

We find talking cheaper than writing, and both easier than

11. Great comparative philologist (1746–1794).

thinking. We talk everlastingly; our magazines are nothing but talk, and that of a flaccid and Polonian fibre. The Spartans banished the unfortunate man who boasted that he could talk all day. With us he had been sure of Congress or the Cabinet. No petty African king is fonder of palaver than the sovereign people. Our national bird is of no kin to the falcon of the Persian poet, whose taciturnity made him of more esteem than the nightingale. We are always in haste; we build a railroad from the cradle to the grave. Our children cannot spare time to learn spelling; they must take the short cut of phonography. In architecture, we cannot abide the slow teachings of the fitness of things; we parody the sacred growth of ages with our inch-board fragilities,

> Their rafters sprouting on the shady side,

and every village boasts its *papier-maché* cathedral. Our railroad-cars are our best effort in this kind yet,—the emblems of hurry. The magnetic telegraph is of our invention, a message upon which, travelling westward, outstrips Time himself. The national trait is aptly symbolized by a gentleman we know of, who has erected his own funeral monument (what a titbit for honest old Weever!) and inscribed upon it an epitaph of his own composing, leaving vacant only the date of his demise. This is to be beforehand with Death himself. We remember only the *occasio celeris* 12 and not the *ars longa* of the adage. Hence a thousand sciolists for one scholar, a hundred improvisators for one poet. Every thing with us ripens so rapidly, that nothing of ours seems very old but our boys.

A sandy diffuseness of style among our speakers and writers is the result of this hurry. We try to grasp a substantial handful here and there, and it runs through our fingers. How our legislators contrive to sit out each other's speeches we could never conceive. Who reads those interminable debates is a question of harder solution than what song the Sirens sang. In our callower years, we sit down beside them, like the clown at the river's edge. But we soon learn the *labitur et labetur.* 13 Providence, which has made nothing that is not food for something else, has doubtless so constituted some systems

12. "Opportunity passes quickly."
13. Figurative, of time, "it slips away and will continue to slip away."

as that they can devour and digest these. The constituency of Buncombe, if it find time to read all that is addressed to it, must be endowed with an unmatched longevity. It must be a community of oldest inhabitants. Yet, with all this tendency to prosing, we love concentration, epigrammatic brevity, antithesis. Hence the potency of phrases among us; a nimble phrase in a trice trips up our judgment; "masterly inactivity," "conquering a peace," "our country right or wrong," and the like. Talleyrand's plan for settling the Restoration on a firm basis would have done for us:— "C'est bien, c'est très bien, et tout ce qu'il faut maintenant, ce sont les feux d'artifice *et un bon mot pour le peuple.*" [14]

Under such circumstances, we need hardly expect a sudden crop of epics. We must have something that we can bolt. And we need not trouble ourselves about the form or the growth of our literature. The law of demand and supply is as inexorable here as in every thing else. The forcing system, we may be sure, is out of place. Art cannot make heartwood under glass. Above all, let not our young authors be seduced into the belief, that there can be any nationality in the great leading ideas of art. The mind has one shape in the Esquimaux and the Anglo-Saxon, and that shape it will strive to impress on its creations. If we evaporate all that is watery, and the mere work of absorption, in the mythologies and early histories of the different races of men, we shall find one invariable residuum at bottom. The legendary age of Greece may find a parallel in our own recent history, and "Old Put," [15] the wolf-killer, at whose door all the un-fathered *derring-does* of the time are laid, is no mean Yankee trans-lation of Theseus. Doubtless, a freer and more untrammelled spirit will be the general characteristic of our literature, and it is to be hoped that it will get its form and pressure before our social life begins (as it inevitably must) to fence itself from the approaches of license behind a stricter and more rigid conventionality. Where external distinctions are wanting, men intrench themselves the more deeply in forms. When this reaction makes itself felt in our litera-ture, let us hope to find the works of our authors as conscientous

14.· "It's fine, fine, and all we need now are fireworks and catch phrases for the masses."

15. Israel Putnam. See note 13, p. 21.

in finish, as they should be bold in design and outline. As for expecting that our mountains and lakes and forests should inoculate our literature with their idiosyncrasies, we may as reasonably look to find the mental results of our corduroy roads there, a speculation which might confirm itself by certain metres we have lately been favored with by our poets. The "surface of the country,"of which we used to read so much in our geographies, never made and never marred a poet. There are mountains as good as Chimborazo and Popocatapetl in the poet's mind. Were Skiddaw and Ben Lomond the lay-figures from which Bunyan painted his Delectable Mountains? Or was the dead marsh-level of parts of *The Excursion* an infection from those hills among which Wordsworth has spent his life? Shakespeare had done better than travel in Egypt when he said,—

> Ye pyramids, built up with newer might,
> To me are nothing novel, nothing strange;
> *Ye are but dressings of a former sight.*[16]

Hitherto our literature has been chiefly imitative and artificial; we have found no better names for our authors than the American Scott, the American Mrs. Hemans, the American Wordsworth.[17] There is nothing to fear from too great license as yet. At present, every English author can see a distorted reflection of himself here,— a something like the eidolons of the Homeric Hades, not ghosts precisely, but unsubstantial counterparts. He finds himself come round again, the Atlantic Ocean taking the function of the Platonic year. Our authors are the best critics of their brethren (or parents) on the other side of the water, catching as they do only what is exaggerated in them. We are in need of a literary declaration of independence; our literature should no longer be colonial.

Let us not be understood as chiming in with that foolish cry of the day, that authors should not profit by example and precedent,— a cry which generally originates with some hardy imitator, the

16. Sonnet 123.

17. Cooper was often called the American Scott; Lydia Huntley Sigourney (1791–1865) the American Mrs. Hemans. Felicia Hemans (1793–1835) was a very popular English poetess. Bryant was most often identified as the American Wordsworth.

"stop thief!" with which he would fain distract attention from himself. It is the tower-stamp of an original mind, that it gives an awakening impulse to other original minds. Memory was the mother of the Muses. Montaigne says, "In my country, when they would decipher a man that has no sense, they say such a one has no memory." But to imitate the works of another is not to profit by them. It is making them our dungeon. It is better to smell of the lamp than of the library. Yet the most original writers have begun in some sort as imitators, and necessarily so. They must first learn to speak by watching the lips and practising the tones of others. This once acquired, the native force within masters and moulds the instrument. Shakespeare's early poems have the trick and accent of Spenser. Milton's *Comus* was written with a quill from the Swan of Avon's wing, dipped in Jonson's ink. But even the imitations of an original mind give no small oracle of originality. The copyist mimics mannerisms only. Like Crashaw's minstrel,

> From this to that, from that to this, he flies.[18]

The original mind is always consistent with itself. Michel Angelo, cramped by the peculiar shape of a piece of marble which another sculptor had roughed out for a conception of his own, conquered something characteristic out of that very restraint, and the finished statue proclaimed its author. The poet, like the sculptor, works in one material, and there, in the formless quarry of the language, lie the divine shapes of gods and heroes awaiting the master's evocation.

North American Review, LXIV (April 1847), 460–467; reprinted in *The Round Table* (Boston: Richard G. Badger, The Gorham Press, 1913), pp. 123–134.

18. Line 119 of "Music's Duel," the first poem in *The Delights of the Muses*. The poem tells of a singing contest between a minstrel and a nightingale. This line mocks the minstrel's capacity to keep pace with the bird.

Nationality in Literature

Lowell seized the occasion to review his friend Longfellow's novel Kavanagh *for the* North American Review *as an opportunity for a long essay on the more hopeful prospects for American literature. The title given this excerpt was the running title used by the* North American Review.

Time is figured with scythe, hour-glass, wallet, and slippery fore-lock. He is allegorized as the devourer of his own offspring. But there is yet one of his functions, and that not the least important, which wants its representative among his emblems. To complete his symbolical outfit, a sieve should be hung at his back. Busy as he must be at his mowing, he has leisure on his hands, scents out the treach-erous saltpetre in the columns of Thebes, and throws a handful of dust over Nineveh, that the mighty hunter Nimrod may not, wanting due rites of sepulture, wander, a terrible shadow, on this side the irrepassable river. A figurative personage, one would say, with quite enough to do already, without imposing any other duty upon him. Yet it is clear that he finds opportunity also thoroughly to sift men and their deeds, winnowing away with the untired motion of his wings, monuments, cities, empires, families, generations, races, as chaff.

We must go to the middle of a child's bunch of cherries to be sure of finding perfect fruit. The outer circles will show unripened halves, stabs of the robin's bill, and rain-cracks, so soon does the ambition of quantity deaden the nice conscience of quality. Indeed, with all of us, men as well as children, amount passes for something of intrinsic value. But Time is more choice, and makes his sieve only the coarser from age to age. One book, one man, one action, shall often be all of a generation busy with sword, pen, and trowel, that has not slipped irrevocably through the ever-widening meshes.

116

We are apt to forget this. In looking at the literature of a nation, we take note only of such names as Dante, Shakespeare, Goethe, not remembering what new acres have been added to the wide chaff-desert of Oblivion, that we may have these great kernels free from hull and husk. We overlook the fact that contemporary literature has not yet been put into the sieve, and quite gratuitously blush for the literary shortcomings of a whole continent. For ourselves, we have long ago got rid of this national (we might call it hemispherical) sensitiveness, as if there were any thing in our western halfworld which stimulated it to produce great rivers, lakes, and mountains, mammoth pumpkins, Kentucky giants, two-headed calves, and what not, yet at the same time rendered it irremediably barren of great poets, painters, sculptors, musicians, and men generally. If there be any such system of natural compensations, whereby geological is balanced against human development, we may, at least, console ourselves with the anticipation, that America can never (from scientifically demonstrable inability) incur the odium of mothering the greatest fool.

There is, nevertheless, something agreeable in being able to shift the responsibility from our own shoulders to the broader ones of a continent. When anxious European friends inquire after our Art and our Literature, we have nothing to do but to refer them to Mount Washington or Lake Superior. It is their concern, not ours. We yield them without scruple to the mercies of foreign reviewers. Let those generously solicitous persons lay on and spare not. There are no such traitors as the natural features of a country which betray their sacred trusts. They should be held strictly to their responsibilities, as, in truth, what spectacle more shameful than that of a huge, lubberly mountain, hiding its talent under a napkin, or a repudiating river? Our geographers should look to it, and instil proper notions on this head. In stating the heights of our mountains and the lengths of our rivers, they should take care to graduate the scale of reproach with a scrupulous regard to every additional foot and mile. They should say, for example, that such a peak is six thousand three hundred feet high, and has never yet produced a poet; that the river so-and-so is a thousand miles long, and has wasted its energies in the manufacture of alligators and flat-boatmen.

On the other hand, they should remember to the credit of the Mississippi, that, being the longest river in the world, it has very properly produced the longest painter, whose single work would overlap by a mile or two the pictures of all the old masters stitched together.[1] We can only hope that it will never give birth to a poet long in proportion.

Since it seems to be so generally conceded, that the form of an author's work is entirely determined by the shape of his skull, and that in turn by the peculiar configuration of his native territory, perhaps a new system of criticism should be framed in accordance with these new developments of science. Want of sublimity would be inexcusable in a native of the mountains, and sameness in one from a diversified region, while flatness could not fairly be objected to a dweller on the prairies, nor could eminent originality be demanded of a writer bred where the surface of the country was only hilly or moderately uneven. Authors, instead of putting upon their title-pages the names of previous works, or of learned societies to which they chance to belong, should supply us with an exact topographical survey of their native districts. The Himalaya mountains are, we believe, the highest yet discovered, and possibly society would find its account in sending the greater part of our poets thither, as to a university, either by subscription or by a tax laid for the purpose. How our literature is likely to be affected by the acquisition of the mountain ranges of California, remains to be seen. Legislators should certainly take such matters into consideration in settling boundary lines, and the General Court of Massachusetts should weigh well the responsibility it may incur to posterity, before transferring to New York the lofty nook of Boston Corner[2] with its potential Homers and Miltons.

But perhaps we have too hastily taken the delinquency of our physical developments for granted. Nothing has hitherto been demanded of rivers and lakes in other parts of the world, except fish

1. Lowell is exaggerating just the slightest bit. Among the many panoramas of the Mississippi, the prize for length goes to Henry Lewis (1819–1904), whose painting of the Mississippi from St. Paul to New Orleans measured 12 feet in height and 3,600 feet in length.

2. This area in western Massachusetts, high in the Berkshires, was the center of a territorial dispute between the two states.

and mill privileges, or, at most, a fine waterfall or a pretty island. The received treatises on mountainous obstetrics give no hint of any parturition to be expected, except of mice. So monstrous a conception as that of a poet is nowhere on record; and what chloroform can we suggest to the practitioner who should be taken unawares by such a phenomenon?

At least, before definitive sentence be passed against us, the period of gestation which a country must go through, ere it bring forth a great poet, should be ascertained with scientific exactness. Let us not be in any hurry to resort to a Caesarian operation. Poets, however valuable in their own esteem, are not, after all, the most important productions of a nation. If we can frame a commonwealth in which it shall not be a misfortune to be born, in which there shall never be a pair of hands nor a mouth too much, we shall be as usefully employed as if we should flower with a Dante or so, and remain a bony stalk forever after. We can, in the meantime, borrow a great poet when we want one, unless the pleasure and profit which we derive from the works of a great master, depend upon the proprietary right in him secured to us by compatriotism. For ourselves, we should be strongly inclined to question any exclusive claim to Shakespeare on the part of our respected relative, John Bull, who could do nothing better than look foolish when the great dramatist was called *bizarre*, and who has never had either the taste or the courage to see a single one of his most characteristic plays acted as he wrote it.

The feeling that it was absolutely necessary to our respectability that we should have a literature, has been a material injury to such as we have had. Our criticism has oscillated between the two extremes of depreciation and overpraise. On the one hand, it has not allowed for the variations of the magnetic needle of taste, and on the other, it has estimated merit by the number of degrees west from Greenwich. It seems never to have occurred to either sect of critics, that there were such things as principles of judgment immutable as those of mathematics. One party has been afraid to commend lest an English Reviewer might afterward laugh; the other has eulogized because it considered so terrible a catastrophe probable. The Stamp Act and the Boston Port Bill scarcely produced a greater excitement in America than the appalling question, *Who reads an American Book*? It is perfectly true, that the amount of enlightenment which a reader will receive from a book depends upon the breadth of surface which he brings within its influence, for we never get *something* for *nothing*; but we would deferentially suggest for the relief of many a still trembling soul, repeating to itself the *quid sum miser tunc dicturus*[3] to that awful question from the Edinburgh judgment-seat, that it is barely possible that the *power* of a book resides in the book itself, and that real books somehow compel an audience without extraneous intervention. From the first, it was impossible that Art should show here the successive stages of growth which have characterized it in the Old World. It is only geographically that we can call ourselves a new nation. However else our literature may avoid the payment of its liabilities, it can surely never be by a plea of infancy. Intellectually, we were full-grown at the start. Shakespeare had been dead five years, and Milton was eleven years old, when Mary Chilton leaped ashore on Plymouth Rock.

In looking backward or forward mentally, we seem to be infected with a Chinese incapacity of perspective. We forget the natural foreshortening, taking objects as they are reflected upon our retina, and neglecting to supply the proper interstices of time. This is equally true whether we are haruspicating the growth of desired opinions and arts, or are contemplating those which are already historical. Thus, we know statistically the amount which any race or nation has stored in its intellectual granaries, but make no account of the years of scarcity, of downright famine even, which have intervened between every full harvest. There is an analogy between the successive stages of a literature and those of a plant. There is, first of all, the seed, then the stalk, and then the seed again. What a length of stalk between Chaucer and Spenser, and again between Milton and Wordsworth! Except in India, perhaps, it would be impossible to affirm confidently an indigenous literature. The seed has been imported, accidentally or otherwise, as the white-weed and Hessian fly into America. Difference of soil, climate, and exposure will have their legitimate influence, but characteristics enough ordinarily remain for the tracing of the pedigree. The locality of its

3. "What, poor miserable wretch, will I answer then?"

original production is as disputable as that of the garden of Eden. Only this is certain, that our search carries us farther and farther eastward.

No literature, of which we have authentic record or remains, can be called national in this limited and strict sense. Nor, if one could be found, would the calling it so be commendation. The best parts of the best authors in all languages can be translated; but, had they this element of exclusive nationality, the idea would demand a lexicon as well as the language which enveloped it. This shell within a shell would give more trouble in the cracking than any author can safely demand of his readers. Only a Dante can compel us to take an interest in the petty local politics of his day. No grubs were ever preserved in such amber. No Smiths and Browns were ever elevated upon so sublime and time-defying pinnacles of love, horror, and pity. The key by which we unlock the great galleries of Art is their common human interest. Nature supplies us with lexicon, commentary, and glossary to the great poems of all ages.

It would be hard to estimate the immediate indebtedness of Grecian literature; easier to reckon how much must have been due to the indirect influence of a religion and philosophy, whose esoteric ideas were of Egyptian derivation. Aristophanes is perhaps the only Grecian poet who is characterized by that quality of nationality of which we are speaking. Nay, it is something intenser than mere nationality in which his comedy is steeped. It is not the spirit of Greece, not even of Attica, but of Athens. It is cockneyism, not nationality. But his humor is more than Athenian. Were it not so, it would be dreary work enough deciphering jokes, as it were, in a mummypit, by the dim light of the scholiast's taper, too choked with dust and smoke to do anything but cough when we are solemnly assured that we have come to the point.

There is a confusion in men's minds upon this subject. Nationality and locality are not distinguished from one another; and, were this jumble fairly cleared up, it would appear that there was a still farther confounding of truth to nature with fidelity of local coloring. Mere nationality is no more nor less than so much provincialism, and will be found but a treacherous antiseptic for any poem. It is because they are men and women, that we are interested in the characters of Homer. The squabbles of a score of petty barbarian chiefs, and the siege of a city which never existed, would have been as barren and fruitless to us as a Welsh genealogy, had the foundations of the *Iliad* been laid no wider and deeper than the Troad.[4] In truth, the only literature which can be called purely national is the Egyptian. What poetry, what philosophy, the torch of the Arab has fruitlessly lighted up for European eyes, we as yet know not; but that any ideas valuable to mankind are buried there, we do not believe. These are not at the mercy of sand, or earthquake, or overflow. No race perishes without intellectual heirs, but whatever was locally peculiar in their literature, their art, or their religious symbols, becomes in time hieroglyphical to the rest of the world, to be, perhaps, painfully deciphered for the verification of useless history, but incapable of giving an impulse to productive thought. Literature survives, not because of its nationality, but in spite of it.

After the United States had achieved their independence, it was forthwith decided that they could not properly be a nation without a literature of their own. As if we had been without one! As if Shakespeare, sprung from the race and the class which colonized New England, had not been also ours! As if we had no share in the puritan and republican Milton, we who had cherished in secret for more than a century the idea of the great puritan effort, and at last embodied it in a living commonwealth! But this ownership in common was not enough for us, and, as partition was out of the question, we must have a drama and an epos of our own. It must be national, too; we must have it all to ourselves. Other nations kept their poets, and so must we. We were to set up a literature as people set up a carriage, in order to be as good as our neighbors. It was even seriously proposed to have a new language. Why not, since we could afford it? Besides, the existing ones were all too small to contain our literature whenever we should get it. One enthusiast suggested the ancient Hebrew, another a firenew tongue of his own invention. Meanwhile, we were busy growing a literature. We watered so freely, and sheltered so carefully, as to make a soil too damp and shaded for any thing but mushrooms; wondered a little why no

4. The landscape of the historical Troy and its environs.

oaks came up, and ended by voting the mushroom an oak, an American variety. Joel Barlow made the lowest bid for the construction of our epos, got the contract, and delivered in due season *The Columbiad*, concerning which we can only regret that it had not been entitled to a still higher praise of nationality by being written in one of the proposed new languages.

One would think that the Barlow experiment should have been enough. But we are still requested by critics, both native and foreign, to produce a national literature, as if it were some school exercise in composition to be handed in by a certain day. The sharp struggle of a day or a year may settle the question of a nation's political independence, but even for that, there must be a long moral preparation. The first furrow drawn by an English plough in the thin soil of Plymouth was truly the first line in our Declaration of Independence. Jefferson was not the prophet looking forth into the future, but the scribe sitting at the feet of the past. But nationality is not a thing to be won by the sword. We may safely trust to the influence of our institutions to produce all of it that is valuable. Let us be content that, if we have been to blame for a *Columbiad*, we have also given form, life, and the opportunity of entire development to social ideas ever reacting with more and more force upon the thought and the literature of the Old World.

The poetry and romance of other nations are assumed to be national, inasmuch as they occupy themselves about local traditions or objects. But we, who never had any proper youth as a nation, never had our mythic period either. We had no cradle and no nursery to be haunted with such bugaboos. One great element of external and immediate influence is therefore wanting to our poets. They cannot, as did Goethe in his *Faust*, imbue an old legend, which already has a hold upon the fancy and early associations of their countrymen, with a modern and philosophical meaning which shall make it interesting to their mature understandings and cultivated imaginations. Whatever be the cause, no race into whose composition so large a Teutonic element has entered is divided by such an impassable chasm of oblivion and unbelief from the ancestral mythology as the English. Their poets accordingly are not popular in any true sense of the word, and have influenced the thought and action of their countrymen less than those of any other nation except those of ancient Rome. Poets in other countries have mainly contributed to the creating and keeping alive of national sentiment; but the English owe theirs wholly to the sea which islands them. Chaucer and Spenser are Normans, and their minds open most fairly southward. Skelton, the Swift of his day, a purely English poet, is forgotten. Shakespeare, thoroughly English as he is, has chosen foreign subjects for the greatest of his dramas, as if to show that genius is cosmopolitan. The first thorough study, criticism, and consequent appreciation of him we owe to the Germans; and he can in no sense be called national except by accident of birth. Even if we grant that he drew his fairy mythology from any then living faith among his countrymen, this formed no bond of union between him and them, and was even regarded as an uncouthness and barbarism till long after every vestige of such faith was obliterated. If we concede any nationality to Milton's great poem, we must at the same time allow to the English an exclusive title to the localities where the scene is laid, a title which they would hardly be anxious to put forward in respect, at least, to one of them. When he was meditating a national poem, it was, he tells us, on the legend of Arthur, who, if he had ever existed at all, would have been English only in the same sense that Tecumseh is American. Coleridge, among his thousand reveries, hovered over the same theme, but settled at last upon the siege of Jerusalem by Titus as the best epical subject remaining. Byron, in his greatest poem, alludes only to England in a rather contemptuous farewell. Those strains of Wordsworth, which have entitled his name to a place on the selecter list of English poets, are precisely the ones in which England has only a common property with the rest of mankind. He could never have swum over Lethe with the sonnets to the river Duddon in his pocket. Whether we look for the cause in the origin of the people, or in their insular position, the English mind has always been characterized by an emigrating tendency. Their most truly national epic was the colonizing of America.

If we admit that it is meritorious in an author to seek for a subject in the superstitions, legends, and historical events of his own peculiar country or district, yet these (unless delocalized by their own intrinsic meaning) are by nature ephemeral, and a wide tract of intervening years makes them as truly foreign as oceans, mountains, or deserts could. Distance of time passes its silent statute of outlawry and alienage against them, as effectually as distance of space. Indeed, in that strictness with which the martinets of nationality use the term, it would be a hard thing for any people to prove an exclusive title to its myths and legends. Take, for example, the story of Wayland the Smith, curious as furnishing the undoubted original of the incident of Tell and the apple, and for its analogies with the Grecian fable of Daedalus. This, after being tracked through the *folklore* of nearly all the nations of Northern Europe, was at last, to the great relief of the archaeologic mind, supposed to be *treed* in Scandinavia, because the word *voelund* was found to mean smith among the Icelanders. Yet even here we cannot rest secure that this piece of mythical property has been restored to its rightful owners. As usual in such cases, investigation points Asia-ward, and the same word is found with the same signification in Ceylon. However unsatisfying in other respects, the search has at least turned up a euphonious synonym for the name Smith, which might be assumed by any member of that numerous patronymic guild desirous of attaining a nearer approach to individuality.

But even the most indisputable proof of original ownership is of no great account in these matters. These tools of fancy cannot be branded with the name of any exclusive proprietor. They are his who can use them. Poor Peter Claus cries out in vain that he has been robbed of himself by the native of a country undiscovered when he took his half-century's nap on the Kypphauser mountains.[5] *Caret vate sacro*,[6] and nobody gives him the least heed. He has become the shadow, and Rip Van Winkle the substance. Perhaps he has made up his mind to it by this time, and contrives to turn an honest penny among the shades by exhibiting himself as the *Original* Rip Van Winkle. We trust, for the honor of our country, that Rip brazens it out there, and denounces the foreign impostor in the purest—American, we were going to say; but here another nationality interposes its claim, and we must put up with Low Dutch.

5. Irving's "Rip Van Winkle" is derived from the story of Peter Klaus.
6. "The proper ceremonies (for prophesy) are missing."

The only element of permanence which belongs to myth, legend, or history, is exactly so much of each as refuses to be circumscribed by provincial boundaries. When once superstitions, customs, and historic personages are dead and buried in antiquarian treatises or county annals, there is no such thing as resurrection for them.The poet who encumbers himself with them takes just that amount of unnecessary burthen upon his shoulders. He is an antiquary, not a creator, and is writing what posterity will read as a catalogue rather than a poem. There is a homeliness about great genius which leads it to glorify the place of its "kindly engendure," (as Chaucer calls it), either by a tender allusion, or by images and descriptions drawn from that fairest landscape in the gallery of memory. But it is a strange confusion of thought to attribute to a spot of earth the inspiration whose source is in a universal sentiment. It is the fine humanity, the muscular sense, and the generous humor of Burns which save him from being merely Scotch, like a score of rhymesters as national as he. The Homers of Little Pedlington die, as their works died before them, and are forgotten; but let a genius get born there, and one touch of his nature shall establish even for Little Pedlington an immortal consanguinity which the whole world shall be eager to claim. The field-mouse and the mountain-daisy are not Scotch, and Tam O'Shanter died the other day within a mile of where we are writing. Measuring Burns by that which is best in him, and which ensures to him a length of life coincident with that of the human heart, he is as little national as Shakespeare, and no more an alien in Iowa than in Ayrshire. There is a vast difference between truth to nature and truth to fact; an impassable gulf between genius, which deals only with the true, and that imitative faculty which patiently and exactly reproduces the actual. This makes the distinction between the works of Fielding, which delight and instruct forever, and those of Smollett, which are of value as affording a clear insight into contemporaneous modes of life, but neither warm the heart nor impregnate the imagination. It is this higher and nobler kind of truth which is said to characterize the portraits of Titian, which gives an indefinable attraction to those of Page, and which inspires the busts of Powers.[7] This excuses meagreness of color

7. William Page (1811–1885) and Hiram Powers (1805–1873), American portrait painter and sculptor, respectively.

and incorrectness of drawing in Hogarth, who was truly rather a great dramatist than a great painter, and gives them that something which even indifferent engraving cannot destroy, any more than bad printing can extinguish Shakespeare.

This demand for a nationality bounded historically and geographically by the independent existence and territory of a particular race or fraction of a race, would debar us of our rightful share in the past and the ideal. It was happily illustrated by that parochially national Gascon, who would have been edified by the sermon had it been his good fortune to belong to the parish. Let us be thankful that there is no court by which we can be excluded from our share in the inheritance of the great poets of all ages and countries, to which our simple humanity entitles us. No great poet has ever sung but the whole human race has been, sooner or later, the wiser and better for it. Above all, let us not tolerate in our criticism a principle which would operate as a prohibitory tariff of ideas. The intellect is a dioecious plant, and books are the bees which carry the quickening pollen from one to another mind. It detracts nothing from Chaucer that we can trace in him the influences of Dante and Boccaccio; nothing from Spenser that he calls Chaucer master; nothing from Shakespeare that he acknowledges how dear Spenser was to him; nothing from Milton that he brought fire from Hebrew and Greek altars. There is no degradation in such indebtedness. Venerable rather is this apostolic succession, and inspiring to see the *vitai lampada*[8] passed thus from consecrated hand to hand.

Nationality, then, is only a less narrow form of provincialism, a sublimer sort of clownishness and ill-manners. It deals in jokes, anecdotes, and allusions of such purely local character that a majority of the company are shut out from all approach to an understanding of them. Yet so universal a demand must have for its basis a more or less solid substratum of truth. There are undoubtedly national, as truly as family, idiosyncrasies, though we think that these will get displayed without any special schooling for that end. The substances with which a nation is compelled to work will modify its results, as well intellectual as material. The still renewing struggle with the unstable desert sands gave to the idea of durability in the Egyptian imagination a preponderance still further increased

8. "The torch of life."

by the necessity of using granite, whose toughness of fibre and vagueness of coloring yielded unwillingly to fineness of outline, but seemed the natural helpmates of massiveness and repose. The out-of-door life of the Greeks, conducing at once to health, and an unconscious education of the eye, and the perfection of physical development resulting from their palaestral exercises and constantly displayed in them, made the Greeks the first to perceive the noble symmetry of the human figure, for embodying the highest types of which Pentelicus[9] supplied the fittest material. Corporeal beauty and strength, therefore, entered largely into their idea of the heroic, and perhaps it was rather policy than dandyism which hindered Alcibiades[10] from learning to play the flute. With us, on the other hand, clothed to the chin in the least graceful costume ever invented by man, and baked half the year with stoves and furnaces, beauty of person has gradually receded from view, and wealth or brain is the essential of the modern novelist's hero. It may not be fanciful to seek in climate, and its resultant effects upon art, the remote cause of that fate-element which entered so largely into the Greek drama. In proportion as sculpture became more perfect, the images of the gods became less and less merely symbolical, and at last presented to the popular mind nothing more than actual representations of an idealized humanity. Before this degradation had taken place, and the divinities had been vulgarized in marble to the common eye, the ideas of the unseen and supernatural came to the assistance of the poet in giving interest to the struggles or connivances between heroes and gods. But presently a new and deeper chord of the imagination must be touched, and the unembodiable shadow of Destiny was summoned up, to move awe and pity as long as the human mind is incapable of familiarizing by precise definition the fearful and the vague. In that more purely objective age, the conflict must be with something external, and the struggles of the mind with itself afforded no sufficient theme for the poet. With us introspection has become a disease, and a poem is a self-dissection.

That Art in America will be modified by circumstances, we have

9. A mountain in Greece, source of the finest marble.

10. Alcibiades (*ca.* 450–404 B.C.) was an unsuccessful student of Socrates famous for his beauty, ability, wealth, and, in youth, his debauchery.

no doubt, though it is impossible to predict the precise form of the moulds into which it will run. New conditions of life will stimulate thought and give new forms to its expression. It may not be our destiny to produce a great literature, as, indeed, our genius seems to find its kindliest development in practicalizing simpler and more perfect forms of social organization. We have yet many problems of this kind to work out, and a continent to subdue with the plough and the railroad, before we are at leisure for aesthetics. Our spirit of adventure will take first a material and practical direction, but will gradually be forced to seek outlet and scope in unoccupied territories of the intellect. In the meantime we may fairly demand of our literature that it should be national to the extent of being as free from outworn conventionalities, and as thoroughly impregnated with humane and manly sentiment, as is the idea on which our political fabric rests. Let it give a true reflection of our social, political, and household life. The *Poems on Man in the Republic*, by Cornelius Mathews,[11] disfigured as they were by gross faults of dialect and metre, had the great merit of presenting the prominent features of our civilization in an American light. The story of *Margaret*[12] is the most emphatically *American* book ever written. The want of plan and slovenliness of construction are characteristic of a new country. The scenery, character, dialect, and incidents mirror New England life as truly as Fresh Pond reflects the sky. The moral, also, pointing forward to a new social order, is the intellectual antitype of that restlessness of disposition, and facility of migration which are among our chief idiosyncrasies. The mistake of our imaginative writers generally is that, though they may take an American subject, they *costume* it in a foreign or antique fashion. The consequence is a painful vagueness and unreality. It is like putting Roman drapery upon a statue of Washington, the absurdity

11. The title is actually "Poems on Man in His Various Aspects Under the American Republic," published in 1843. For a discussion of this work and of Mathews generally, see the introduction to *A Fable for Critics*, below, pp. 153–155.

12. A novel (1845) by Sylvester Judd (1813–1853), a Unitarian minister and author. *Margaret* has for its subtitle *A Tale of the Real and the Ideal*, and was self-consciously intended to reflect the tenets of transcendentalism. The remarks Lowell makes about it here, both positive and negative, may be verified by any reader of the book; it is an amazing production, as fascinating in its flaws as in its delights.

of which does not strike us so forcibly because we are accustomed to it, but which we should recognize at once were the same treatment applied to Franklin. The old masters did exactly the reverse of this. They took ancient or foreign subjects, but selected their models from their own immediate neighborhood. When Shakespeare conceived his Athenian mechanics, he did not cram with Grecian antiquities in order to make them real in speech and manners. Their unconscious prototypes were doubtless walking Stratford streets, and demonstrating to any one who had clear enough eyes, that stupidity and conceit 'were precisely the same thing on the banks of the Avon and those of the Ilissus. Here we arrive at the truth which is wrapped up and concealed in the demand for nationality in literature. It is neither more nor less than this, that authors should use their own eyes and ears, and not those of other people. We ask of them human nature as it appears in man, not in books; and scenery not at second hand from the canvas of painter or poet, but from that unmatched landscape painted by the Great Master upon the retina of their own eyes. Though a poet should make the bobolink sing in Attica, the *anachorism* is nothing, provided he can only make it truly sing so that we can hear it. He will have no difficulty in making his peace with posterity. The error of our advocates of nationality lies in their assigning geographical limits to the poet's range of historical characters as well as to his natural scenery. There is no time or place in human nature, and Prometheus, Coriolanus, Tasso, and Tell are ours if we can use them, as truly as Washington or Daniel Boone. Let an American author make a living character, even if it be antediluvian, and nationality will take care of itself. The newspaper, the railroad, and the steamship are fast obliterating the externals of distinct and hostile nationality. The Turkish soldier has shrunk into coat and pantaloons, and reads Dickens. But human nature is everywhere the same, and everywhere inextinguishable. If we only insist that our authors shall be good, we may cease to feel nervous about their being national. Excellence is an alien nowhere. And even if, as we hear it lamented, we have no literature, there are a thousand other ways of making ourselves useful. If the bobolink and mockingbird find no poet to sing them, they can afford, like Kepler, to wait; and in the meantime they themselves will sing as if nothing had happened. For ourselves, we confess, we have hopes. The breed of poets is not extinct, nor has Apollo shot away all the golden, singing arrows in his quiver. We have a very strong persuasion, amounting even to faith, that eyes and ears will yet open on this Western Continent, and find adequate utterance. If some of our birds have a right to feel neglected, yet other parts of our natural history have met with due civility; and if the pine tree complain of the tribute which Emerson has paid it, we surrender it to the lumberer and the saw-mill without remorse. It must be an unreasonable tree, wooden at head and heart.

Nay, how are we to know what is preparing for us at this very moment? What herald had Chaucer, singing the matins of that grand cathedral-service whose vespers we have not yet heard, in England? What external circumstance controlled the sweet influence of Spenser? Was *Gorboduc* a prologue that should have led us to expect *Hamlet*? Did the Restoration furnish the score for those organ-strains of Milton, breaking in with a somewhat unexpected voluntary to drown the thin song of pander and parasite with its sublime thunders of fervor and ascription? What collyrium of nationality was it that enabled those pleasant Irish eyes of Goldsmith to pierce through the artificial tinsel and frippery of his day to that little clump of primroses at Wakefield? England had long been little better than a province of France in song, when Wordsworth struck the note of independence, and led the people back to the old worship. While we are waiting for our literature, let us console ourselves with the following observation with which Dr. Newman[13] commences his *History of the Hebrew Monarchy*. "Few nations," he says, "which have put forth a wide and enduring influence upon others, proclaim themselves to have been indigenous on the land of their celebrity." Or, if the worst come, we can steal a literature like the Romans, and thus acquire another point of similarity to that remarkable people, whom we resemble so much, according to the *Quarterly Review*, in our origin.

North American Review, LXIX (July 1849), 196–211; reprinted in *The Round Table* (Boston: Richard G. Badger, The Gorham Press, 1913), pp. 9–32.

13. Francis William Newman (1805–1897) published the work in 1847.

"A Great Public Character"

Two events of 1867 allowed Lowell to cast that retrospective glance over the phenomenon of American provincialism which served to balance his many comments on the subject. The first of these, a review of a biography of the American politician Josiah Quincy (1772–1864), for the Atlantic Monthly, *1867, allowed Lowell to produce a list, like those of Hawthorne in the preface to* The Marble Faun *and James in his study of Hawthorne, of the factors missing from American life which are conducive to literature. Lowell's list is specifically directed toward seriousness in historical writing, but it may surely be applied to literature.*

It is the misfortune of American biography that it must needs be more or less provincial, and that, contrary to what might have been predicted, this quality in it predominates in proportion as the country grows larger. Wanting any great and acknowledged centre of national life and thought, our expansion has hitherto been rather aggregation than growth; reputations must be hammered out thin to cover so wide a surface, and the substance of most hardly holds out to the boundaries of a single state. Our very history wants unity, and down to the Revolution the attention is wearied and confused by having to divide itself among thirteen parallel threads, instead of being concentred on a single clue. A sense of remoteness and seclusion comes over us as we read, and we cannot help asking ourselves, "Were *not* these things done in a corner?" Notoriety may be achieved in a narrow sphere, but fame demands for its evidence a more distant and prolonged reverberation. To the world at large we were but a short column of figures in the corner of a blue-book, New England exporting so much salt-fish, timber, and Medford rum, Virginia so many hogsheads of tobacco, and buying with the proceeds a certain amount of English manufactures. The story of our early colonization had a certain moral interest, to be sure, but was altogether inferior in picturesque fascination to that of Mexico or Peru. The lives of our worthies, like that of our nation, are bare of those foregone and far-reaching associations with names, the divining-rods of fancy, which the soldiers and civilians of the Old World get for nothing by the mere accident of birth. Their historians and biographers have succeeded to the good-will, as well as to the long-established stand, of the shop of glory. Time is, after all, the greatest of poets, and the sons of Memory stand a better chance of being the heirs of Fame. The philosophic poet may find a proud solace in saying,—

> Avia Pieridum peragro loca nullius ante
> Trita solo;[1]—

but all the while he has the splendid centuries of Greece and Rome behind him, and can begin his poem with invoking a goddess from whom legend derived the planter of his race. His eyes looked out on a landscape saturated with glorious recollections; he had seen Caesar, and heard Cicero. But who shall conjure with Saugus or Cato Four Corners,—with Israel Putnam or Return Jonathan Meigs?[2] We have been transplanted, and for us the long hierarchical succession of history is broken. The Past has not laid its venerable hands upon us in consecration, conveying to us that mysterious influence whose force is in its continuity. We are to Europe as the Church of England to her of Rome. The latter old lady may be the Scarlet Woman, or the Beast with ten horns, if you will, but hers are all the heirlooms, hers that vast spiritual estate of tradition, nowhere yet everywhere, whose revenues are none the less fruitful for being levied on the imagination. We may claim that England's history is also ours, but it is a *de jure*, and not a *de facto* property that we have in it,—something that may be proved indeed, yet is a merely intellectual satisfaction, and does not savor of the realty.

·1. "I wander alone through untrodden places of the muses, worn away by nobody's foot" (Lucretius, *De Rerum Natura*, I, 929).

2. Meigs (1801–1891) was an American lawyer. Saugus and Cato Four Corners are place names in Massachusetts.

Have we not seen the mockery crown and sceptre of the exiled Stuarts in St. Peter's? the medal struck so lately as 1784 with its legend, HEN IX MAG BRIT ET HIB REX,[3] whose contractions but faintly typify the scantness of the fact?

As the novelist complains that our society wants that sharp contrast of character and costume which comes of caste, so in the narrative of our historians we miss what may be called background and perspective, as if the events and the actors in them failed of that cumulative interest which only a long historical entail can give. Relatively, the crusade of Sir William Pepperell was of more consequence than that of St. Louis, and yet forgive me, injured shade of the second American baronet, if I find the narrative of Joinville more interesting than your despatches to Governor Shirley.[4] Relatively, the insurrection of that Daniel whose Irish patronymic Shea was euphonized into Shays, as a set-off for the debasing of French *chaise* into *shay*, was more dangerous than that of Charles Edward;[5] but for some reason or other (as vice sometimes has the advantage of virtue) the latter is more enticing to the imagination, and the least authentic relic of it in song or story has a relish denied to the painful industry of Minot. Our events seem to fall short of that colossal proportion which befits the monumental style. Look grave as we will, there is something ludicrous in Counsellor Keane's pig being the pivot of a revolution. We are of yesterday, and it is to no purpose that our political augurs divine from the flight of our eagles that to-morrow shall be ours, and flatter us with an all-hail hereafter. Things do really gain in greatness by being acted on a great and cosmopolitan stage, because there is inspiration in the thronged audience and the nearer match that puts men on their mettle. Webster was more largely endowed by nature than

3. "Henry IX, of Great Britain and Scotland, King."

4. Pepperell (1696–1759) forced the capitulation of Louisburg in French Canada in 1745; Jean de Joinville (1224?–1317), French historian, chronicled the crusade of Louis IX (1214–1270), St. Louis. William Shirley (1694–1771) was governor of Massachusetts Bay Colony at the time of Pepperell's expedition.

5. Daniel Shays (1747?–1825) led the rebellion of western Massachusetts farmers against the federal government in 1786; Charles Edward, "Bonnie Prince Charlie" (1720–1788), was the "Young Pretender" of the abortive revolution of 1745.

Fox, and Fisher Ames not much below Burke as a talker[6]; but what a difference in the intellectual training, in the literary culture and associations, in the whole social outfit, of the men who were their antagonists and companions! It should seem that, if it be collision with other minds and with events that strikes or draws the fire from a man, then the quality of those might have something to do with the quality of the fire,—whether it shall be culinary or electric. We have never known the varied stimulus, the inexorable criticism, the many-sided opportunity of a great metropolis, the inspiring reinforcement of an undivided national consciousness. In everything but trade we have missed the invigoration of foreign rivalry. We may prove that we are this and that and the other; our Fourth-of-July orators have proved it time and again; the census has proved it; but the Muses are women, and have no great fancy for statistics, though easily silenced by them. We are great, we are rich, we are all kinds of good things; but did it never occur to you that somehow we are not interesting, except as a phenomenon? It may safely be affirmed that for one cultivated man in this country who studies American history, there are fifty who study European, ancient or modern.

Works, II, 3–7.

6. Daniel Webster (1782–1852) and Fisher Ames (1758–1808) were American politicians; Charles James Fox (1749–1806) and Edmund Burke (1729–1797), English politicians. Lowell's point is that the Americans may have been superior men, but lacking the English context, they could not be tested to their limits.

James Gates Percival

Lowell's review of Julius H. Ward's The Life and Letters of James Gates Percival *for the* North American Review, *1866, gave him an opportunity to examine once more the phenomenon of American provincialism while dissecting the one man who was undoubtedly the perfect symbol of it. Percival (1795–1856) was the most popular poet of his day, before Bryant. The contradiction of Percival's enormous popularity and the mediocrity of his verse demands precisely the wide-ranging explanation Lowell gives in this essay.*

This is an interesting and in many respects instructive book. Mr. Ward has done his work, as is fitting, in a loving spirit; and if he overestimate both what Percival was and what he did, he enables us to form our own judgment by letting him so far as possible speak for himself. The book gives a rather curious picture of what the life of a man of letters is likely to be in a country not yet ripe for literary production, especially if he be not endowed with the higher qualities which command and can wait for that best of all successes which comes slowly. In a generation where everybody can write verses, and where certain modes of thought and turns of phrase have become so tyrannous that it is as hard to distinguish between the productions of one minor poet and another as among those of so many Minne-singers or Troubadours, there is a demand for only two things,—for what chimes with the moment's whim of popular sentiment and is forgotten when that has changed, or for what is never an anachronism, because it slakes or seems to slake the eternal thirst of our nature for those ideal waters that glimmer before us and still before us in ever-renewing mirage. Percival met neither of these conditions. With a nature singularly unplastic, unsympathetic, and self-involved, he was incapable of receiving into his own mind the ordinary emotions of men and giving them back in music; and with a lofty conception of the object and purposes of poesy, he had neither the resolution nor the power which might have enabled him to realize it. He offers as striking an example as could be found of the poetic temperament unballasted with those less obvious qualities which make the poetic faculty. His verse carries every inch of canvas that diction and sentiment can crowd, but the craft is cranky, and we miss that deep-grasping keel of reason which alone can steady and give direction. His mind drifts, too waterlogged to answer the helm, and in his longer poems, like "Prometheus," half the voyage is spent in trying to make up for a leeway which becomes at last irretrievable. If he had a port in view when he set out, he seems soon to give up all hope of ever reaching it; and wherever we open the log-book, we find him running for nowhere in particular, as the wind happens to lead, or lying to in the merest gale of verbiage. The truth is, that Percival was led to the writing of verse by a sentimental desire of the mind, and not by that concurring instinct of all the faculties which is a self-forgetting passion of the entire man. Too excitable to possess his subject fully, as a man of mere talent even may often do, he is not possessed by it as the man of genius is, and seems helplessly striving, the greater part of the time, to make out what, in the name of common or uncommon sense, he is after. With all the stock properties of verse whirling and dancing about his ears puffed out to an empty show of life, the reader of much of his blank verse feels as if a mob of well-draperied clothes-lines were rioting about him in all the unwilling ecstasy of a thunder-gust.

Percival, living from 1795 to 1856, arrived at manhood just as the last war with England had come to an end. Poor, shy, and proud, there is nothing in his earlier years that might not be paralleled in those of hundreds of sensitive boys who gradually get the nonsense shaken out of them in the rough school of life. The length of the schooling needful in his case is what makes it peculiar. Not till after he was fifty, if even then, did he learn that the world never takes a man at his own valuation, and never pays money for what it does not want, or think it wants. It did not want his poetry, simply because it was not, is not, and by no conceivable power of argument can be made, interesting,—the first duty of every artistic product.

Percival, who would have thought his neighbors mad if they had insisted on his buying twenty thousand refrigerators merely because they had been at the trouble of making them, and found it convenient to turn them into cash, could never forgive the world for taking this business view of the matter in his own case. He went on doggedly, making refrigerators of every possible pattern, and comforted himself with the thought of a wiser posterity, which should have learned that the purpose of poetry is to cool and not to kindle. His "Mind," which is on the whole perhaps the best of his writings, vies in coldness with the writings of his brother doctor, Akenside, whose "Pleasures of Imagination" are something quite other than pleasing of reality. If there be here and there a semblance of pale fire, it is but the reflection of moonshine upon ice. Akenside is respectable, because he really had something new to say, in spite of his pompous, mouthing way of saying it; but when Percival says it over again, it is a little too much. In his more ambitious pieces, and it is curious how literally the word "pieces" applies to all he did, he devotes himself mainly to telling us what poetry ought to be, as if mankind were not always more than satisfied with any one who fulfils the true office of poet, by showing them, with the least possible fuss, what it is. Percival was a professor of poetry rather than a poet, and we are not surprised at the number of lectures he reads us, when we learn that in early life he was an excellent demonstrator of anatomy, whose subject must be dead before his business with it begins. His interest in poetry was always more or less scientific. He was forever trying experiments in matter and form, especially the latter. And these were especially unhappy, because it is plain that he had no musical ear, or at best a very imperfect one. His attempts at classical metres are simply unreadable, whether as verse or prose. He contrives to make even the Sapphic so, which when we read it in Latin moves featly to our modern accentuation. Let any one who wishes to feel the difference between ear and no ear compare Percival's specimens with those in the same kind of Coleridge, who had the finest metrical sense since Milton. We take this very experimenting to be a sufficient proof that Percival's faculty, such as it was, and we do not rate it highly, was artificial, and not innate. The true poet is much rather experimented upon by life and nature, by joy and sorrow, by beauty and defect, till it be found out whether he have any hidden music in him that can sing them into an accord with the eternal harmony which we call God.

It is easy to trace the literary influences to which the mind of Percival was in turn subjected. Early in life we find a taint of Byronism, which indeed does not wholly disappear to the last. There is among his poems "An Imprecation," of which a single stanza will suffice as a specimen:—

> Wrapped in sheets of gory lightning,
> While cursed night-hags ring thy knell,
> May the arm of vengeance bright'ning,
> O'er thee wave the sword of hell!

If we could fancy Laura Matilda shut up tipsy in the watch-house, we might suppose her capable of this melodious substitute for swearing. We confess that we cannot read it without laughing, after learning from Mr. Ward that its Salmoneus thunderbolts were launched at the comfortable little city of Hartford, because the poet fancied that the inhabitants thereof did not like him or his verses so much as he himself did. There is something deliciously ludicrous in the conception of night-hags ringing the orthodox bell of the Second Congregational or First Baptist Meeting-house to summon the parishioners to witness these fatal consequences of not reading Percival's poems. Nothing less than the fear of some such catastrophe could compel the perusal of the greater part of them. Next to Byron comes Moore, whose cloying sentimentalism and too facile melody are recalled by the subject and treatment of very many of the shorter lyrics of Percival. In "Prometheus" it is Shelley who is paramount for the time, and Shelley at his worst period, before his unwieldy abundance of incoherent words and images, that were merely words and images without any meaning of real experience to give them solidity, had been compressed in the stricter moulds of thought and study. In the blank verse again, we encounter Wordsworth's tone and sentiment. These were no good models for Percival, who always improvised, and who seems to have thought verse the great distinction between poetry and prose. Percival got nothing from Shelley but the fatal copiousness which is his vice, nothing from Wordsworth but that tendency to preach at every corner about a sympathy with nature which is not his real distinction, and which becomes a wearisome cant at second-hand. Shelley and Wordsworth are both stilted, though in different ways. Shelley wreathed his stilts with flowers; while Wordsworth, protesting against the use of them as sinful, mounts his solemnly at last, and stalks away conscientiously eschewing whatever would serve to hide the naked wood,—nay, was it not Gray's only that were scandalous, and were not his own, modelled upon those of the sainted Cowper, of strictly orthodox pattern after all? Percival, like all imitators, is caught by the defects of what he copies, and exaggerates them. With him the stilts are the chief matter; and getting a taller pair than either of his predecessors, he lifts his commonplace upon them only to make it more drearily conspicuous. Shelley has his gleams of unearthly wildfire; Wordsworth is by fits the most deeply inspired man of his generation; but Percival has no lucid interval. He is pertinaciously and unappeasably dull,—as dull as a comedy of Goethe. He never in his life wrote a rememberable verse. I should not have thought this of any consequence now, for we need not try to read him, did not Mr. Ward with amusing gravity all along assume that he was a great poet. There was scarce timber enough in him for the making of a Tiedge or a Hagedorn,[1] both of whom he somewhat resembles.

Percival came to maturity at an unfortunate time for a man so liable to self-delusion. Leaving college with so imperfect a classical training (in spite of the numerous "testimonials" cited by Mr. Ward) that he was capable of laying the accent on the second syllable of Pericles, he seems never to have systematically trained even such faculty as was in him, but to have gone on to the end mistaking excitability of brain for wholesome exercise of thought. The consequence is a prolonged immaturity which makes his latest volume, published in 1843, as crude and as plainly wanting in enduring quality as the first number of his "Clio." We have the same old complaints of neglected genius, as if genius could ever be neglected so long as it has the perennial consolation of its own divine society, the same wilted sentiment, the same feeling about for topics

1. Christoph August Tiedge (1752–1841) and Friedrich von Hagedorn (1708–1754) German poets, very popular in their day.

of verse in which he may possibly find that inspiration from without which the true poet cannot flee from in himself. These tedious wailings about heavenly powers suffocating in the heavy atmosphere of an uncongenial, unrecognizing world, and Percival is profuse of them, are simply an advertisement, to whoever has ears, of some innate disability in the man who utters them. Heavenly powers know very well how to take care of themselves. The poor "World," meaning thereby that small fraction of society which has any personal knowledge of an author or his affairs, has had great wrong done it in such matters. It is not, and never was, the powers of a man that it neglects,—it could not if it would,—but his weaknesses, and especially the publication of them, of which it grows weary. It can never supply any man with what is wanting in himself, and the attempt to do so only makes bad worse. If a man can find the proof of his own genius only in public appreciation, still worse, if his vanity console itself with taking it as an evidence of rare qualities in himself that his fellow mortals are unable to see them, it is all up with him. The "World" resolutely refused to find Wordsworth entertaining, and it refuses still, on good grounds; but the genius that was in him bore up unflinchingly, would take no denial, got its claim admitted on all hands, and impregnated at last the literature of an entire generation, though *habitans in sicco*,[2] if ever genius did. But Percival seems to have satisfied himself with a syllogism something like this: Men of genius are neglected; the more neglect, the more genius; I am altogether neglected,—*ergo*, wholly made up of that priceless material.

The truth was that he suffered rather from over-appreciation; and "when," says a nameless old Frenchman, "I see a man go up like a rocket, I expect before long to see the stick come down." The times were singularly propitious to mediocrity. As in Holland one had only to

Invent a shovel and be a magistrate,

so here to write a hundred blank verses was to be immortal, till somebody else wrote a hundred and fifty blanker ones. It had been resolved unanimously that we must and would have a national literature. England, France, Spain, Italy, each already had one,

2. "Dwelling in dryness" (Pliny).

Germany was getting one made as fast as possible, and Ireland vowed that she once had one far surpassing them all. To be respectable, we must have one also, and that speedily. We forgot that artistic literature, the only literature possible under our modern conditions, thrives best in an air laden with tradition, in a soil mellow with immemorial culture, in the temperature steady yet stimulating of historic and national associations. We had none of these, but Sydney Smith's scornful question, "Who reads an American book?"[3] tingled in our ears. Surely never was a young nation setting forth jauntily to seek its fortune so dumfounded as Brother Jonathan when John Bull cried gruffly from the roadside, "Stand, and deliver a national literature!" After fumbling in his pockets, he was obliged to confess that he had n't one about him at the moment, but vowed that he had left a first-rate one at home which he would have fetched along—only it was so everlasting heavy.

If the East should fail, as judged by European standards it seemed to have done, it was resolved that a poet should come out of the West, fashioned on a scale somewhat proportioned to our geographical pretensions. Our rivers, forests, mountains, cataracts, prairies, and inland seas were to find in him their antitype and voice. Shaggy he was to be, brown-fisted, careless of proprieties, unhampered by tradition, his Pegasus of the half-horse, half-alligator breed. By him at last the epos of the New World was to be fitly sung, the great tragi-comedy of democracy put upon the stage for all time. It was a cheap vision, for it cost no thought; and like all judicious prophecy, it muffled itself from criticism in the loose drapery of its terms. Till the advent of this splendid apparition, who should dare affirm positively that he would never come? that, indeed, he was impossible? And yet his impossibility was demonstrable, nevertheless.

Supposing a great poet to be born in the West, though he would naturally levy upon what had always been familiar to his eyes for his images and illustrations, he would almost as certainly look for his

3. This rallying cry, so often cited in Lowell's writings, as in other American writings of the period, first appeared in Smith's review of Seybert's *Annals of the United States* in the January, 1820, issue of the *Edinburgh Review*, which Smith (1771–1845) founded in 1802.

ideal somewhere outside of the life that lay immediately about him. Life in its large sense, and not as it is temporarily modified by manners or politics, is the only subject of the poet; and though its elements lie always close at hand, yet in its unity it seems always infinitely distant, and the difference of angle at which it is seen in India and in Minnesota is almost inappreciable. Moreover, a rooted discontent seems always to underlie all great poetry, if it be not even the motive of it. The *Iliad* and the *Odyssey* paint manners that are only here and there incidentally true to the actual, but which in their larger truth had either never existed or had long since passed away. Had Dante's scope been narrowed to contemporary Italy, the *Divina Commedia* would have been a picture-book merely. But his theme was Man, and the vision that inspired him was of an Italy that never was nor could be, his political theories as abstract as those of Plato or Spinoza. Shakespeare shows us less of the England that then was than any other considerable poet of his time. The struggle of Goethe's whole life was to emancipate himself from Germany, and fill his lungs for once with a more universal air.

Yet there is always a flavor of the climate in these rare fruits, some gift of the sun peculiar to the region that ripened them. If we are ever to have a national poet, let us hope that his nationality will be of this subtle essence, something that shall make him unspeakably nearer to us, while it does not provincialize him for the rest of mankind. The popular recipe for compounding him would give us, perhaps, the most sublimely furnished bore in human annals. The novel aspects of life under our novel conditions may give some freshness of color to our literature; but democracy itself, which many seem to regard as the necessary Lucina[4] of some new poetic birth, is altogether too abstract an influence to serve for any such purpose. If any American author may be looked on as in some sort the result of our social and political ideal, it is Emerson, who, in his emancipation from the traditional, in the irresponsible freedom of his speculation, and his faith in the absolute value of his own individuality, is certainly, to some extent, typical; but if ever author was inspired by the past, it is he, and he is as far as possible from the shaggy hero of prophecy. Of the sham shaggy, who have tried the trick of Jacob

4. The Roman goddess who presided over childbirth.

upon us, we have had quite enough, and may safely doubt whether this satyr of masquerade is to be our representative singer. Were it so, it would not be greatly to the credit of democracy as an element of esthetics. But we may safely hope for better things.

The themes of poetry have been pretty much the same from the first; and if a man should ever be born among us with a great imagination, and the gift of the right word,—for it is these, and not sublime spaces, that make a poet,—he will be original rather in spite of democracy than in consequence of it, and will owe his inspiration quite as much to the accumulations of the Old World as to the promises of the New. But for a long while yet the proper conditions will be wanting, not, perhaps, for the birth of such a man, but for his development and culture. At present, with the largest reading population in the world, perhaps no country ever offered less encouragement to the higher forms of art or the more thorough achievements of scholarship. Even were it not so, it would be idle to expect us to produce any literature so peculiarly our own as was the natural growth of ages less communicative, less open to every breath of foreign influence. Literature tends more and more to become a vast commonwealth, with no dividing lines of nationality. Any more *Cids*, or *Songs of Roland*, or *Nibelungens*, or *Kalewalas*[5] are out of the question,—nay, anything at all like them; for the necessary insulation of race, of country, of religion, is impossible, even were it desirable. Journalism, translation, criticism, and facility of intercourse tend continually more and more to make the thought and turn of expression in cultivated men identical all over the world. Whether we like it or not, the costume of mind and body is gradually becoming of one cut. When, therefore, the young Lochinvar comes out of the West, his steed may be the best in all the wide border, but his pedigree will run back to Arabia, and there will be no cross of the saurian in him. *A priori*, we should expect of the young Western poet that he would aim rather at elegance and refinement than at a display of the rude vigor that is supposed to be his birthright; for to him culture will seem the ideal thing, and, in a country without a past, tradition will charm all the more that it speaks with a foreign accent, and stirs the gypsy blood of imagination.

5. These are the national poems of Spain, France, Germany, and Finland.

Sixty years ago, our anxiety to answer Sydney Smith's question showed that we felt keenly the truth implied in it,—that a nation was not to be counted as a moral force which had not fulfilled the highest demands of civilization. In our hurry to prove that we had done so, we forgot the conditions that rendered it impossible. That we were not yet, in any true sense, a nation; that we wanted that literary and social atmosphere which is the breath of life to all artistic production; that our scholarship, such as it was, was mostly of that theological sort which acts like a prolonged drouth upon the brain; that our poetic fathers were Joel Barlow and Timothy Dwight; all this was nothing to the purpose; a literature adapted to the size of the country was what we must and would have. Given the number of square miles, the length of the rivers, the size of the lakes, and you have the greatness of the literature we were bound to produce without further delay. If that little dribble of an Avon had succeeded in engendering Shakespeare, what a giant might we not look for from the mighty womb of Mississippi! Physical Geography for the first time took her rightful place as the tenth and most inspiring Muse. A glance at the map would satisfy the most incredulous that she had done her best for us, and should we be wanting to the glorious opportunity? Not we indeed! So surely as Franklin invented the art of printing, and Fulton the steam-engine, we would invent us a great poet in time to send the news by the next packet to England, and teach her that we were her masters in arts as well as in arms.

Percival was only too ready to be invented, and he forthwith produced his bale of verses from a loom capable of turning off a hitherto unheard-of number of yards to the hour, and perfectly adapted to the amplitude of our territory, inasmuch as it was manufactured on the theory of covering the largest surface with the least possible amount of meaning that would hold words together. He was as ready to accept the perilous emprise, and as loud in asserting his claim thereto, as Sir Kay used to be, and with much the same result. Our critical journals—and America certainly *has* led the world in a department of letters which of course requires no outfit but the power to read and write, gratuitously furnished by our public schools— received him with a shout of welcome. Here came the true deliverer at last, mounted on a steed to which he himself had given the new name of "Pegasus,"—for we were to be original in everything,— and certainly blowing his own trumpet with remarkable vigor of lungs. Solitary enthusiasts, who had long awaited this sublime avatar, addressed him in sonnets which he accepted with a gravity beyond all praise. (To be sure, even Mr. Ward seems to allow that his sense of humor was hardly equal to his other transcendent endowments.) His path was strewn with laurel—of the native variety, altogether superior to that of the Old World, at any rate not precisely like it. Verses signed "P.," as like each other as two peas, and as much like poetry as that vegetable is like a peach, were watched for in the corner of a newspaper as an astronomer watches for a new planet. There was never anything so comically unreal since the crowning in the Capitol of Messer Francesco Petrarca, Grand Sentimentalist in Ordinary at the Court of King Robert of Sicily.[6] Unhappily, Percival took it all quite seriously. There was no praise too ample for the easy elasticity of his swallow. He believed himself as gigantic as the shadow he cast on these rolling mists of insubstantial adulation, and life-long he could never make out why *his* fine words refused to butter his parsnips for him, nay, to furnish both parsnips and sauce. While the critics were debating precisely how many of the prime qualities of the great poets of his own and preceding generations he combined in his single genius, and in what particular respects he surpassed them all,—a point about which he himself seems never to have had any doubts,—the public, which could read Scott and Byron with avidity, and which was beginning even to taste Words-worth, found his verses inexpressibly wearisome. They would not throng to subscribe for a collected edition of those works which singly had been too much for them. With whatever dulness of sense they may be charged, they have a remarkably keen scent for tediousness, and will have none of it unless in a tract or sermon, where, of course, it is to be expected and is also edifying. Percival never forgave the public; but it was the critics that he never should have forgiven, for of all the maggots that can make their way into the brains through the ears, there is none so disastrous as the persua-

6. Petrarch (1304–1374), Italian poet and humanist, was made poet laureate at Rome in 1341.

sion that you are a great poet. There is surely something in the construction of the ears of small authors which lays them specially open
to the inroads of this pest. It tickles pleasantly while it eats away the
fibre of will, and incapacitates a man for all honest commerce with
realities. Unhappily its insidious titillation seems to have been
Percival's one great pleasure during life.

I began by saying that the book before me was interesting and instructive; but I meant that it was so not so much from any positive
merits of its own as by the lesson which almost every page of it
suggests. To those who have some knowledge of the history of
literature, or some experience in life ,it is from beginning to end a
history of weakness mistaking great desires for great powers. If
poetry, in Bacon's noble definition of it, "adapt the shows of things
to the desires of the mind," sentimentalism is equally skilful in
making realities shape themselves to the cravings of vanity. The
theory that the poet is a being above the world and apart from it is
true of him as an observer only who applies to the phenomena about
him the test of a finer and more spiritual sense. That he is a creature
divinely set apart from his fellow men by a mental organization that
makes them mutually unintelligible to each other is in flat contradiction with the lives of those poets universally acknowledged as
greatest. Dante, Shakespeare, Cervantes, Calderon, Milton, Molière,
Goethe,—in what conceivable sense is it true of them that they
wanted the manly qualities which made them equal to the demands
of the world in which they lived? That a poet should assume, as
Victor Hugo used to do, that he is a reorganizer of the moral world,
and that works cunningly adapted to the popular whim of the time
form part of some mysterious system which is to give us a new
heaven and a new earth, and to remodel laws of art which are as
unchangeable as those of astronomy, can do no very great harm
to any one but the author himself, who will thereby be led astray
from his proper function, and from the only path to legitimate and
lasting success. But when the theory is carried a step further, and we
are asked to believe, as in Percival's case, that, because a man can
write verses, he is exempt from that inexorable logic of life and circumstance to which all other men are subjected, and to which
it is wholesome for them that they should be, then it becomes

mischievous, and calls for a protest from all those who have at heart the interests of good morals and healthy literature. It is the theory of idlers and *dilettanti*, of fribbles in morals and declaimers in verse, which a young man of real power may dally with during some fit of mental indigestion, but which when accepted by a mature man, and carried along with him through life, is a sure mark of feebleness and of insincere dealing with himself. Percival is a good example of a class of authors unhappily too numerous in these latter days. In Europe the natural growth of a world ill at ease with itself and still nervous with the frightful palpitation of the French Revolution, they are but feeble exotics in our healthier air. Without faith or hope, and deprived of that outward support in the habitual procession of events and in the authoritative limitations of thought which in ordinary times gives steadiness to feeble and timid intellects, they are turned inward, and forced, like Hudibras's sword,—

> To eat into themselves, for lack
> Of other thing to hew and hack.[7]

Compelled to find within them that stay which had hitherto been supplied by creeds and institutions, they learned to attribute to their own consciousness the grandeur which belongs of right only to the mind of the human race, slowly endeavoring after an equilibrium between its desires and the external conditions under which they are attainable. Hence that exaggeration of the individual, and depreciation of the social man, which has become the cant of modern literature. Abundance of such phenomena accompanied the rise of what was called Romanticism in Germany and France, reacting to some extent even upon England, and consequently upon America. The smaller poets erected themselves into a kind of guild, to which all were admitted who gave proof of a certain feebleness of character which rendered them superior to their grosser fellow men. It was a society of cripples undertaking to teach the new generation how to walk. Meanwhile, the object of their generous solicitude, what with clinging to Mother Past's skirts, and helping itself by every piece of household furniture it could lay hands on, learned, after many a tumble, to get on its legs and to use them as other generations

7. Part 1, Canto 1, ll. 361–362.

had done before it. Percival belonged to this new order of bards, weak in the knees, and thinking it healthy exercise to climb the peaks of Dreamland. To the vague and misty views attainable from those sublime summits into his own vast interior, his reports in blank verse and otherwise did ample justice, but failed to excite the appetite of mankind. He spent his life, like others of his class, in proclaiming himself a neglected Columbus, ever ready to start on his voyage when the public would supply the means of building his ships. Meanwhile, to be ready at a moment's warning, he packs his mind pell-mell like a carpet-bag, wraps a geologist's hammer in a shirt with a Byron collar, does up Volney's *Ruins* with an odd volume of Wordsworth, and another of Bell's *Anatomy* in a loose sheet of Webster's Dictionary, jams Moore's poems between the leaves of Bopp's Grammar,—and forgets only such small matters as combs and brushes.[8] It never seems to have entered his head that the gulf between genius and its new world is never too wide for a stout swimmer. Like all sentimentalists, he reversed the process of nature, which makes it a part of greatness that it is a simple thing to itself, however much of a marvel it may be to other men. He discovered his own genius, as he supposed,—a thing impossible had the genius been real. Donne, who wrote more profound verses than any other English poet save one only, never wrote a profounder verse than

Who knows his virtue's name and place, hath none.

Percival's life was by no means a remarkable one, except, perhaps, in the number of chances that seem to have been offered him to make something of himself, if anything were possibly to be made. He was never without friends, never without opportunities, if he could have availed himself of them. It is pleasant to see Mr. Ticknor[9] treating

8. This list amounts to a thumbnail biography of Percival via metaphor. Percival was a doctor of medicine as well as a geologist; his poems are studiously Byronic, with a good deal of Romantic topography and sighing idealism (Wordsworthian); he worked on Webster's dictionary and had quite a reputation as a philologist and linguist (he was reputed to speak seventeen languages fluently and wrote poems in Sanskrit, Persian, Arabic, Greek, Italian, French, German, Gaelic, Welsh, Danish, Swedish, Scottish, Norse, Flemish, Finnish, Bohemian, Servian, and Russian). Withal, he was personally vulgar and unkempt.

9. William D. Ticknor (1810–1864), Percival's publisher.

him with that considerate kindness which many a young scholar can remember as shown so generously to himself. But nothing could help Percival, whose nature had defeat worked into its every fibre. He was not a real, but an imaginary man. His early attempt at suicide (as Mr. Ward seems to think it) is typical of him. He is not the first young man who, when crossed in love, has spoken of "loupin o'er a linn," nor will he be the last. But that any one who really meant to kill himself should put himself so resolutely in the way of being prevented, as Percival did, is hard to believe. Châteaubriand, the arch sentimentalist of these latter days, had the same harmless velleity of self-destruction, enough to scare his sister and so give him a smack of sensation, but a very different thing from the settled will which would be really perilous. Shakespeare, always true to Nature, makes Hamlet dally with the same exciting fancy. Alas! self is the one thing the sentimentalist never truly wishes to destroy! One remarkable gift Percival seems to have had, which may be called memory of the eye. What he saw he never forgot, and this fitted him for a good geological observer. How great his power of combination was, which alone could have made him a great geologist, we cannot determine. But he seems to have shown but little in other directions. His faculty of acquiring foreign tongues I do not value so highly as Mr. Ward, having known many otherwise inferior men who possessed it. Indeed the power to express the same nothing in ten different languages is something to be dreaded rather than admired. It gives a horrible advantage to dulness. The best thing to be learned from Percival's life is that he was happy for the first time when taken away from his vague pursuit of a vaguer ideal, and set to practical work.

Works, II, 104–127.

IV

AMERICAN CONTEMPORARIES

A Fable for Critics

Lowell's doggerel summary of American letters halfway through the nine-
teenth century might have quickly slipped into obscurity. Its faults are almost
overwhelming: the farfetched "classical" frame, the sophomoric humor of its
macaronic puns, the distressing regularity of its anapests, the straining for
rhyme, the obscurity of so many of the butts of Lowell's humor. Still, it does
survive, and remains an extraordinary vantage point from which one may
observe the provincial character of American literature and some few of its suc-
cesses. For the critical viewpoint is coherent; the organic standards, when they
are seriously applied, are meaningful and appropriate; critical distance is, for
the most part, achieved; and Lowell's good taste in writing is just as apparent
as, unfortunately, his doubtful taste in what he thought was comic technique.

The background to the poem suggests Lowell's considerable achievement
in the writing of it. American writing was split into four quite distinct camps
based on geography, politics, and provincialism (hardly at all on critical
theory). The geographical division was between Boston and New York,
Boston representing tradition and culture and the Anglo-American heritage;
New York, the new, driving, materialistic American spirit. There were as
yet no significant western writers, and efforts to make the South a center of
culture had largely failed. The best southern writers, William Gilmore Simms
and Edgar Allan Poe, were satellites of New York. But both cities were also
sharply divided within themselves. Literary Boston was split between the
Brahmins and the transcendentalists, while literary New York suffered from
what has been quite justly called by Perry Miller the "war of words and
wits" between the Knickerbockers and the "Young America" group. Lowell's
first impulse was to write as a partisan Bostonian about the upstart New York
writers, pausing to throw a dart here and there at the transcendentalists.
As he began writing seriously, however, he overcame this kind of partisanship
and, with a few exceptions, dealt justly with members of all four parties.

It was hardest to deal with the group to which he himself belonged, the
Brahmins. In general, he solved the problem by cutting short his comments
and making them more analytical than evaluative, as he did with Longfellow,

Whittier, and Holmes. Chivalry and his close friendship drove him to the opposite tack with Lydia Maria Child; his digressive and uncritical eulogy of her is a testament of friendship, not criticism, and its rhetoric makes that clear. The transcendental writers, major and minor, called forth some fine criticism from Lowell. The only figure about whom he could not be objective was "Miranda," Margaret Fuller (1810–1850), who is unquestionably a victim of Lowell's spite and more a subject of cruel wit than sharp criticism. But she is an exception. Although Lowell had little sympathy with the vagaries of transcendental ideas, he could understand their organicism and still point out when it became merely eccentric that

> *Roots, wood, bark, and leaves singly perfect may be,*
> *But, clapt hodge-podge together, they don't make a tree.*

But it was with the New York writers that Lowell achieved his best criticism in A Fable. At a time when criticism was hopelessly provincial in America, when works of poetry or fiction were either praised or damned, inevitably according to the political leanings of their authors, when one party listened for a pure English skylark in all new poems while the other party could be satisfied with nothing but the roar of Niagara—at that time, Lowell somehow managed at least appropriate and sometimes brilliant criticism on a wide range of writers, from Cooper to Briggs, from Bryant to Mathews. Many of these men are completely forgotten today, but they were powers to be reckoned with in Lowell's time. The Democrat, Evert Augustus Duyckinck (1816–1878), as founder of the Arcturus *and editor of the* Literary World *from 1846 to 1847, and as the center of the "Young America" group in New York, must have loomed like a new Dr. Johnson upon the American literary scene. His protégé, Cornelius Mathews (1817–1889), the author of* Poems on Man, in His Various Aspects Under the American Republic *(1843) and a half-dozen other works by 1848, including the drama* Witchcraft, *all promising works by a young man, had enormous pretensions to literary significance. In the* Fable, *Lowell manages, fairly consistently, to compute the specific gravity of each man and many others like them, generally distinguishing the amount of brass plating on each.*

The excerpts given in this selection include all the critical material in the poem, no matter how obscure the subject. I have deleted only some noncritical digressions and the groaning machinery of the plot, which Lowell himself admitted was "slender and slippery." The frame may be quickly summarized. Apollo, seated beneath a laurel tree, is glancing at some of his verses. He has with him a pedantic critic who serves as a buffer between the god and the writers who pester him. However, Apollo discovers that he needs a lily to complete a metaphor, and he sends the critic to fetch one for him. He is then virtually assaulted by a stream of American writers, led by Duyckinck and Mathews. Much later, the critic returns, bearing a thistle, which he has mistaken for a lily. Apollo then lectures the assembled American writers on criticism, apparently to no avail, for as soon as he is through, Miranda is ready to address him again, at which point Apollo flees.

The text is taken from the first edition, although I have added the preface to the second edition. Lowell's revisions and excisions for later editions (his manner, you see, is finally inescapable) were, in my opinion, unfortunate. However, I have noted certain changes where they substantially effect his estimate of a writer. I have given bracketed titles to the various sections of the poem, and as is customary, I am reproducing the rhyming title page.

READER! *walk up at once (it will soon be too late) and buy*
at a perfectly ruinous rate

A
FABLE FOR CRITICS
OR
Better—
I like, as a thing that the reader's first fancy may strike,
an old fashioned title-page,
such as presents a tabular view of the volume's contents—

A GLANCE

AT A FEW OF OUR LITERARY PROGENIES

(*Mrs. Malaprop's word*)

FROM

THE TUB OF DIOGENES;

A VOCAL AND MUSICAL MEDLEY,

THAT IS,

A SERIES OF JOKES

By a Wonderful Quiz,
who accompanies himself with a rub-a-dub-dub, full of spirit and grace,
on the top of a tub.

SET FORTH IN

October, the 21st day in the year '48,

BY

G. P. PUTNAM, BROADWAY

[Preface to the first edition]

It being the commonest mode of procedure, I premise a few candid remarks

TO THE READER:

This trifle, begun to please only myself and my own private fancy, was laid on the shelf. But some friends, who had seen it, induced me, by dint of saying they liked it, to put it in print. That is, having come to that very conclusion, I consulted them when it could make no confusion. For (though in the gentlest of ways) they had hinted it was scarce worth the while, I should doubtless have printed it.

I began it, intending a Fable, a frail, slender thing, rhyme-ywinged, with a sting in its tail. But, by addings and alterings not previously planned,—digressions chance-hatched, like birds' eggs in the sand,— and dawdlings to suit every whimsy's demand (always freeing the bird which I held in my hand, for the two perched, perhaps out of reach, in the tree)—it grew by degrees to the size which you see. I was like the old woman that carried the calf, and my neighbors, like hers, no doubt, wonder and laugh, and when, my strained arms with their grown burthen full, I call it my Fable, they call it a bull.

Having scrawled at full gallop (as far as that goes) in a style that is neither good verse nor bad prose, and being a person whom nobody knows, some people will say I am rather more free with my readers than it is becoming to be, that I seem to expect them to wait on my leisure in following wherever I wander at pleasure, that, in short, I take more than a young author's lawful ease, and laugh in a queer way so like Mephistopheles, that the public will doubt, as they grope through my rhythm, if in truth I am making fun *at* them or *with* them.

So the excellent Public is hereby assured that the sale of my book is already secured. For there is not a poet throughout the whole land, but will purchase a copy or two out of hand, in the fond expectation of being amused in it, by seeing his betters cut-up and abused in it. Now, I find, by a pretty exact calculation, there are something like ten thousand bards in the nation, of that special variety whom the Review and Magazine critics call *lofty* and *true*, and about thirty thousand (*this* tribe is increasing) of the kinds who are termed *full of promise* and *pleasing*. The Public will see by a glance at this schedule, that they cannot expect me to be over-sedulous about courting *them*, since it seems I have got enough fuel made sure of for boiling my pot.

As for such of our poets as find not their names mentioned once in my pages, with praises or blames, let them SEND IN THEIR CARDS, without farther DELAY, to my friend G. P. PUTNAM, Esquire, in Broadway, where a LIST will be kept with the strictest regard to the day and the hour of receiving the card. Then, taking them up as I chance to have time (that is, if their names can be twisted in rhyme), I will honestly give each his PROPER POSITION, at the rate of ONE AUTHOR to each NEW EDITION. Thus a PREMIUM is offered sufficiently HIGH (as the magazines say when they tell their best lie) to induce bards to CLUB their resources and buy the balance of every edition, until they have all of them fairly been run through the mill.

One word to such readers (judicious and wise) as read books with something behind the mere eyes, of whom in the country, perhaps, there are two, including myself, gentle reader, and you. All the characters sketched in this slight *jeu d'esprit*, though, it may be, they seem, here and there, rather free, and drawn from a Mephisto-phelian stand-point, are *meant* to be faithful, and that is the grand point, and none but an owl would feel sore at a rub from a jester who tells you, without any subterfuge, that he sits in Diogenes' tub.

A PRELIMINARY NOTE TO THE SECOND EDITION,

though it well may be reckoned, of all composition, the species at once most delightful and healthy, is a thing which an author, unless he be wealthy and willing to pay for that kind of delight, is not, in all instances, called on to write. Though there are, it is said, who, their spirits to cheer, slip in a new title-page three times a year, and in this way snuff up an imaginary savor of that sweetest of dishes, the popular favor,—much as if a starved painter should fall to and treat the Ugolino [1] inside to a picture of meat.

You remember (if not, pray turn backward and look) that, in

1. Count Ugolino of Gheradesca perished of hunger in 1288. His fate is described by Dante in *Inferno*, xxxiii.

writing the preface which ushered my book, I treated you, excellent Public, not merely with a cool disregard, but downright cavalierly. Now I would not take back the least thing I then said, though I thereby could butter both sides of my bread, for I never could see that an author owed aught to the people he solaced, diverted, or taught; and, as for mere fame, I have long ago learned that the persons by whom it is finally earned, are those with whom *your* verdict weighed not a pin, unsustained by the higher court sitting within.

But I wander from what I intended to say—that you have, namely, shown such a liberal way of thinking, and so much esthetic perception of anonymous worth in the handsome reception you gave to my book, spite of some private piques (having bought the first thousand in barely two weeks), that I think, past a doubt, if you measured the phiz of yours most devotedly, Wonderful Quiz, you would find that its vertical section was shorter, by an inch and two tenths, or 'twixt that and a quarter.

You have watched a child playing—in those wondrous years when belief is not bound to the eyes and the ears, and the vision divine is so clear and unmarred, that each baker of pies in the dirt is a bard? Give a knife and a shingle, he fits out a fleet, and, on that little mud-puddle over the street, his invention, in purest good faith, will make sail round the globe with a puff of his breath for a gale, will visit, in barely ten minutes, all climes, and find Northwestern passages hundreds of times. Or, suppose the young Poet fresh stored with delights from that Bible of childhood the Arabian Nights, he will turn to a crony and cry, "Jack, let's play that I am a Genius!" Jacky straightway makes Aladdin's lamp out of a stone, and, for hours, they enjoy each his own supernatural powers. This is all very pretty and pleasant, but then suppose our two urchins have grown into men, and both have turned authors,—one says to his brother, "Let's play we're the American somethings or other (only let them be big enough, no matter what). Come you shall be Goethe or Pope, which you choose; I'll be Coleridge, and both shall write mutual reviews." So they both (as mere strangers) before many days, send each other a cord of anonymous bays. Each, in piling his epithets, smiles in his sleeve to see what his friend can be made to believe; each, in reading the other's unbiased review, thinks—Here's pretty high praise, but no more than is true. Well, we laugh at them both, and yet make no great fuss when the same farce is acted to benefit us. Even I, who, if asked, scarce a month since, what Fudge meant, should have answered, the dear Public's critical judgment, begin to think sharpwitted Horace spoke sooth when he said, that the Public *sometimes* hit the truth.

In reading these lines, you perhaps have a vision of a person in pretty good health and condition, and yet, since I put forth my primary edition, I have been crushed, scorched, withered, used up and put down (by Smith with the cordial assistance of Brown), in all, if you put any faith in my rhymes, to the number of ninety-five several times, and, while I am writing—I tremble to think of it, for I may at this moment be just on the brink of it—Molybdostom, angry at being omitted, has begun a critique,—am I not to be pitied?[2]

Now I shall not crush *them* since, indeed, for that matter, no pressure I know of could render them flatter; nor wither, nor scorch them,—no action of fire could make either them or their articles drier; nor waste time in putting them down—I am thinking not their own self-inflation will keep them from sinking; for there's this contradiction about the whole bevy—though without the least weight, they are awfully heavy. No, my dear honest bore, *surdo fabulam narras,*[3] they are no more to me than a rat in the arras. I can walk with the Doctor, get facts from the Don, or draw out the Lambish quintessence of John, and feel nothing more than a half-comic sorrow, to think that they all will be lying tomorrow tossed carelessly up on the waste-paper shelves, and forgotten by all but their half-dozen selves. Once snug in my attic, my fire in a roar, I leave the whole pack of them outside the door. With Hakluyt or Purchas[4] I wander away to the black northern seas or barbaric

2. The wise Scandinavians probably called their bards by the queer-looking title of Scald in a delicate way, as it were, just to hint to the world the hot water they always get into. [Lowell's note.]

3. "Deaf to the story as told" (Terence, *Heautontimorumenos*, II. i. 10).

4. Richard Hakluyt (1552?–1616) published his *Principall Navigations, Voiages and Discoveries of the English Nation* in three volumes, 1598–1600. For Samuel Purchas, see above, p. 19, note 12.

Cathay; get *fou* with O'Shanter, and sober me then with that builder of brick-kilnish dramas, rare Ben; snuff Herbert, as holy as a flower on a grave; with Fletcher wax tender, o'er Chapman grow brave; with Marlowe or Kyd take a fine poet-rave;[5] in Very,[6] most Hebrew of Saxons, find peace; with Lycidas welter on vext Irish seas; with Webster grow wild, and climb earthward again, down by mystical Browne's Jacob's-ladder-like brain, to that spiritual Pepys (Cotton's version) Montaigne; find a new depth in Wordsworth, undreamed of before,—that divinely-inspired, wise, deep, tender, grand,—bore. Or, out of my study, the scholar thrown off, nature holds up her shield 'gainst the sneer and the scoff; the landscape, forever consoling and kind, pours her wine and her oil on the smarts of the mind. The waterfall, scattering its vanishing gems; the tall grove of hemlocks, with moss on their stems, like plashes of sunlight; the pond in the woods, where no foot but mine and the bittern's intrudes; these are all my kind neighbors, and leave me no wish to say aught to you all, my poor critics, but—pish! I have buried the hatchet; I am twisting an allumette out of one of you now, and relighting my calumet. In your private capacities, come when you please, I will give you my hand and a fresh pipe a-piece.

As I ran through the leaves of my poor little book, to take a fond author's first tremulous look, it was quite an excitement to hunt the *errata*, sprawled in as birds' tracks are in some kinds of strata (only these made things crookeder). Fancy an heir, that a father had seen born well-featured and fair, turning suddenly wry-nosed, club-footed, squint-eyed, hare-lipped, wapper-jawed, carrot-haired, from a pride become an aversion,—my case was yet worse. A club-foot (by way of a change) in a verse, I might have forgiven, an *o*'s being wry, a botch in an *e*, or a cock in an *i*,—but to have the sweet babe of my brain served in *pi*! I am not queasy-stomached, but such a Thyestean banquet[7] as that was quite out of the question.

---

5. Lowell's first prose work was on the Elizabethan dramatists, *Conversations on Some of the Old Poets* (1845), and his admiration for them never faded.

6. Jones Very (1813–1880), American transcendentalist poet. His appearance in the sublime company of this list would be surprising to all modern critics except Yvor Winters.

7. Thyestes was served his own children.

In the edition now issued, no pains are neglected, and my verses, as orators say, stand corrected. Yet some blunders remain of the public's own make, which I wish to correct for my personal sake. For instance, a character drawn in pure fun and condensing the traits of a dozen in one, has been, as I hear by some persons applied to a good friend of mine, whom to stab in the side, as we walked along chatting and joking together, would not be *my* way.[8] I can hardly tell whether a question will ever arise in which he and I should by any strange fortune agree, but meanwhile my esteem for him grows as I know him, and, though not the best judge upon earth of a poem, he knows what it is he is saying and why, and is honest and fearless, two good points which I have not found so rife I can easily smother my love for them, whether on my side or 'tother.

For my other *anonymi*, you may be sure that I know what is meant by a caricature, and what by a portrait. There *are* those who think it is capital fun to be spattering their ink on quiet unquarrelsome folk, but the minute the game changes sides and the others begin it, they see something savage and horrible in it. As for me I respect neither women or men for their gender, nor own any sex in a pen. I choose just to hint to some causeless unfriends that, as far as I know, there are always two ends (and one of them heaviest, too) to a staff, and two parties also to every good laugh.

[Apollo on Inspiration]

* * *

At some poems he glanced, had been sent to him lately,
And the metre and sentiment puzzled him greatly;
"Mehercle! I'd make such proceedings felonious,—
Have they all of them slept in the cave of Trophonius?[9]
Look well to your seat, 'tis like taking an airing
On a corduroy road, and that out of repairing;

8. The reference is too vague to be certain, but it is possible that Lowell is here referring to his friend Francis James Child (1825–1896), Harvard scholar most famous for his definitive collection, *English and Scottish Popular Ballads* (10 vols.; Cambridge: Harvard University Press, 1882–1898).

9. The frightening oracle in this cave in Boeotia was supposed to deafen its hearers.

It leads one, 'tis true, through the primitive forest,
Grand natural features—but, then, one has no rest;
You just catch a glimpse of some ravishing distance,
When a jolt puts the whole of it out of existence,—
Why not use their ears, if they happen to have any?"
—Here the laurel-leaves murmured the name of poor Daphne.

"O, weep with me, Daphne," he sighed, "for you know it's
A terrible thing to be pestered with poets!
But, alas, she is dumb, and the proverb holds good,
She never will cry till she's out of the wood!
What wouldn't I give if I never had known of her?
'Twere a kind of relief had I something to groan over;
If I had but some letters of hers, now, to toss over,
I might turn for the nonce a Byronic philosopher,
And bewitch all the flats by bemoaning the loss of her.
One needs something tangible, though, to begin on—
A loom, as it were, for the fancy to spin on;
What boots all your grist? it can never be ground
Till a breeze makes the arms of the windmill go round
(Or, if 'tis a water-mill, alter the metaphor,
And say it won't stir, save the wheel be well wet afore,
Or lug in some stuff about water "so dreamily,"—
It is not a metaphor, though, 'tis a simile);
A lily, perhaps, would set *my* mill agoing,
For just at this season, I think, they are blowing,
Here, somebody, fetch one, not very far hence
They're in bloom by the score, 'tis but climbing a fence;
There's a poet hard by, who does nothing but fill his
Whole garden, from one end to t'other, with lilies;
A very good plan, were it not for satiety,
One longs for a weed here and there, for variety;
Though a weed is no more than a flower in disguise,
Which is seen through at once, if love give a man eyes.

[THE PEDANTIC CRITIC]

Now there happened to be among Phoebus's followers,

A gentleman, one of the omnivorous swallowers
Who bolt every book that comes out of the press,
Without the least question of larger or less,
Whose stomachs are strong at the expense of their head,—
For reading new books is like eating new bread,
One can bear it at first, but by gradual steps he
Is brought to death's door of a mental dyspepsy.
On a previous stage of existence, our Hero
Had ridden outside, with the glass below zero;
He had been, 'tis a fact you may safely rely on,
Of a very old stock a most eminent scion,—
A stock all fresh quacks their fierce boluses ply on,
Who stretch the new boots Earth's unwilling to try on,
Whom humbugs of all shapes and sorts keep their eye on,
Whose hair's in the mortar of every new Zion,
Who, when whistles are dear, go directly and buy one,
Who think Slavery a crime that we must not say fie on,
Who hunt, if they e'er hunt at all, with the lion
(Though they hunt lions also, whenever they spy one),
Who contrive to make every good fortune a wry one,
And at last choose the hard bed of honor to die on,
Whose pedigree, traced to earth's earliest years,
Is longer than anything else but their ears;—
In short, he was sent into life with the wrong key,
He unlocked the door, and stept forth a poor donkey.
Though kicked and abused by his bipedal betters,
Yet he filled no mean place in the kingdom of letters;
Far happier than many a literary hack,
He bore only paper-mill rags on his back;
(For it makes a vast difference which side the mill
One expends on the paper his labor and skill);
So, when his soul waited a new transmigration,
And Destiny balanced 'twixt this and that station,
Not having much time to expend upon bothers,
Remembering he'd had some connexion with authors,
And considering his four legs had grown paralytic,—
She set him on two, and he came forth a critic.

Through his babyhood no kind of pleasure he took
In any amusement but tearing a book;
For him there was no intermediate stage,
From babyhood up to straight-laced middle age;
There were years when he didn't wear coat-tails behind,
But a boy he could never be rightly defined;
Like the Irish Good Folk, though in length scarce a span,
From the womb he came gravely, a little old man;
While other boys' trowsers demanded the toil
Of the motherly fingers on all kinds of soil,
Red, yellow, brown, black, clayey, gravelly, loamy,
He sat in a corner and read *Viri Romae*.[10]
He never was known to unbend or to revel once
In base, marbles, hockey, or kick up the devil once;
He was just one of those who excite the benevolence
Of old prigs who sound the soul's depths with a ledger,
And are on the look-out for some young men to "edger-
-cate," as they call it, who won't be too costly,
And who'll afterward take to the ministry mostly;
Who always wear spectacles, always look bilious,
Always keep on good terms with each *mater-familias*
Throughout the whole parish, and manage to rear
Ten boys like themselves, on four hundred a year;
Who, fulfilling in turn the same fearful conditions,
Either preach through their noses, or go upon missions.

In this way our hero got safely to College,
Where he bolted alike both his commons and knowledge;
A reading-machine, always wound up and going,
He mastered whatever was not worth the knowing,
Appeared in a gown, and a vest of black satin,
To spout such a Gothic oration in Latin,
That Tully could never have made out a word in it
(Though himself was the model the author preferred in it),
And grasping the parchment which gave him in fee,
All the mystic and-so-forths contained in A. B.,

10. *Men of Rome*, a grammar school Latin text.

He was launched (life is always compared to a sea),
With just enough learning, and skill for the using it,
To prove he'd a brain, by forever confusing it.
So worthy Saint Benedict, piously burning
With the holiest zeal against secular learning,
Nesciensque scienter, as writers express it,
Indoctusque sapienter à Româ recessit.[11]

'Twould be endless to tell you the things that he knew,
All separate facts, undeniably true,
But with him or each other they'd nothing to do;
No power of combining, arranging, discerning,
Digested the masses he learned into learning;
There was one thing in life he had practical knowledge for,
(And this, you will think, he need scarce go to college for),
Not a deed would he do, nor a word would he utter,
Till he'd weighed its relations to plain bread and butter.
When he left Alma Mater, he practised his wits
In compiling the journals' historical bits,—
Of shops broken open, men falling in fits,
Great fortunes in England bequeathed to poor printers,
And cold spells, the coldest for many past winters,—
Then, rising by industry, knack, and address,
Got notices up for an unbiased press,
With a mind so well poised, it seemed equally made for
Applause or abuse, just which chanced to be paid for;
From this point his progress was rapid and sure,
To the post of a regular heavy reviewer.[12]

And here I must say, he wrote excellent articles
On the Hebraic points, or the force of Greek particles,
They filled up the space nothing else was prepared for,
And nobody read that which nobody cared for;
If any old book reached a fiftieth edition,
He could fill forty pages with safe erudition;

11. "The ignorant man wisely, the learned man foolishly retires from Rome."
12. Lowell is describing here the typical manner by which many, if not most, of the critics of his time proceeded from journalism to "literature."

He could gauge the old books by the old set of rules,
And his very old nothings pleased very old fools;
But give him a new book, fresh out of the heart,
And you put him at sea without compass or chart,—
His blunders aspired to the rank of an art;
For his lore was engraft, something foreign that grew in him,
Exhausting the sap of the native and true in him,
So that when a man came with a soul that was new in him,
Carving new forms of truth out of Nature's old granite,
New and old at their birth, like Le Verrier's planet,[13]
Which, to get a true judgment; themselves must create
In the soul of their critic the measure and weight,
Being rather themselves a fresh standard of grace,
To compute their own judge, and assign him his place,
Our reviewer would crawl all about it and round it,
And, reporting each circumstance just as he found it,
Without the least malice,—his record would be
Profoundly esthetic as that of a flea,
Which, supping on Wordsworth, should print, for our sakes,
Recollections of nights with the Bard of the Lakes,
Or, borne by an Arab guide, ventured to render a
General view of the ruins at Denderah.

As I said, he was never precisely unkind,
The defect in his brain was mere absence of mind;
If he boasted, 'twas simply that he was self-made,
A position which I, for one, never gainsaid,
My respect for my Maker supposing a skill
In his works which our hero would answer but ill;
And I trust that the mould which he used may be cracked, or he,
Made bold by success, may make broad his phylactery,
And set up a kind of a man-manufactory,
An event which I shudder to think about, seeing
That Man is a moral, accountable being.

He meant well enough, but was still in the way,

13. The planet Neptune, discovered and named by the French astronomer
Leverrier in 1846.

As a dunce always is, let him be where he may;
Indeed, they appear to come into existence
To impede other folks with their awkward assistance;
If you set up a dunce on the very North pole,
All alone with himself, I believe, on my soul,
He'd manage to get betwixt somebody's shins,
And pitch him down bodily, all in his sins,
To the grave polar bears sitting round on the ice,
All shortening their grace, to be in for a slice;
Or, if he found nobody else there to pother,
Why, one of his legs would just trip up the other,
For there's nothing we read of in torture's inventions,
Like a well-meaning dunce, with the best of intentions.

A terrible fellow to meet in society,
Not the toast that he buttered was ever so dry at tea;
There he'd sit at the table and stir in his sugar,
Crouching close for a spring, all the while, like a cougar;
Be sure of your facts, of your measures and weights,
Of your time—he's as fond as an Arab of dates;—
You'll be telling, perhaps, in your comical way,
Of something you've seen in the course of the day;
And, just as you're tapering out the conclusion,
You venture an ill-fated classic allusion,—
The girls have all got their laughs ready, when, whack!
The cougar comes down on your thunderstruck back;
You had left out a comma,—your Greek's put in joint,
And pointed at cost of your story's whole point.
In the course of the evening, you venture on certain
Soft speeches to Anne, in shade of the curtain;
You tell her your heart can be likened to *one* flower,
"And that, oh most charming of women, 's the sunflower,
Which turns"—here a clear nasal voice, to your terror,
From outside the curtain, says "that's all an error."
As for him, he's—no matter, he never grew tender,
Sitting after a ball, with his feet on the fender,
Shaping somebody's sweet features out of cigar smoke
(Though he'd willingly grant you that such doings are smoke);

All women he damns with *mutabile semper*,[14]
And if ever he felt something like love's distemper,
'Twas toward a young lady who spoke ancient Mexican,
And assisted her father in making a lexicon;
Though I recollect hearing him get quite ferocious
About one Mary Clausum, the mistress of Grotius,[15]
Or something of that sort,—but, no more to bore ye
With character-painting, I'll turn to my story.

Now, Apollo, who finds it convenient sometimes
To get his court clear of the makers of rhymes,
The *genus*, I think it is called, *irritabile*,[16]
Every one of whom thinks himself treated most shabbily,
And nurses a—what is it?—*immedicabile*,[17]
Which keeps him at boiling-point, hot for a quarrel,
As bitter as wormwood, and sourer than sorrel,
If any poor devil but look at a laurel;—
Apollo, I say, being sick of their rioting
(Though he sometimes acknowledged their verse had a quieting
Effect after dinner, and seemed to suggest a
Retreat to the shrine of a tranquil siesta),
Kept our Hero at hand, who, by means of a bray,
Which he gave to the life, drove the rabble away;
And if that wouldn't do, he was sure to succeed,
If he took his review out and offered to read;
Or, failing in plans of this milder description,
He would ask for their aid to get up a subscription,
Considering that authorship wasn't a rich craft,
To print the "American drama of Witchcraft."[18]

14. "Always fickle."

15. A recondite pun. Hugh de Groot, or Hugo Grotius (1583–1645), Dutch humanist and scholar, published his lengthy study of maritime law, *Mare Clausum*, in 1632.

16. "Irritable race" (Horace, *Epistles II*, 2. 102).

17. "Incurable."

18. Cornelius Mathews' play *Witchcraft* was puffed by Margaret Fuller and by the "Young America" group, but failed disastrously when it was performed in Philadelphia in 1846.

"Stay, I'll read you a scene,"—but he hardly began,
Ere Apollo shrieked "Help!" and the authors all ran:
And once, when these purgatives acted with less spirit,
And the desperate case asked a remedy desperate,
He drew from his pocket a foolscap epistle,
As calmly as if 'twere a nine-barrelled pistol,
And threatened them all with the judgment to come,
Of "A wandering Star's first impressions of Rome."[19]
"Stop! stop!" with their hands o'er their ears, screamed the Muses,
"He may go off and murder himself, if he chooses,
'Twas a means self-defence only sanctioned his trying,
'Tis mere massacre now that the enemy's flying;
If he's forced to 't again, and we happen to be there,
Give us each a large handkerchief soaked in strong ether."

[The Sonnet]

* * *

He was gone a long time, and Apollo meanwhile,
Went over some sonnets of his with a file,
For of all compositions, he thought that the sonnet
Best repaid all the toil you expended upon it;
It should reach with one impulse the end of its course,
And for one final blow collect all of its force;
Not a verse should be salient, but each one should tend
With a wave-like up-gathering to burst at the end;—

[The Parade of American Writers]

So, condensing the strength here, there smoothing a wry kink,
He was killing the time, when up walked Mr. [Duyckinck];

19. Lowell probably does not have a specific poem in mind here; one of the most common clichés of poetry of this period was the American traveler's verses of straining sensationalism on Rome. Many such works were written, ranging in literary reputation (but not merit) from Emerson's "Written at Rome" to Samuel Rogers' "I Am in Rome!," not to mention Harriet Beecher Stowe's "Day in the Pamfili Doria." All such effusions ultimately derived from "Childe Harold."

At a few steps behind him, a small man in glasses,[20]
Went dodging about, muttering "murderers! asses!"
From out of his pocket a paper he'd take,
With the proud look of martyrdom tied to its stake,
And, reading a squib at himself, he'd say, "Here I see
'Gainst American letters a bloody conspiracy,
They are all by my personal enemies written;
I must post an anonymous letter to Britain,
And show that this gall is the merest suggestion
Of spite at my zeal on the Copyright question,
For, on this side the water, 'tis prudent to pull
O'er the eyes of the public their national wool,
By accusing of slavish respect to John Bull,
All American authors who have more or less
Of that anti-American humbug—success,
While in private we're always embracing the knees
Of some twopenny editor over the seas,
And licking his critical shoes, for you know 'tis
The whole aim of our lives to get one English 'notice';
My American puffs I would willingly burn all
(They're all from one source, monthly, weekly, diurnal),
To get but a kick from a transmarine journal!"

So, culling the jibes of each critical scorner
As if they were plums, and himself were Jack Horner,
He came cautiously on, peeping round every corner,
And into each hole where a weasel might pass in,
Expecting the knife of some critic assassin,
Who stabs to the heart with a caricature,
Not so bad as those daubs of the Sun, to be sure,
Yet done with a dagger-o'-type, whose vile portraits
Disperse all one's good, and condense all one's poor traits.

Apollo looked up, hearing footsteps approaching,
And slipped out of sight the new rhymes he was broaching,—
"Good day, Mr. [Duyckinck], I'm happy to meet
With a scholar so ripe, and a critic so neat,

20. Cornelius Mathews, Duyckinck's protégé.

Who through Grub street the soul of a gentleman carries,—
What news from that suburb of London and Paris
Which latterly makes such shrill claims to monopolize
The credit of being the New World's metropolis?" [21]

"Why, nothing of consequence, save this attack
On my friend there, behind, by some pitiful hack,
Who thinks every national author a poor one,
That isn't a copy of something that's foreign,
And assaults the American Dick—"
                                        "Nay, 'tis clear
That your Damon there 's fond of a flea in his ear,
And, if no one else furnished them gratis, on tick
He would buy some himself, just to hear the old click;
Why, I honestly think, if some fool in Japan
Should turn up his nose at the "Poems on Man," [22]
Your friend there by some inward instinct would know it,
Would get it translated, reprinted, and show it;
As a man might take off a high stock to exhibit
The autograph round his own neck of the gibbet;
Nor would let it rest so, but fire column after column,
Signed Cato, or Brutus, or something as solemn,
By way of displaying his critical crosses,
And tweaking that poor trans-atlantic proboscis,
His broadsides resulting (and this there's no doubt of)
In successively sinking the craft they're fired out of.
Now nobody knows when an author is hit,
If he don't have a public hysterical fit;
Let him only keep close in his snug garret's dim aether,
And nobody'd think of his critics—or him either;
If an author have any least fibre of worth in him,
Abuse would but tickle the organ of mirth in him,

21. That is, New York, which was then replacing Boston as the cultural center of the United States.
22. See above, p. 129, note 11. Subsequent editions of the *Fable* added this couplet here: "(Which contain many verses as fine, by the bye, / As any that lately came under my eye.)"

All the critics on earth cannot crush with their ban,
One word that's in tune with the nature of man."

"Well, perhaps so; meanwhile I have brought you a book,
Into which if you'll just have the goodness to look,
You may feel so delighted, when you have got through it,
As to think it not unworth your while to review it,
And I think I can promise your thoughts, if you do,
A place in the next *Democratic Review*." 23

"The most thankless of gods you must surely have tho't me,
For this is the forty-fourth copy you've brought me,
I have given them away, or at least I have tried,
But I've forty-two left, standing all side by side
(The man who accepted that one copy, died)—
From one end of a shelf to the other they reach,
'With the author's respects' neatly written in each.
The publisher, sure, will proclaim a Te Deum,
When he hears of that order the British Museum
Has sent for one set of what books were first printed
In America, little or big,—for 'tis hinted
That this is the first truly tangible hope he
Has ever had raised for the sale of a copy.
I've thought very often 'twould be a good thing
In all public collections of books, if a wing
Were set off by itself, like the seas from the dry lands,
Marked *Literature suited to desolate islands*,
And filled with such books as could never be read
Save by readers of proofs, forced to do it for bread,—
Such books as one's wrecked on in small country-taverns,
Such as hermits might mortify over in caverns,
Such as Satan, if printing had then been invented,
As the climax of woe, would to Job have presented,

23. There is a hint of spite here in an otherwise rather sympathetic portrait of
Duyckinck. Duyckinck had recently refused an article of Lowell's for the *Demo-cratic Review*. Lowell is perhaps striking back at him with the comments that follow
in the next paragraph on Mathews' *Big Abel and the Little Manhattan* (1845), which
Duyckinck had been puffing unsuccessfully.

Such as Crusoe might dip in, although there are few so
Outrageously cornered by fate as poor Crusoe;
And since the philanthropists just now are banging
And gibbetting all who're in favor of hanging—
(Though Cheever[24] has proved that the Bible and Altar
Were let down from Heaven at the end of a halter,
And that vital religion would dull and grow callous,
Unrefreshed, now and then, with a sniff of the gallows)—
And folks are beginning to think it looks odd,
To choke a poor scamp for the glory of God;
And that He who esteems the Virginia reel
A bait to draw saints from their spiritual weal,
And regards the quadrille as a far greater knavery
Than crushing His African children with slavery,—
Since all who take part in a waltz or cotillon
Are mounted for hell on the Devil's own pillion,
Who, as every true orthodox Christian well knows,
Approaches the heart through the door of the toes,—
That He, I was saying, whose judgments are stored
For such as take steps in despite of his word,
Should look with delight on the agonized prancing
Of a wretch who has not the least ground for his dancing,
While the State, standing by, sings a verse from the Psalter
About offering to God on his favorite halter,
And, when the legs droop from their twitching divergence,
Sells the clothes to a Jew, and the corpse to the surgeons.

Now, instead of all this, I think I can direct you all
To a criminal code both humane and effectual;—
I propose to shut up every doer of wrong
With these desperate books, for such term, short or long,
As by statute in such cases made and provided,
Shall be by your wise legislators decided
Thus:—Let murderers be shut, to grow wiser and cooler,

24. George B. Cheever (1807–1890), American clergyman and writer, had
recently written *A Defence of Capital Punishment* (1846). Cheever's illiberal position
was anathema to Lowell, and provoked this long digression on the hypocrisy of those
favoring capital punishment.

At hard labor for life on the works of Miss [Fuller];
Petty thieves, kept from flagranter crimes by their fears,
Shall peruse *Yankee Doodle*[25] a blank term of years,—
That American *Punch*, like the English, no doubt—
Just the sugar and lemons and spirit left out.

"But stay, here comes Tityrus Griswold,[26] and leads on
The flocks whom he first plucks alive, and then feeds on,—
A loud cackling swarm, in whose feathers warm-drest,
He goes for as perfect a—swan, as the rest.

"There comes Emerson first, whose rich words, every one,
Are like gold nails in temples to hang trophies on,
Whose prose is grand verse, while his verse, the Lord knows,
Is some of it pr——No, 'tis not even prose;
I'm speaking of metres; some poems have welled
From those rare depths of soul that have ne'er been excelled;
They're not epics, but that doesn't matter a pin,
In creating, the only hard thing 's to begin;
A grass-blade 's no easier to make than an oak,
If you've once found the way, you've achieved the grand stroke;
In the worst of his poems are mines of rich matter,
But thrown in a heap with a crash and a clatter;
Now it is not one thing nor another alone
Makes a poem, but rather the general tone,
The something pervading, uniting the whole,
The before unconceived, unconceivable soul,
So that just in removing this trifle or that, you
Take away, as it were, a chief limb of the statue;
Roots, wood, bark, and leaves, singly perfect may be,
But, clapt hodge-podge together, they don't make a tree.

"But, to come back to Emerson (whom, by the way,
I believe we left waiting)—his is, we may say,

25. A short-lived American humor magazine (1846–1847), edited by Mathews.
26. Rufus Wilmot Griswold (1815–1857), journalist and anthologist. Lowell's ambivalent feelings about Griswold are clear from these four lines: he is "Tityrus" Griswold, a name which is an archetype for pastoral character, yet what he does to his "flocks"—the writers he anthologizes—is far from pastoral.

A Greek head on right Yankee shoulders, whose range
Has Olympus for one pole, for t'other the Exchange;
He seems, to my thinking (although I'm afraid
The comparison must, long ere this, have been made),
A Plotinus-Montaigne,[27] where the Egyptian's gold mist
And the Gascon's shrewd wit cheek-by-jowl co-exist;
All admire, and yet scarcely six converts he's got
To I don't (nor they either) exactly know what;
For though he builds glorious temples, 'tis odd
He leaves never a doorway to get in a god.
'Tis refreshing to old-fashioned people like me,
To meet such a primitive Pagan as he,
In whose mind all creation is duly respected
As parts of himself—just a little projected;
And who's willing to worship the stars and the sun,
A convert to—nothing but Emerson.
So perfect a balance there is in his head,
That he talks of things sometimes as if they were dead;
Life, nature, love, God, and affairs of that sort,
He looks at as merely ideas; in short,
As if they were fossils stuck round in a cabinet,
Of such vast extent that our Earth's a mere dab in it;
Composed just as he is inclined to conjecture her,
Namely, one part pure earth, ninety-nine parts pure lecturer;
You are filled with delight at his clear demonstration,
Each figure, word, gesture, just fits the occasion,
With the quiet precision of science he'll sort 'em,
But you can't help suspecting the whole a *post mortem*.

   "There are persons, mole-blind to the soul's make and style,
Who insist on a likeness 'twixt him and Carlyle;
To compare him with Plato would be vastly fairer,
Carlyle's the more burly, but E. is the rarer;
He sees fewer objects, but clearlier, trulier,
If C.'s as original, E.'s more peculiar;

27. Plotinus (A.D. 205–270), neo-Platonic philosopher, and Montaigne, the
great skeptical thinker, well define Emerson's breadth. Lowell takes up Emerson's
ideas more seriously in "Emerson the Lecturer," pp. 206–215.

That he's more of a man you might say of the one,
Of the other he's more of an Emerson;
C.'s the Titan, as shaggy of mind as of limb,—
E. the clear-eyed Olympian, rapid and slim;
The one's two-thirds Norseman, the other half Greek,
Where the one's most abounding, the other's to seek;
C.'s generals require to be seen in the mass,—
E.'s specialties gain if enlarged by the glass;
C. gives Nature and God his own fits of the blues,
And rims common-sense things with mystical hues,—
E. sits in the mystery calm and intense,
And looks coolly around him with sharp common-sense;
C. shows you how every-day matters unite
With the dim transdiurnal recesses of night,—
While E., in a plain, preternatural way,
Makes mysteries matters of mere every day;
C. draws all his characters quite _à la_ Fuseli,—[28]
He don't sketch their bundles of muscles and thews illy,
But he paints with a brush so untamed and profuse,
They seem nothing but bundles of muscles and thews;
E. is rather like Flaxman,[29] lines strait and severe,
And a colorless outline, but full, round, and clear;—
To the men he thinks worthy he frankly accords
The design of a white marble statue in words.
C. labors to get at the centre, and then
Take a reckoning from there of his actions and men;
E. calmly assumes the said centre as granted,
And, given himself, has whatever is wanted.

"He has imitators in scores, who omit
No part of the man but his wisdom and wit,—
Who go carefully o'er the sky-blue of his brain,

28. John Heinrich Fuseli (1742–1825), Swiss-English painter and illustrator.
Like Carlyle, he was fond of chiaroscuro and, as the text states, physical exaggeration by illustration at moments of stress.

29. John Flaxman (1755–1826), English sculptor and engraver; although the modern student of Flaxman might not agree with Lowell's comment that he is colorless, it is surely true of him when contrasted with Fuseli.

And when he has skimmed it once, skim it again;
If at all they resemble him, you may be sure it is
Because their shoals mirror his mists and obscurities,
As a mud-puddle seems deep as heaven for a minute,
While a cloud that floats o'er is reflected within it.

"There comes [Channing],[30] for instance; to see him's rare sport,
Tread in Emerson's tracks with legs painfully short;
How he jumps, how he strains, and gets red in the face,
To keep step with the mystagogue's natural pace!
He follows as close as a stick to a rocket,
His fingers exploring the prophet's each pocket.
Fie, for shame, brother bard; with good fruit of your own,
Can't you let neighbor Emerson's orchards alone?
Besides, 'tis no use, you'll not find e'en a core,—
[Thoreau] has picked up all the windfalls before.
They might strip every tree, and E. never would catch 'em,
His Hesperides have no rude dragon to watch 'em;
When they send him a dish-full, and ask him to try 'em,
He never suspects how the sly rogues came by 'em;
He wonders why 'tis there are none such his trees on,
And thinks 'em the best he has tasted this season.

"Yonder, calm as a cloud, Alcott[31] stalks in a dream,
And fancies himself in thy groves, Academe,
With the Parthenon nigh, and the olive-trees o'er him,
And never a fact to perplex him or bore him,
With a snug room at Plato's, when night comes, to walk to,
And people from morning till midnight to talk to,
And from midnight till morning, nor snore in their listening;—

30. This and the following identification are disputed, but E. J. Nichols'
"Identification of Characters in Lowell's *A Fable for Critics*" (*American Literature*, IV
[May 1932], 191–194) gives some good evidence that Lowell intended William
Ellery Channing (1818–1901) as the first of Emerson's followers and Thoreau as
the second. See also Perry Miller, *The Transcendentalists* (Cambridge: Harvard
University Press, 1950), pp. 375–383.

31. Amos Bronson Alcott (1799–1888), transcendental reformer, writer of
Orphic sayings for the *Dial*, and perhaps most famous as the father of Louisa May
Alcott.

So he muses, his face with the joy of it glistening,
For his highest conceit of a happiest state is
Where they'd live upon acorns, and hear him talk gratis;
And indeed, I believe, no man ever talked better—
Each sentence hangs perfectly poised to a letter;
He seems piling words, but there's royal dust hid
In the heart of each sky-piercing pyramid.
While he talks he is great, but goes out like a taper,
If you shut him up closely with pen, ink, and paper;
Yet his fingers itch for 'em from morning till night,
And he thinks he does wrong if he don't always write;
In this, as in all things, a lamb among men,
He goes to sure death when he goes to his pen.

  "Close behind him is Brownson,[32] his mouth very full
With attempting to gulp a Gregorian bull;
Who contrives, spite of that, to pour out as he goes
A stream of transparent and forcible prose;
He shifts quite about, then proceeds to expound
That 'tis merely the earth, not himself, that turns round,
And wishes it clearly impressed on your mind,
That the weather-cock rules and not follows the wind;
Proving first, then as deftly confuting each side,
With no doctrine pleased that's not somewhere denied,
He lays the denier away on the shelf,
And then—down beside him lies gravely himself.
He's the Salt River boatman, who always stands willing
To convey friend or foe without charging a shilling,
And so fond of the trip that, when leisure's to spare,
He'll row himself up, if he can't get a fare.
The worst of it is, that his logic's so strong,
That of two sides he commonly chooses the wrong;
If there *is* only one, why, he'll split it in two,
And first pummel this half, then that, black and blue.
That white's white needs no proof, but it takes a deep fellow

  32. Orestes A. Brownson (1803–1876), transcendentalist writer whose conversion
to Catholicism in 1844 shocked the movement.

To prove it jet-black, and that jet-black is yellow.
He offers the true faith to drink in a sieve,—
When it reaches your lips there's naught left to believe
But a few silly- (syllo-, I mean,) -gisms that squat 'em,
Like tadpoles, o'erjoyed with the mud at the bottom.

"There is Willis,[33] so *natty* and jaunty and gay,
Who says his best things in so foppish a way,
With conceits and pet phrases so thickly o'erlaying 'em,
That one hardly knows whether to thank him for saying 'em;
Over-ornament ruins both poem and prose,
Just conceive of a muse with a ring in her nose!
His prose had a natural grace of its own,
And enough of it, too, if he'd let it alone;
But he twitches and jerks so, one fairly gets tired,
And is forced to forgive where he might have admired;
Yet whenever it slips away free and unlaced,
It runs like a stream, with a musical waste,
And gurgles along with the liquidest sweep;—
'Tis not deep as a river, but who'd have it deep?
In a country where scarcely a village is found
That has not its author sublime and profound,
For some one to be slightly shoal is a duty,
And Willis's shallowness makes half his beauty.
His prose winds along with a blithe, gurgling error,
And reflects all of Heaven it can see in its mirror.
'Tis a narrowish strip, but it is not an artifice,—
'Tis the true out-of-doors with its genuine hearty phiz;
It is Nature herself, and there's something in that,
Since most brains reflect but the crown of a hat.
No volume I know to read under a tree,
More truly delicious than his *A l'Abri*,
With the shadows of leaves flowing over your book,
Like ripple-shades netting the bed of a brook;

33.· Nathaniel Parker Willis (1806–1867), journalist and author, chiefly of travel
books and nature descriptions. His *A l'Abri* (1839), mentioned below, was written
quite literally "in the shade" of a tent Willis pitched in the Susquehanna Valley.

With June coming softly your shoulder to look over,
Breezes waiting to turn every leaf of your book over,
And Nature to criticise still as you read,—
The page that bears that is a rare one indeed.

"He's so innate a cockney, that had he been born
Where plain bare-skin 's the only full-dress that is worn,
He'd have given his own such an air that you'd say
'T had been made by a tailor to lounge in Broadway.
His nature 's a glass of champagne with the foam on 't,
As tender as Fletcher, as witty as Beaumont;
So his best things are done in the flush of the moment,
If he wait, all is spoiled; he may stir it and shake it,
But, the fixed air once gone, he can never re-make it.
He might be a marvel of easy delightfulness,
If he would not sometimes leave the *r* out of spritefulness;
And he ought to let Scripture alone—'tis self-slaughter,
For nobody likes inspiration-and-water.
He'd have been just the fellow to sup at the Mermaid,
Cracking jokes at rare Ben, with an eye to the bar-maid,
His wit running up as Canary ran down,—
The topmost bright bubble on the wave of The Town.

"Here comes Parker,[34] the Orson of parsons, a man
Whom the Church undertook to put under her ban—
(The Church of Socinus, I mean)—his opinions
Being So- (ultra) -cinian, they shocked the Socinians;
They believed—faith, I'm puzzled—I think I may call
Their belief a believing in nothing at all,
Or something of that sort; I know they all went
For a general union of total dissent:
He went a step farther; without cough or hem,
He frankly avowed he believed not in them;

34. Theodore Parker (1810–1860), the most brilliant and heretical of the
transcendentalist ministers. "Orson" refers to the fifteenth-century romance
Valentin et Orson, in which Orson, whose name derives from *ourson*, "little bear," is
nurtured wild in the forest. Lowell is being somewhat flippant in identifying
Parker's transcendentalism with the Socinian heresy, and then suggesting that he
was less orthodox still.

And, before he could be jumbled up or prevented,
From their orthodox kind of dissent he dissented.
There was heresy here, you perceive, for the right
Of privately judging means simply that light
Has been granted to *me*, for deciding on *you*,
And, in happier times, before Atheism grew,
The deed contained clauses for cooking you, too.
Now at Xerxes and Knut[35] we all laugh, yet our foot
With the same wave is wet that mocked Xerxes and Knut;
And we all entertain a sincere private notion,
That our *Thus far!* will have a great weight on the ocean.
'Twas so with our liberal Christians: they bore
With sincerest conviction their chairs to the shore;
They brandished their worn theological birches,
Bade natural progress keep out of the Churches,
And expected the lines they had drawn to prevail
With the fast-rising tide to keep out of their pale;
They had formerly dammed the Pontifical See,
And the same thing, they thought, would do nicely for P.;
But he turned up his nose at their mumming and shamming,
And cared (shall I say?) not a d— for their damming;
So they first read him out of their Church, and next minute
Turned round and declared he had never been in it.
But the ban was too small or the man was too big,
For he recks not their bells, books, and candles a fig;
(He don't look like a man who would *stay* treated shabbily,
Sophroniscus' son's head o'er the features of Rabelais;)—
He bangs and bethwacks them,—their backs he salutes
With the whole tree of knowledge torn up by the roots;
His sermons with satire are plenteously verjuiced,
And he talks in one breath of Confutzee, Cass, Zerduscht,
Jack Robinson, Peter the Hermit, Strap, Dathan,
Cush, Pit (not the bottomless, *that* he's no faith in),
Pan, Pillicock, Shakespeare, Paul, Toots, Monsieur Tonson,
Aldebaran, Alcander, Ben Khorat, Ben Jonson,

35. Both Xerxes the Great (519?–465 B.C.) and Canute II (994?–1035) are
supposed to have ordered the sea whipped after they suffered naval defeats.

Thoth, Richter, Joe Smith, Father Paul, Judah Monis,
Musaeus, Muretus, hem—μ Scorpionis,
Maccabee, Maccaboy, Mac—Mac—ah! Machiavelli,
Condorcet, Count d'Orsay, Conder, Say, Ganganelli,
Orion, O'Connell, the Chevalier D'O
(Whom the great Sully speaks of), το παν, the great toe
Of the statue of Jupiter, now made to pass
For that of Jew Peter by good Romish brass—36
(You may add for yourselves, for I find it a bore,
All the names you have ever, or not, heard before,
And when you've done that—why, invent a few more).
His hearers can't tell you on Sunday beforehand,
If in that day's discourse they'll be Bibled or Koraned,
For he's seized the idea (by his martyrdom fired),
That all men (not orthodox) *may be* inspired;
Yet, though wisdom profane with his creed he may weave in,
He makes it quite clear what he *doesn't* believe in,
While some, who decry him, think all Kingdom Come
Is a sort of a, kind of a, species of Hum,
Of which, as it were, so to speak, not a crumb
Would be left, if we didn't keep carefully mum,
And, to make a clean breast, that 'tis perfectly plain
That *all* kinds of wisdom are somewhat profane;
Now P.'s creed than this may be lighter or darker,
But in one thing, 'tis clear, he has faith, namely—Parker;
And this is what makes him the crowd-drawing preacher,
There's a back-ground of god to each hard-working feature,
Every word that he speaks has been fierily furnaced
In the blast of a life that has struggled in earnest:
There he stands, looking more like a ploughman than priest,
If not dreadfully awkward, not graceful at least,
His gestures all downright and same, if you will,
As of brown-fisted Hobnail in hoeing a drill,
But his periods fall on you, stroke after stroke,

36. Since this list is only a tour de force, I have not annotated it. Parker had this
kind of erudition, and Lowell was the one man who could appreciate his learning,
even though he here pokes fun at it.

Like the blows of a lumberer felling an oak,
You forget the man wholly, you're thankful to meet
With a preacher who smacks of the field and the street,
And to hear, you're not over-particular whence,
Almost Taylor's profusion, quite Latimer's sense.[37]

"There is Bryant, as quiet, as cool, and as dignified,
As a smooth, silent iceberg, that never is ignified,
Save when by reflection 'tis kindled o' nights
With a semblance of flame by the chill Northern Lights.
He may rank (Griswold says so) first bard of your nation
(There's no doubt that he stands in supreme ice-olation),
Your topmost Parnassus he may set his heel on,
But no warm applauses come, peal following peal on,—
He's too smooth and too polished to hang any zeal on:
Unqualified merits, I'll grant, if you choose, he has 'em,
But he lacks the one merit of kindling enthusiasm;
If he stir you at all, it is just, on my soul,
Like being stirred up with the very North Pole.

"He is very nice reading in summer, but *inter*
Nos, we don't want *extra* freezing in winter;
Take him up in the depth of July, my advice is,
When you feel an Egyptian devotion to ices.
But, deduct all you can, there's enough that's right good in him,
He has a true soul for field, river, and wood in him;
And his heart, in the midst of brick walls, or where'er it is;
Glows, softens, and thrills with the tenderest charities,—
To you mortals that delve in this trade-ridden planet?
No, to old Berkshire's hills, with their limestone and granite.
If you're one who *in loco* (add *foco* here) *desipis*,[38]

37. Bishop Jeremy Taylor (1613–1667), English prelate and author of some
fifteen volumes of sermons; Hugh Latimer (1485?–1555) English protestant
martyr who, though he never took the doctorate, often corrected bishops during
his long lifetime.

38. A very complicated pun; the Latin is from Horace, *Odes*, IV. 12, 28: "to
trifle may be pleasant in the right place." A locofoco was originally a self-igniting
match, but the name was most often applied to members of the Democratic party;
Lowell plays on all these senses.

You will get of his outermost heart (as I guess) a piece;
But you'd get deeper down if you came as a precipice,
And would break the last seal of its inwardest fountain,
If you only could palm yourself off for a mountain.
Mr. Quivis,[39] or somebody quite as discerning,
Some scholar who's hourly expecting his learning,
Calls B. the American Wordsworth; but Wordsworth
Is worth near as much as your whole tuneful herd's worth.
No, don't be absurd, he's an excellent Bryant;
But, my friends, you'll endanger the life of your client,
By attempting to stretch him up into a giant:
If you choose to compare him, I think there are two per-
-sons fit for a parallel—Thomson and Cowper;[40]
I don't mean exactly,—there's something of each,
There's T.'s love of nature, C.'s penchant to preach;
Just mix up their minds so that C.'s spice of craziness
Shall balance and neutralize T.'s turn for laziness,
And it gives you a brain cool, quite frictionless, quiet,
Whose internal police nips the buds of all riot,—
A brain like a permanent strait-jacket put on
The heart which strives vainly to burst off a button,—
A brain which, without being slow or mechanic,
Does more than a larger less drilled, more volcanic;
He's a Cowper condensed, with no craziness bitten,
And the advantage that Wordsworth before him has written.

"But, my dear little bardlings, don't prick up your ears,
Nor suppose I would rank you and Bryant as peers;
If I call him an iceberg, I don't mean to say
There is nothing in that which is grand, in its way;

39. "Mr. Anybody."
40.

> To demonstrate quickly and easily how per-
> -versely absurd 'tis to sound this name *Cowper*,
> As people in general call him named super,
> I just add that he rhymes it himself with horse-trooper.

[Lowell's note.]

James Thomson (1700–1748) and William Cowper (1731–1800) were both English
poets who, like Bryant, wrote nature poetry of a certain formal and tender sort.

He is almost the one of your poets that knows
How much grace, strength, and dignity lie in Repose;
If he sometimes fall short, he is too wise to mar
His thought's modest fulness by going too far;
'Twould be well if your authors should all make a trial
Of what virtue there is in severe self-denial,
And measure their writings by Hesiod's[41] staff,
Which teaches that all has less value than half.

"There is Whittier, whose swelling and vehement heart
Strains the strait-breasted drab of the Quaker apart,
And reveals the live Man, still supreme and erect
Underneath the bemummying wrappers of sect;
There was ne'er a man born who had more of the swing
Of the true lyric bard and all that kind of thing;
And his failures arise (though perhaps he don't know it)
From the very same cause that has made him a poet,—
A fervor of mind, which knows no separation
'Twixt simple excitement and pure inspiration,
As my Pythoness erst sometimes erred from not knowing
If 'twere I or mere wind through her tripod was blowing;
Let his mind once get head in its favorite direction
And the torrent of verse bursts the dams of reflection,
While, borne with the rush of the metre along,
The poet may chance to go right or go wrong,
Content with the whirl and delirium of song;
Then his grammar's not always correct, nor his rhymes,
And he's prone to repeat his own lyrics sometimes,
Not his best, though, for those are struck off at white-heats
When the heart in his breast like a trip-hammer beats,
And can ne'er be repeated again any more
Than they could have been carefully plotted before:
Like old what's-his-name[42] there at the battle of Hastings

41. In "Works and Days," line 40: "Fools all! who never learned how much better than the whole the half is." The context is that the statement is true if strife is to be avoided.

42. Taillefer, a minstrel who participated in the Battle of Hastings (1066), and was allowed to strike the first blow.

(Who, however, gave more than mere rhythmical bastings),
Our Quaker leads off metaphorical fights
For reform and whatever they call human rights,
Both singing and striking in front of the war
And hitting his foes with the mallet of Thor;
Anne haec, one exclaims, on beholding his knocks,
Vestis filii tui, O, leather-clad Fox?[43]
Can that be thy son, in the battle's mad din,
Preaching brotherly love and then driving it in
To the brain of the tough old Goliath of sin,
With the smoothest of pebbles from Castaly's spring[44]
Impressed on his hard moral sense with a sling?

   "All honor and praise to the right-hearted bard
Who was true to The Voice when such service was hard,
Who himself was so free he dared sing for the slave
When to look but a protest in silence was brave;
All honor and praise to the women and men
Who spoke out for the dumb and the down-trodden then!
I need not to name them, already for each
I see History preparing the statue and niche;
They were harsh, but shall *you* be so shocked at hard words
Who have beaten your pruning-hooks up into swords,
Whose rewards and hurrahs men are surer to gain
By the reaping of men and of women than grain?
Why should *you* stand aghast at their fierce wordy war, if
You scalp one another for Bank or for Tariff?
You're calling them cut-throats and knaves all day long
Don't prove that the use of hard language is wrong;
While the World's heart beats quicker to think of such men
As signed Tyranny's doom with a bloody steel-pen,
While on Fourth-of-Julys beardless orators fright one
With hints at Harmodius and Aristogeiton,[45]
You need not look shy at your sisters and brothers

   43. "Can this be the coat of your son?" (*Genesis,* 32:33); George Fox (1624–1691) founded the Society of Friends.
   44. A sacred spring on Mount Parnassus; hence, a source of inspiration.
   45. Two Athenian youths who assassinated the tyrant Hipparchus in 514 B.C.

Who stab with sharp words for the freedom of others;—
No, a wreath, twine a wreath for the loyal and true
Who, for sake of the many, dared stand with the few,
Not of blood-spattered laurel for enemies braved,
But of broad, peaceful oak-leaves for citizens saved!

"Here comes Dana,[46] abstractedly loitering along,
Involved in a paulo-post-future of song,
Who'll be going to write what'll never be written
Till the Muse, ere he thinks of it, gives him the mitten,—
Who is so well aware of how things should be done,
That his own works displease him before they're begun,—
Who so well all that makes up good poetry knows,
That the best of his poems is written in prose;
All saddled and bridled stood Pegasus waiting,
He was booted and spurred, but he loitered debating,
In a very grave question his soul was immersed,—
Which foot in the stirrup he ought to put first;
And, while this point and that he judicially dwelt on,
He, somehow or other, had written *Paul Felton*,
Whose beauties or faults, whichsoever you see there,
You'll allow only genius could hit upon either.
That he once was the *Idle Man* none will deplore,
But I fear he will never be anything more;
The ocean of song heaves and glitters before him,
The depth and the vastness and longing sweep o'er him,
He knows every breaker and shoal on the chart,
He has the Coast Pilot and so on by heart,
Yet he spends his whole life, like the man in the fable,
In learning to swim on his library-table.

"There swaggers John Neal,[47] who has wasted in Maine
The sinews and cords of his pugilist brain,

46. Richard Henry Dana, Sr. (1787–1879), poet and essayist, editor of the *North American Review*; it is his son who was the author of *Two Years before the Mast*. *Paul Felton* was a tale by Dana published in 1821; the *Idle Man* was a periodical he edited in 1821–1822.

47. Author and critic (1793–1876) noted for his sharp criticisms of American writers.

Who might have been poet, but that, in its stead, he
Preferred to believe that he was so already;
Too hasty to wait till Art's ripe fruit should drop,
He must pelt down an unripe and colicky crop;
Who took to the law, and had this sterling plea for it,
It required him to quarrel, and paid him a fee for it;
A man who's made less than he might have, because
He always has thought himself more than he was,—
Who, with very good natural gifts as a bard,
Broke the strings of his lyre out by striking too hard,
And cracked half the notes of a truly fine voice,
Because song drew less instant attention than noise.
Ah, men do not know how much strength is in poise,
That he goes the farthest who goes far enough,
And that all beyond that is just bother and stuff.
No vain man matures, he makes too much new wood;
His blooms are too thick for the fruit to be good;
'Tis the modest man ripens, 'tis he that achieves,
Just what's needed of sunshine and shade he receives;
Grapes, to mellow, require the cool dark of their leaves;
Neal wants balance; he throws his mind always too far,
And whisks out flocks of comets, but never a star;
He has so much muscle, and loves so to show it,
That he strips himself naked to prove he's a poet,
And, to show he could leap Art's wide ditch, if he tried,
Jumps clean o'er it, and into the hedge t'other side.
He has strength, but there's nothing about him in keeping;
One gets surelier onward by walking than leaping;
He has used his own sinews himself to distress,
And had done vastly more had he done vastly less;
In letters, too soon is as bad as too late,
Could he only have waited he might have been great,
But he plumped into Helicon up to the waist,
And muddied the stream ere he took his first taste.

"There is Hawthorne, with genius so shrinking and rare
That you hardly at first see the strength that is there;
A frame so robust, with a nature so sweet,

So earnest, so graceful, so solid, so fleet,
Is worth a descent from Olympus to meet;
'Tis as if a rough oak that for ages had stood,
With his gnarled bony branches like ribs of the wood,
Should bloom, after cycles of struggle and scathe,
With a single anemone trembly and rathe;
His strength is so tender, his wildness so meek,
That a suitable parallel sets one to seek,—
He's a John Bunyan Fouqué, a Puritan Tieck;[48]
When Nature was shaping him, clay was not granted
For making so full-sized a man as she wanted,
So, to fill out her model, a little she spared
From some finer-grained stuff for a woman prepared,
And she could not have hit a more excellent plan
For making him fully and perfectly man.
The success of her scheme gave her so much delight,
That she tried it again, shortly after, in Dwight;[49]
Only, while she was kneading and shaping the clay,
She sang to her work in her sweet childish way,
And found, when she'd put the last touch to his soul,
That the music had somehow got mixed with the whole.

"Here's Cooper, who's written six volumes to show
He's as good as a lord: well, let's grant that he's so;
If a person prefer that description of praise,
Why, a coronet's certainly cheaper than bays;
But he need take no pains to convince us he's not
(As his enemies say) the American Scott.
Choose any twelve men, and let C. read aloud
That one of his novels of which he's most proud,

48. Baron de la Motte Fouqué (1777–1843) and Ludwig Tieck (1773–1853),
French and German writers of romances. Lowell is careful to point out the Puritan
cast of Hawthorne's romantic writing; Poe, in a review of Hawthorne that appeared (in *Godey's Lady's Book*, XXXV [November 1847]) only a few months
before the *Fable*, remarked that Tieck's manner "in *some* of his works, is absolutely
identical with that *habitual* to Hawthorne." Hawthorne had almost certainly not
read Tieck, Poe was rather careless with such accusations, and Lowell is certainly
correct in emphasizing the Puritan cast of Hawthorne's fiction.

49. John Sullivan Dwight (1813–1893), Boston composer; Lowell's comparison
would seem only to attest to the lovable nature of both men.

And I'd lay any bet that, without ever quitting
Their box, they'd be all, to a man, for acquitting.
He has drawn you one character, though, that is new,
One wildflower he's plucked that is wet with the dew
Of this fresh Western world, and, the thing not to mince,
He has done naught but copy it ill ever since;
His Indians, with proper respect be it said,
Are just Natty Bumppo daubed over with red,
And his very Long Toms[50] are the same useful Nat,
Rigged up in duck pants and a sou'-wester hat
(Though, once in a Coffin, a good chance was found
To have slipt the old fellow away underground).
All his other men-figures are clothes upon sticks,
The *dernière chemise* of a man in a fix
(As a captain besieged, when his garrison's small,
Sets up caps upon poles to be seen o'er the wall);
And the women he draws from one model don't vary,
All sappy as maples and flat as a prairie,
When a character's wanted, he goes to the task
As a cooper would do in composing a cask;
He picks out the staves, of their qualities heedful,
Just hoops them together as tight as is needful,
And, if the best fortune should crown the attempt, he
Has made at the most something wooden and empty.

"Don't suppose I would underrate Cooper's abilities,
If I thought you'd do that, I should feel very ill at ease;
The men who have given to *one* character life
And objective existence, are not very rife,
You may number them all, both prose-writers and singers,
Without overrunning the bounds of your fingers,
And Natty won't go to oblivion quicker
Than Adams the parson or Primrose the vicar.[51]

"There is one thing in Cooper I like, too, and that is

50. Long Tom Coffin was a character in *The Pilot* (1823).
51. Parson Adams appears prominently in Fielding's *Joseph Andrews*; Dr. Primrose is the title character in Goldsmith's *The Vicar of Wakefield*.

That on manners he lectures his countrymen gratis;
Not precisely so either, because, for a rarity,
He is paid for his tickets in unpopularity.
Now he may overcharge his American pictures,
But you'll grant there's a good deal of truth in his strictures;
And I honor the man who is willing to sink
Half his present repute for the freedom to think,
And, when he has thought, be his cause strong or weak,
Will risk t'other half for the freedom to speak,
Caring naught for what vengeance the mob has in store,
Let that mob be the upper ten thousand or lower.

"There are truths you Americans need to be told,
And it never'll refute them to swagger and scold;
John Bull, looking o'er the Atlantic, in choler
At your aptness for trade, says you worship the dollar;
But to scorn such i-dollar-try's what very few do,
And John goes to that church as often as you do.
No matter what John says, don't try to outcrow him,
'Tis enough to go quietly on and outgrow him;
Like most fathers, Bull hates to see Number One
Displacing himself in the mind of his son,
And detests the same faults in himself he'd neglected
When he sees them again in his child's glass reflected;
To love one another you're too like by half,
If he is a bull, you're a pretty stout calf,
And tear your own pasture for naught but to show
What a nice pair of horns you're beginning to grow.

[INDEPENDENCE IN LITERATURE]

"There are one or two things I should just like to hint,
For you don't often get the truth told you in print;
The most of you (this is what strikes all beholders)
Have a mental and physical stoop in the shoulders;
Though you ought to be free as the winds and the waves,
You've the gait and the manners of runaway slaves;

Tho' you brag of your New World, you don't half believe in it,
And as much of the Old as is possible weave in it;
Your goddess of freedom, a tight, buxom girl,
With lips like a cherry and teeth like a pearl,
With eyes bold as Hera's, and hair floating free,
And full of the sun as the spray of the sea,
Who can sing at a husking or romp at a shearing,
Who can trip through the forests alone without fearing,
Who can drive home the cows with a song through the grass,
Keeps glancing aside into Europe's cracked glass,
Hides her red hands in gloves, pinches up her lithe waist,
And makes herself wretched with transmarine taste;
She loses her fresh country charm when she takes
Any mirror except her own rivers and lakes.

"You steal Englishmen's books and think Englishmen's
        thought,
With their salt on her tail your wild eagle is caught;
Your literature suits its each whisper and motion
To what will be thought of it over the ocean;
The cast clothes of Europe your statesmanship tries
And mumbles again the old blarneys and lies;—
Forget Europe wholly, your veins throb with blood
To which the dull current in hers is but mud;
Let her sneer, let her say your experiment fails,
In her voice there's a tremble e'en now while she rails,
And your shore will soon be in the nature of things
Covered thick with gilt driftwood of runaway kings,
Where alone, as it were in a Longfellow's *Waif*,[52]
Her fugitive pieces will find themselves safe.
O, my friends, thank your God, if you have one, that he
'Twixt the Old World and you set the gulf of a sea;
Be strong-backed, brown-handed, upright as your pines,
By the scale of a hemisphere shape your designs,
Be true to yourselves and this new nineteenth age,
As a statue by Powers, or a picture by Page,

52. An anthology of poetry edited by Longfellow in 1845.

Plough, dig, sail, forge, build, carve, paint, make all things new,
To your own New-World instincts contrive to be true,
Keep your ears open wide to the Future's first call,
Be whatever you will, but yourselves first of all,
Stand fronting the dawn on Toil's heaven-scaling peaks,
And become my new race of more practical Greeks.—
Hem! your likeness at present, I shudder to tell o't,
Is that you have your slaves, and the Greek had his helot.

* * *

"But there comes Miranda, Zeus! where shall I flee to?
She has such a penchant for bothering me too!
She always keeps asking if I don't observe a
Particular likeness 'twixt her and Minerva;
She tells me my efforts in verse are quite clever;—
She's been travelling now, and will be worse than ever;
One would think, though, a sharp-sighted noter she'd be
Of all that's worth mentioning over the sea,
For a woman must surely see well, if she try,
The whole of whose being's a capital I:
She will take an old notion, and make it her own,
By saying it o'er in her Sybilline tone,
Or persuade you 'tis something tremendously deep,
By repeating it so as to put you to sleep;
And she well may defy any mortal to see through it,
When once she has mixed up her infinite *me* through it.
There is one thing she owns in her own single right,
It is native and genuine—namely, her spite;
Though, when acting as Censor, she privately blows
A censer of vanity 'neath her own nose."

    Here Miranda came up, and said, "Phoebus! you know
That the Infinite Soul has its infinite woe,
As I ought to know, having lived cheek by jowl,
Since the day I was born, with the Infinite Soul;
I myself introduced, I myself, I alone,
To my Land's better life authors solely my own,
Who the sad heart of earth on their shoulders have taken,

Whose works sound a depth by Life's quite unshaken,
Such as Shakespeare, for instance, the Bible, and Bacon,
Not to mention my own works; Time's nadir is fleet,
And, as for myself, I'm quite out of conceit,"

"Quite out of conceit! I'm enchanted to hear it,"
Cried Apollo aside, "Who'd have thought she was near it?
To be sure one is apt to exhaust those commodities
He uses too fast, yet in this case as odd it is
As if Neptune should say to his turbots and whitings,
'I'm as much out of salt as Miranda's own writings'
(Which, as she in her own happy manner has said,
Sound a depth, for 'tis one of the functions of lead).
She often has asked me if I could not find
A place somewhere near me that suited her mind;
I know but a single one vacant, which she,
With her rare talent that way, would fit to a T,
And it would not imply any pause or cessation
In the work she esteems her peculiar vocation,—
She may enter on duty to-day, if she chooses,
And remain Tiring-woman for life to the Muses."

(Miranda meanwhile has succeeded in driving
Up into a corner, in spite of their striving,
A small flock of terrified victims, and there,
With an I-turn-the-crank-of-the-Universe air
And a tone which, at least to *my* fancy, appears
Not so much to be entering as boxing your ears,
Is unfolding a tale (of herself, I surmise),
For 'tis dotted as thick as a peacock's with I's.)

* * *

"There comes Harry Franco,[53] and, as he draws near,
You find that's a smile which you took for a sneer;

53. Pseudonym of Charles Frederick Briggs (1804–1877), New York writer and journalist and close friend of Lowell. Lowell donated the royalties of *A Fable for Critics* as a dowry for Briggs's daughter. The mention at the end of the paragraph of the letters of Pinto and the pun on "liar" refer to another pseudonym of Briggs, his letters of "Ferdinand Mendez Pinto," which appeared in the New York *Mirror* in 1846 and 1847. Their satire is based upon elaborate mendacity.

One half of him contradicts t'other, his wont
Is to say very sharp things and do very blunt;
His manner 's as hard as his feelings are tender,
And a *sortie* he'll make when he means to surrender;
He's in joke half the time when he seems to be sternest,
When he seems to be joking, be sure he's in earnest;
He has common sense in a way that's uncommon,
Hates humbug and cant, loves his friends like a woman,
Builds his dislikes of cards and his friendships of oak,
Loves a prejudice better than aught but a joke,
Is half upright Quaker, half downright Come-outer,
Loves Freedom too well to go stark mad about her,
Quite artless himself, is a lover of Art,
Shuts you out of his secrets and into his heart,
And though not a poet, yet all must admire
In his letters of Pinto his skill on the liar.

"There comes Poe with his raven, like Barnaby Rudge,[54]
Three-fifths of him genius and two-fifths sheer fudge,
Who talks like a book of iambs and pentameters,
In a way to make people of common-sense damn metres,
Who has written some things quite the best of their kind,
But the heart somehow seems all squeezed out by the mind,
Who—but hey-day! What's this? Messieurs Mathews and Poe,
You mustn't fling mud-balls at Longfellow so,
Does it make a man worse that his character's such
As to make his friends love him (as you think) too much?
Why, there is not a bard at this moment alive
More willing than he that his fellows should thrive;
While you are abusing him thus, even now
He would help either one of you out of a slough;
You may say that he's smooth and all that till you're hoarse,
But remember that elegance also is force;
After polishing granite as much as you will,
The heart keeps its tough old persistency still;
Deduct all you can that still keeps you at bay,—

54. Title character of Dickens' novel, who had a raven.

Why, he'll live till men weary of Collins and Gray;
I'm not over-fond of Greek metres in English,
To me rhyme 's a gain, so it be not too jinglish,
And your modern hexameter verses are no more
Like Greek ones than sleek Mr. Pope is like Homer;
As the roar of the sea to the coo of a pigeon is
So, compared to your moderns sounds old Melesigenes;[55]
I may be too partial, the reason, perhaps, o't is
That I've heard the old blind man recite his own rhapsodies,
And my ear with that music impregnate may be,
Like the poor exiled shell with the soul of the sea,
Or as one can't bear Strauss when his nature is cloven
To its deeps within deeps by the stroke of Beethoven;
But, set that aside, and 'tis truth that I speak,
Had Theocritus written in English, not Greek,
I believe that his exquisite sense would scarce change a line
In that rare, tender, virgin-like pastoral *Evangeline.*
That's not ancient nor modern, its place is apart
Where Time has no sway, in the realm of pure Art,
'Tis a shrine of retreat from Earth's hubbub and strife
As quiet and chaste as the author's own life.

"There comes Philothea,[56] her face all aglow,
She has just been dividing some poor creature's woe,
And can't tell which pleases her most, to relieve
His want, or his story to hear and believe;
No doubt against many deep griefs she prevails,
For her ear is the refuge of destitute tales;
She knows well that silence is sorrow's best food,
And that talking draws off from the heart its black blood,
So she'll listen with patience and let you unfold
Your bundle of rags as 'twere pure cloth of gold,

55. That is, Homer.
56. Lydia Maria Child (1802–1880), Boston author and daughter of Francis James Child, Lowell's very close friend. Her novel *Philothea* appeared in 1836. The extravagant remarks that follow about Miss Child's virtues as a writer ought not to be taken as anything more than evidence of Lowell's friendship for her and his chivalry.

Which, indeed, it all turns to as soon as she's touched it,
And (to borrow a phrase from the nursery) *muched* it;
She has such a musical taste, she will go
Any distance to hear one who draws a long bow;
She will swallow a wonder by mere might and main
And thinks it geometry's fault if she's fain
To consider things flat, inasmuch as they're plain;
Facts with her are accomplished, as Frenchmen would say,
They will prove all she wishes them to—either way,
And, as fact lies on this side or that, we must try,
If we're seeking the truth, to find where it don't lie;
I was telling her once of a marvellous aloe
That for thousands of years had looked spindling and sallow
And, though nursed by the fruitfullest powers of mud,
Had never vouchsafed e'en so much as a bud,
Till its owner remarked, as a sailor, you know,
Often will in a calm, that it never would blow,
For he wished to exhibit the plant, and designed
That its blowing should help him in raising the wind;
At last it was told him that if he should water
Its roots with the blood of his unmarried daughter
(Who was born, as her mother, a Calvinist, said,
With a Baxter's[57] effectual caul on her head),
It would blow as the obstinate breeze did when by a
Like decree of her father died Iphigenia;
At first he declared he himself would be blowed
Ere his conscience with such a foul crime he would load,
But the thought, coming oft, grew less dark than before,
And he mused, as each creditor knocked at his door,
If *this* were but done they would dun me no more;
I told Philothea his struggles and doubts
And how he considered the ins and the outs,
Of the visions he had, and the dreadful dyspepsy,
How he went to the seer that lives at ·Po'keepsie,[58]
How the seer advised him to sleep on it first

57. Richard Baxter (1615–1691), English Puritan divine.
58. The seer is unidentified—perhaps present for the rhyme only.

And to read his big volume in case of the worst,
And further advised he should pay him five dollars
For writing ℌum ℌum on his wristbands and collars;
Three years and ten days these dark words he had studied
When the daughter was missed, and the aloe had budded;
I told how he watched it grow large and more large,
And wondered how much for the show he should charge,—
She had listened with utter indifference to this, till
I told how it bloomed, and, discharging its pistil
With an aim the Eumenides dictated, shot
The botanical filicide dead on the spot;
It had blown, but he reaped not his horrible gains,
For it blew with such force as to blow out his brains,
And the crime was blown also, because on the wad,
Which was paper, was writ 'Visitation of God,'
As well as a thrilling account of the deed
Which the coroner kindly allowed me to read.

"Well, my friend took this story up just, to be sure,
As one might a poor foundling that's laid at one's door;
She combed it and washed it and clothed it and fed it,
And as if 'twere her own child most tenderly bred it,
Laid the scene (of the legend, I mean) far away a-
-mong the green vales underneath Himalaya,
And by artist-like touches, laid on here and there,
Made the whole thing so touching, I frankly declare
I have read it all thrice, and, perhaps I am weak,
But I found every time there were tears on my cheek.
The pole, science tells us, the magnet controls,
But she is a magnet to emigrant Poles,
And folks with a mission that nobody knows,
Throng thickly about her as bees round a rose;
She can fill up the *carets* [59] in such, make their scope
Converge to some focus of rational hope,
And, with sympathies fresh as the morning, their gall
Can transmute into honey,—but this is not all;

59. "Vacancies."

Not only for these she has solace, oh, say,
Vice's desperate nurseling adrift in Broadway,
Who clingest, with all that is left of the human,
To the last slender spar from the wreck of the woman,
Hast thou not found one shore where those tired drooping feet
Could reach firm mother-earth, one full heart on whose beat
The soothed head in silence reposing could hear
The chimes of far childhood throb thick on the ear?
Ah, there's many a beam from the fountain of day
That, to reach us unclouded, must pass, on its way,
Through the soul of a woman, and hers is wide ope
To the influence of Heaven as the blue eyes of Hope;
Yes, a great soul is hers, one that dares to go in
To the prison, the slave-hut, the alleys of sin,
And to bring into each, or to find there, some line
Of the never completely out-trampled divine;
If her heart at high floods swamps her brain now and then,
'Tis but richer for that when the tide ebbs agen,
As, after old Nile has subsided, his plain
Overflows with a second broad deluge of grain;
What a wealth would it bring to the narrow and sour
Could they be as a Child but for one little hour!

"What! Irving? thrice welcome, warm heart and fine brain,
You bring back the happiest spirit from Spain,
And the gravest sweet humor, that ever were there
Since Cervantes met death in his gentle despair;
Nay, don't be embarrassed, nor look so beseeching,—
I shan't run directly against my own preaching,
And, having just laughed at their Raphaels and Dantes,
Go to setting you up beside matchless Cervantes;
But allow me to speak what I honestly feel,—
To a true poet-heart add the fun of Dick Steele,
Throw in all of Addison, *minus* the chill,
With the whole of that partnership's stock and good will,
Mix well, and, while stirring, hum o'er, as a spell,
The fine *old* English Gentleman, simmer it well,

Sweeten just to your own private liking, then strain,
That only the finest and clearest remain,
Let it stand out of doors till a soul it receives
From the warm lazy sun loitering down through green leaves,
And you'll find a choice nature, not wholly deserving
A name either English or Yankee,—just Irving.

"There goes,—but *stet nominis umbra*,[60]—his name
You'll be glad enough, some day or other, to claim,
And will all crowd about him and swear that you knew him
If some English hack-critic should chance to review him;
The old *porcos ante ne projiciatis*
MARGARITAS,[61] for him you have verified gratis;
What matters his name? Why, it may be Sylvester,
Judd, Junior, or Junius, Ulysses, or Nestor,
For aught *I* know or care; 'tis enough that I look
On the author of *Margaret*, the first Yankee book
With the *soul* of Down East in't, and things farther East,
As far as the threshold of morning, at least,
Where awaits the fair dawn of the simple and true,
Of the day that comes slowly to make all things new.
'T has a smack of pine woods, of bare field and bleak hill
Such as only the breed of the Mayflower could till;
The Puritan 's shown in it, tough to the core,
Such as prayed, smiting Agag[62] on red Marston moor;
With an unwilling humour, half-choked by the drouth
In brown hollows about the inhospitable mouth;
With a soul full of poetry, though it has qualms
About finding a happiness out of the Psalms;
Full of tenderness, too, though it shrinks in the dark,
Hamadryad-like, under the coarse, shaggy bark;
That sees visions, knows wrestlings of God with the Will,

60. "Let the shadow of the name stand."
61. "Do not cast your pearls before swine," *Matthew*, 7:6. The pun is complicated, since *margaritas* ("pearls") is a latinizing of the title of Sylvester Judd's
anonymous novel *Margaret*. See above, p. 129, note 12.
62. In Dryden's *Absalom and Achitophel*, Agag is Sir Edmundbury Godfrey,
murdered in a ditch near Primrose Hill.

And has its own Sinais and thunderings still."—

* * *

"There's Holmes, who is matchless among you for wit;
A Leyden-jar [63] always full-charged, from which flit
The electrical tingles of hit after hit;
In long poems 'tis painful sometimes and invites
A thought of the way the new Telegraph writes,
Which pricks down its little sharp sentences spitefully
As if you got more than you'd title to rightfully,
And you find yourself hoping its wild father Lightning
Would flame in for a second and give you a fright'ning.
He has perfect sway of what *I* call a sham metre,
But many admire it, the English pentameter,
And Campbell, I think wrote most commonly worse,
With less nerve, swing, and fire in the same kind of verse,
Nor e'er achieved aught in't so worthy of praise
As the tribute of Holmes to the grand *Marseillaise.*[64]
You went crazy last year over Bulwer's *New Timon*;—
Why, if B., to the day of his dying, should rhyme on,
Heaping verses on verses and tomes upon tomes,
He could ne'er reach the best point and vigor of Holmes.
His are just the fine hands, too, to weave you a lyric
Full of fancy, fun, feeling, or spiced with satyric
In so kindly a measure, that nobody knows
What to do but e'en join in the laugh, friends and foes.

"There is Lowell, who's striving Parnassus to climb
With a whole bale of *isms* tied together with rhyme,
He might get on alone, spite of brambles and boulders,
But he can't with that bundle he has on his shoulders,
The top of the hill he will ne'er come nigh reaching
Till he learns the distinction 'twixt singing and preaching;
His lyre has some chords that would ring pretty well,
But he'd rather by half make a drum of the shell,
And rattle away till he's old as Methusalem,
At the head of a march to the last New Jerusalem.

63. A jar used for electrical experiments.
64. In section II of Holmes' *Poetry: A Metrical Essay* (1836).

"There goes Halleck, whose Fanny's a pseudo Don Juan,[65]
With the wickedness out that gave salt to the true one,
He's a wit, though, I hear, of the very first order,
And once made a pun on the words soft Recorder;
More than this, he's a very great poet, I'm told,
And has had his works published in crimson and gold,
With something they call "Illustrations," to wit,
Like those with which Chapman obscured Holy Writ,[66]
Which are said to illustrate, because, as I view it,
Like *lucus a non*,[67] they precisely don't do it;
Let a man who can write what himself understands
Keep clear, if he can, of designing men's hands,
Who bury the sense, if there's any worth having,
And then very honestly call it engraving.
But, to quit *badinage*, which there isn't much wit in,
No doubt Halleck's better than all he has written;
In his verse a clear glimpse you will frequently find,
If not of a great, of a fortunate mind,
Which contrives to be true to its natural loves
In a world of back-offices, ledgers, and stoves.
When his heart breaks away from the brokers and banks,
And kneels in its own private shrine to give thanks,
There's a genial manliness in him that earns
Our sincerest respect (read, for instance, his "Burns")
And we can't but regret (seek excuse where we may)
That so much of a man has been peddled away.

"But what's that? a mass-meeting? No, there come in lots
The American Disraelis, Bulwers, and Scotts,
And in short the American everything-elses'

65. Fitz-Greene Halleck's *Fanny* was published in 1819. See Lowell's review of his *Alnwick Castle*, above, pp. 103–106.

66. (Cuts rightly called wooden, as all must admit.) [Lowell's note.] John Gadsby Chapman (1808–1889) was a prolific and mediocre American artist. He produced over 1400 drawings for the Bible published by Harper's in 1846.

67. "... *lucendo*," another complex pun of Lowell's. The phrase is a famous bit of folk etymology by Isadore of Seville, in which he derives *lucus* (a grove of trees) from *lucêo* (to shine) because they "don't do it," as Lowell says.

Each charging the others with envies and jealousies;—
By the way, 'tis a fact that displays what profusions
Of all kinds of greatness bless free institutions,
That while the Old World has produced barely eight
Of such poets as all men agree to call great,
And of other great characters hardly a score
(One might safely say less than that rather than more),
With you every year a whole crop is begotten,
They're as much of a staple as corn, or cotton;
Why, there's scarcely a huddle of log-huts and shanties
That has not brought forth its own Miltons and Dantes;
I myself know ten Byrons, one Coleridge, three Shelleys,
Two Raphaels, six Titians (I think) one Apelles,
Leonardos and Rubenses plenty as lichens,
One (but that one is plenty) American Dickens,[68]
A whole flock of Lambs, any number of Tennysons,—
In short, if a man has the luck to have any sons,
He may feel pretty certain that one out of twain
Will be some very great person over again.

[ON CRITICISM]

* * *

"My friends, in the happier days of the muse,
We were luckily free from such things as reviews;
Then naught came between with its fog to make clearer
The heart of the poet to that of his hearer;
Then the poet brought heaven to the people, and they
Felt that they, too, were poets in hearing his lay;
Then the poet was prophet, the past in his soul
Pre-created the future, both parts of one whole;
Then for him there was nothing too great or too small,
For one natural deity sanctified all;
Then the bard owned no clipper and meter of moods
Save the spirit of silence that hovers and broods
O'er the seas and the mountains, the rivers and woods;

68. That is, Cornelius Mathews. The other trans-Atlantic identifications are
Lowell's invention.

He asked not earth's verdict, forgetting the clods,
His soul soared and sang to an audience of gods;
'Twas for them that he measured the thought and the line,
And shaped for their vision the perfect design,
With as glorious a foresight, a balance as true,
As swung out the worlds in the infinite blue;
Then a glory and greatness invested man's heart,
The universal, which now stands estranged and apart,
In the free individual moulded, was Art;
Then the forms of the Artist seemed thrilled with desire
For something as yet unattained, fuller, higher,
As once with her lips, lifted hands, and eyes listening,
And her whole upward soul in her countenance glistening,
Eurydice [69] stood,—like a beacon unfired,
Which, once touch'd with flame, will leap heav'nward inspired,—
And waited with answering kindle to mark
The first gleam of Orpheus that pained the red Dark;
Then painting, song, sculpture, did more than relieve
The need that men feel to create and believe,
And as, in all beauty, who listens with love,
Hears these words oft repeated—'beyond and above,'
So these seemed to be but the visible sign
Of the grasp of the soul after things more divine;
They were ladders the Artist erected to climb
O'er the narrow horizon of space and of time,
And we see there the footsteps by which men had gained
To the one rapturous glimpse of the never-attained,
As shepherds could erst sometimes trace in the sod
The last spurning print of a sky-cleaving god.

"But now, on the poet's dis-privacied moods
With *do this* and *do that* the pert critic intrudes;
While he thinks he's been barely fulfilling his duty
To interpret 'twixt men and their own sense of beauty,
And has striven, while others sought honor or pelf,
To make his kind happy as he was himself,
He finds he's been guilty of horrid offences

69. Orpheus and Eurydice here are the poet and his reader ideally represented.

In all kinds of moods, numbers, genders, and tenses;
He's been *ob*jective, *sub*jective, what Kettle calls Pot,
Precisely, at all events, what he ought not,
You have done this, says one judge; *done that*, says another;
You should have done this, grumbles one; *that* says t'other;
Never mind what he touches, one shrieks out *Taboo!*
And while he is wondering what he shall do,
Since each suggests opposite topics for song,
They all shout together *you're right!* or *you're wrong!*

"Nature fits all her children with something to do,
He who would write and can't write, can surely review,
Can set up a small booth as critic and sell us his
Petty conceit and his pettier jealousies;
Thus a lawyer's apprentice, just out of his teens,
Will do for the Jeffrey[70] of six magazines;
Having read Johnson's *Lives of the Poets* half through,
There's nothing on earth he's not competent to;
He reviews with as much nonchalance as he whistles,—
He goes through a book and just picks out the thistles,
It matters not whether he blame or commend,
If he's bad as a foe, he's far worse as a friend;
Let an author but write what's above his poor scope,
And he'll go to work gravely and twist up a rope,
And, inviting the world to see punishment done,
Hang himself up to bleach in the wind and the sun;
'Tis delightful to see, when a man comes along
Who has anything in him peculiar and strong,
Every cockboat that swims clear its fierce (pop-) gundeck at him
And make as he passes its ludicrous Peck[71] at him,"—

Here Miranda came up and began, "As to that,"—
Apollo at once seized his gloves, cane, and hat,
And, seeing the place getting rapidly cleared,
I, too, snatched my notes and forthwith disappeared.

A Fable for Critics (G. P. Putnam, 1848), first edition, pp. i–iii, 7–18, 20–51,
51–54, 56–64, 67–71, 74–78; second edition, pp. vi–xi.

70. Francis, Lord Jeffrey (1773–1850), founder of the *Edinburgh Review*.
71. George Washington Peck (1817–1859), New York reviewer.

Emerson the Lecturer

Explaining the greatness of Emerson has always presented a major problem to critics. If Lowell is unable to account adequately for the "singular fact" he notes in his first sentence, he is not alone. Some twenty years after Lowell's remarks, Henry James was to duck in a similar fashion the problem of accounting for Emerson: "I have assumed his importance and continuance, and shall probably not be gainsaid by those who read him. . . . He did something better than any one else; he had a particular faculty, which has not been surpassed, for speaking to the soul in a voice of direction and authority."

Lowell was, in general, unsympathetic to Emerson's transcendental idealism, as this essay and the essay on Thoreau amply illustrate. What he did appreciate in Emerson (and what rubbed him the wrong way in Thoreau) was the combination of matter and manner, the blend of Yankee truth and oracular presentation. In Emerson, the combination was diffident and unassuming; in Thoreau—at least for Lowell—it was egotistical. Both men treated truth as if they had invented the concept, but Emerson asked the hearer to share in his glee of discovery.

This essay, first published in the Nation *in 1868, is probably Lowell's best-known and most admired piece of criticism, while the essay on Thoreau is hardly less well known, but receives scant admiration, especially from admirers of Thoreau. Read together, they indicate Lowell's perception of a phenomenon of his time, and suggest certain limitations in his critical stance.*

It is a singular fact that Mr. Emerson is the most steadily attractive lecturer in America. Into that somewhat cold-waterish region adventures of the sensational kind come down now and then with a splash, to become disregarded King Logs[1] before the next season. But Mr. Emerson always draws. A lecturer now for something like a

1. In the fable by Aesop, the frogs are given a log as their king, which they happily accept until they discover its true nature.

third of a century, one of the pioneers of the lecturing system, the charm of his voice, his manner, and his matter has never lost its power over his earlier hearers, and continually winds new ones in its enchanting meshes. What they do not fully understand they take on trust, and listen, saying to themselves, as the old poet[2] of Sir Philip Sidney,—

> A sweet, attractive, kind of grace,
> A full assurance given by looks,
> Continual comfort in a face,
> The lineaments of gospel books.

We call it a singular fact, because we Yankees are thought to be fond of the spread-eagle style, and nothing can be more remote from that than his. We are reckoned a practical folk, who would rather hear about a new air-tight stove than about Plato; yet our favorite teacher's practicality is not in the least of the Poor Richard variety. If he have any Buncombe constituency, it is that unrealized commonwealth of philosophers which Plotinus proposed to establish; and if he were to make an almanac, his directions to farmers would be something like this: "OCTOBER: *Indian Summer*; now is the time to get in your early Vedas." What, then, is his secret? Is it not that he out-Yankees us all? that his range includes us all? that he is equally at home with the potato-disease and original sin, with pegging shoes and the Over-Soul? that, as we try all trades, so has he tried all cultures? and above all, that his mysticism gives us a counterpoise to our super-practicality?

There is no man living to whom, as a writer, so many of us feel and thankfully acknowledge so great an indebtedness for ennobling impulses,—none whom so many cannot abide. What does he mean? ask these last. Where is his system? What is the use of it all? What the deuce have we to do with Brahma? I do not propose to write an essay on Emerson at this time. I will only say that one may find grandeur and consolation in a starlit night without caring to ask what it means, save grandeur and consolation; one may like Montaigne, as some ten generations before us have done, without thinking him so systematic as some

2. Matthew Royden (*ca.* 1580–1622), minor English poet. The lines are from his "Elegie" to Sidney, first published in *The Phoenix Nest* (1593).

more eminently tedious (or shall we say tediously eminent?) authors; one may think roses as good in their way as cabbages, though the latter would make a better show in the witness box, if cross-examined as to their usefulness; and as for Brahma, why, he can take care of himself, and won't bite us at any rate.

The bother with Mr. Emerson is, that, though he writes in prose, he is essentially a poet. If you undertake to paraphrase what he says, and to reduce it to words of one syllable for infant minds, you will make as sad work of it as the good monk with his analysis of Homer in the "Epistolae Obscurorum Virorum."[3] We look upon him as one of the few men of genius whom our age has produced, and there needs no better proof of it than his masculine faculty of fecundating other minds. Search for his eloquence in his books and you will perchance miss it, but meanwhile you will find that it has kindled all your thoughts. For choice and pith of language he belongs to a better age than ours, and might rub shoulders with Fuller and Browne,[4]— though he does use that abominable word *reliable*. His eye for a fine, telling phrase that will carry true is like that of a backwoodsman for a rifle; and he will dredge you up a choice word from the mud of Cotton Mather himself. A diction at once so rich and so homely as his I know not where to match in these days of writing by the page; it is like homespun cloth-of-gold. The many cannot miss his meaning, and only the few can find it. It is the open secret of all true genius. It is wholesome to angle in those profound pools, though one be rewarded with nothing more than the leap of a fish that flashes his freckled side in the sun and as suddenly absconds in the dark and dreamy waters again. There is keen excitement, though there be no ponderable acquisition. If we carry nothing home in our baskets, there is ample gain in dilated lungs and stimulated blood. What does he mean, quotha? He means inspiring hints, a divining-rod to your deeper nature. No doubt, Emerson, like all original men, has his peculiar audience, and yet I know none that can hold a promiscuous crowd in pleased attention so long as he. As in all

3. "Letters of Obscure Men," an anonymous work of the sixteenth century.
4. Thomas Fuller (1608–1661), English divine; Sir Thomas Browne (1605–1682), English mystical writer. The observation appears casual, but it succinctly describes Emerson's sources and style.

original men, there is something for every palate. "Would you know," says Goethe, "the ripest cherries? Ask the boys and the blackbirds."

The announcement that such a pleasure as a new course of lectures by him is coming, to people as old as I am, is something like those forebodings of spring that prepare us every year for a familiar novelty, none the less novel, when it arrives, because it is familiar. We know perfectly well what we are to expect from Mr. Emerson, and yet what he says always penetrates and stirs us, as is apt to be the case with genius, in a very unlooked-for fashion. Perhaps genius is one of the few things which we gladly allow to repeat itself,—one of the few that multiply rather than weaken the force of their impression by iteration? Perhaps some of us hear more than the mere words, are moved by something deeper than the thoughts? If it be so, we are quite right, for it is thirty years and more of "plain living and high thinking" that speak to us in this altogether unique lay-preacher. We have shared in the beneficence of this varied culture, this fearless impartiality in criticism and speculation, this masculine sincerity, this sweetness of nature which rather stimulates than cloys, for a generation long. If ever there was a standing testimonial to the cumulative power and value of Character (and we need it sadly in these days), we have it in this gracious and dignified presence. What an antiseptic is a pure life! At sixty-five (or two years beyond his grand climacteric, as he would prefer to call it) he has that privilege of soul which abolishes the calendar, and presents him to us always the unwasted contemporary of his own prime. I do not know if he seem old to his younger hearers, but we who have known him so long wonder at the tenacity with which he maintains himself even in the outposts of youth. I suppose it is not the Emerson of 1868 to whom we listen. For us the whole life of the man is distilled in the clear drop of every sentence, and behind each word we divine the force of a noble character, the weight of a large capital of thinking and being. We do not go to hear what Emerson says so much as to hear Emerson. Not that we perceive any falling-off in anything that ever was essential to the charm of Mr. Emerson's peculiar style of thought or phrase. The first lecture, to be sure, was more disjointed even than common. It was as if, after vainly trying to get his paragraphs into sequence and order, he had at last tried the desperate expedient of *shuffling* them. It was chaos come again, but it was a chaos full of shooting-stars, a jumble of creative forces. The second lecture, on "Criticism and Poetry," was quite up to the level of old times, full of that power of strangely subtle association whose indirect approaches startle the mind into almost painful attention, of those flashes of mutual understanding between speaker and hearer that are gone ere one can say it lightens. The vice of Emerson's criticism seems to be, that while no man is so sensitive to what is poetical, few men are less sensible than he of what makes a poem. He values the solid meaning of thought above the subtler meaning of style. He would prefer Donne, I suspect, to Spenser, and sometimes mistakes the queer for the original.

To be young is surely the best, if the most precarious, gift of life; yet there are some of us who would hardly consent to be young again, if it were at the cost of our recollection of Mr. Emerson's first lectures during the consulate of Van Buren. We used to walk in from the country to the Masonic Temple (I think it was), through the crisp winter night, and listen to that thrilling voice of his, so charged with subtle meaning and subtle music, as shipwrecked men on a raft to the hail of a ship that came with unhoped-for food and rescue. Cynics might say what they liked. Did our own imaginations transfigure dry remainder-biscuit into ambrosia? At any rate, he brought us *life*, which, on the whole, is no bad thing. Was it all transcendentalism? magic-lantern pictures on mist? As you will. Those, then, were just what we wanted. But it was not so. The delight and the benefit were that he put us in communication with a larger style of thought, sharpened our wits with a more pungent phrase, gave us ravishing glimpses of an ideal under the dry husk of our New England; made us conscious of the supreme and everlasting originality of whatever bit of soul might be in any of us; freed us, in short, from the stocks of prose in which we had sat so long that we had grown well-nigh contented in our cramps. And who that saw the audience will ever forget it, where every one still capable of fire, or longing to renew in himself the half-forgotten sense of it, was gathered? Those faces, young and old, agleam with pale intellectual light, eager with pleased attention, flash upon me once more from the deep recesses of the years with an exquisite pathos. Ah, beautiful young eyes, brimming with love and hope, wholly vanished now in that other world we call the Past, or peering doubtfully through the pensive gloaming of memory, your light impoverishes these cheaper days! I hear again that rustle of sensation, as they turned to exchange glances over some pithier thought, some keener flash of that humor which always played about the horizon of his mind like heat-lightning, and it seems now like the sad whisper of the autumn leaves that are whirling around me. But would my picture be complete if I forgot that ample and vegete countenance of Mr. R—— of W——, —how, from its regular post at the corner of the front bench, it turned in ruddy triumph to the profaner audience as if he were the inexplicably appointed fugleman of appreciation? I was reminded of him by those hearty cherubs in Titian's Assumption that look at you as who should say, "Did you ever see a Madonna like *that*? Did you ever behold one hundred and fifty pounds of womanhood mount heavenward before like a rocket?"

To some of us that long-past experience remains as the most marvellous and fruitful we have ever had. Emerson awakened us, saved us from the body of this death. It is the sound of the trumpet that the young soul longs for, careless what breath may fill it. Sidney heard it in the ballad of "Chevy Chase,"[5] and we in Emerson. Nor did it blow retreat, but called to us with assurance of victory. Did they say he was disconnected? So were the stars, that seemed larger to our eyes, still keen with that excitement, as we walked homeward with prouder stride over the creaking snow. And were *they* not knit together by a higher logic than our mere sense could master? Were we enthusiasts? I hope and believe we were, and am thankful to the man who made us worth something for once in our lives. If asked what was left? what we carried home? we should not have been careful for an answer. It would have been enough if we had said that something beautiful had passed that way. Or we might have asked in return what one brought away from a symphony of

5. In his *Defense of Poetry* (1595), Sir Philip Sidney noted the remarkable effect of the ballad: "I never heard the old song of Percy and Douglas that I found not my heart moved more than with a trumpet; and yet is it sung but by some blind crowder, with no rougher voice than rude style."

Beethoven? Enough that he had set that ferment of wholesome discontent at work in us. There is one, at least, of those old hearers, so
many of whom are now in the fruition of that intellectual beauty of
which Emerson gave them both the desire and the foretaste, who
will always love to repeat:—

> Che in la mente m' è fitta, ed or m' acuora
> La cara e buona immagine paterna
> Di voi, quando nel mondo ad ora ad ora
> M' insegnavaste come l' uom s' eterna.[6]

I am unconsciously thinking, as I write, of the third lecture of the
present course, in which Mr. Emerson gave some delightful reminiscences of the intellectual influences in whose movement he had
shared. It was like hearing Goethe read some passages of the
Wahrheit aus seinem Leben.[7] Not that there was not a little *Dichtung*,
too, here and there, as the lecturer built up so lofty a pedestal under
certain figures as to lift them into a prominence of obscurity, and
seem to masthead them there. Everybody was asking his neighbor
who this or that recondite great man was, in the faint hope that
somebody might once have heard of him. There are those who call
Mr. Emerson cold. Let them revise their judgment in presence of this
loyalty of his that can keep warm for half a century, that never forgets
a friendship, or fails to pay even a fancied obligation to the uttermost
farthing. This substantiation of shadows was but incidental, and
pleasantly characteristic of the man to those who know and love
him. The greater part of the lecture was devoted to reminiscences of
things substantial in themselves. He spoke of Everett, fresh from
Greece and Germany; of Channing; of the translations of Margaret

---

6. Dante, *Inferno*, xv. 82–85.

> For in my mind is fixed, and touches now
>   My heart, the dear and good paternal image
> Of you, when in the world from hour to hour
>   You taught me how a man becomes eternal.

>   (Longfellow's translation,
>   Boston: Houghton Mifflin and Co., 1865.)

7. *Truth from His Life*. The full title is *Dichtung* [Poetry] *und Warheit aus meinem
Leben*.

Fuller, Ripley, and Dwight; of *The Dial* and Brook Farm.[8] To what he said of the latter an undertone of good-humored irony gave special zest. But what every one of his hearers felt was that the protagonist in the drama was left out. The lecturer was no Aeneas to babble the *quorum magna pars fui*,[9] and, as one of his listeners, I cannot help wishing to say how each of them was commenting the story as it went along, and filling up the necessary gaps in it from his own private store of memories. His younger hearers could not know how much they owed to the benign impersonality, the quiet scorn of everything ignoble, the never-sated hunger of self-culture, that were personified in the man before them. But the older knew how much the country's intellectual emancipation was due to the stimulus of his teaching and example, how constantly he had kept burning the beacon of an ideal life above our lower region of turmoil. To him more than to all other causes together did the young martyrs of our civil war owe the sustaining strength of thoughtful heroism that is so touching in every record of their lives. Those who are grateful to Mr. Emerson, as many of us are, for what they feel to be most valuable in their culture, or perhaps I should say their impulse, are grateful not so much for any direct teachings of his as for that inspiring lift which only genius can give, and without which all doctrine is chaff.

This was something like the *caret*[10] which some of us older boys wished to fill up on the margin of the master's lecture. Few men have been so much to so many, and through so large a range of aptitudes and temperaments, and this simply because all of us value manhood

8. The list spans the major figures in the transcendental movement, with some of the more spectacular (and disreputable) figures—like Alcott, Brownson, and Thoreau—left out. Edward Everett (1794–1865) was one of the first Americans to become acquainted with the "new truth" from Germany; three Channings were connected with the movement: William Ellery the Elder (1780–1842), his nephew William Ellery (1818–1901), and William Henry Channing (1810–1884). Margaret Fuller (1810–1850), George Ripley (1802–1880), and the composer John Sullivan Dwight (1813–1893) all contributed to the *Dial* (1840–1844), the magazine of the movement, and had something to do with the utopian community established at Brook Farm.

9. "Of which I took great part" (*Aeneid*, ii. 6).

10. "Something missing."

beyond any or all other qualities of character. We may suspect in him, here and there, a certain thinness and vagueness of quality, but let the waters go over him as they list, this masculine fibre of his will keep its lively color and its toughness of texture. I have heard some great speakers and some accomplished orators, but never any that so moved and persuaded men as he. There is a kind of undertow in that rich baritone of his that sweeps our minds from their foothold into deeper waters with a drift we cannot and would not resist. And how artfully (for Emerson is a long-studied artist in these things) does the deliberate utterance, that seems waiting for the fit word, appear to admit us partners in the labor of thought and make us feel as if the glance of humor were a sudden suggestion, as if the perfect phrase lying written there on the desk were as unexpected to him as to us! In that closely filed speech of his at the Burns centenary dinner, every word seemed to have just dropped down to him from the clouds. He looked far away over the heads of his hearers, with a vague kind of expectation, as into some private heaven of invention, and the winged period came at last obedient to his spell. "My dainty Ariel!" [11] he seemed murmuring to himself as he cast down his eyes as if in deprecation of the frenzy of approval and caught another sentence from the Sibylline leaves that lay before him, ambushed behind a dish of fruit and seen only by nearest neighbors. Every sentence brought down the house, as I never saw one brought down before,—and it is not so easy to hit Scotsmen with a sentiment that has no hint of native brogue in it. I watched, for it was an interesting study, how the quick sympathy ran flashing from face to face down the long tables, like an electric spark thrilling as it went, and then exploded in a thunder of plaudits. I watched till tables and faces vanished, for I, too, found myself caught up in the common enthusiasm, and my excited fancy set me under the *bema*[12] listening to him who fulmined over Greece. I can never help applying to him what Ben Jonson said of Bacon: "There happened in my time one noble speaker, who was full of gravity in his speaking. His language was nobly censorious. No man ever spake more neatly, more pressly, more weightily, or suffered less emptiness, less idleness, in what he

11. See *The Tempest*, V. i. 95.
12. In Athens, the tribune from which one spoke to the people.

uttered. No member of his speech but consisted of his own graces.
His hearers could not cough, or look aside from him, without loss.
He commanded where he spoke." Those who heard him while their
natures were yet plastic, and their mental nerves trembled under
the slightest breath of divine air, will never cease to feel and say:—

> Was never eye did see that face,
>   Was never ear did hear that tongue,
> Was never mind did mind his grace,
>   That ever thought the travail long;
> But eyes, and ears, and every thought,
> Were with his sweet perfections caught.[13]

Works, II, 391–404.

13. This also is quoted from Royden's "Elegie"; see note 2, above.

Thoreau

Lowell was constitutionally unsuited to criticize Henry David Thoreau in a manner satisfactory to the modern reader. Unsympathetic to the ideas lying behind Thoreau's work, he places transcendentalism in its historic context better in this essay than any critic had yet done, and then proceeds to demolish the most eccentric exponent of those ideas. This essay, unlike the preceding one, "Emerson the Lecturer," makes no effort to distinguish the baby from the bath water; Lowell's position is simply that Thoreau's matter cannot be distinguished from his manner, and therefore, if the principle of organic form has any validity, his whole production is suspect. The modern reader is not likely to agree with many of the conclusions of this essay, written in 1865, but he must see the brilliance of observations like "He wishes always to trump your suit and to ruff when you least expect it," and "A greater familiarity with ordinary men would have done Thoreau good, by showing him how many fine qualities are common to the race."

If one admits that there may be two sides to the question of Thoreau, Lowell presents that other side in a classic piece of criticism. It was first published in the North American Review *in 1865.*

What contemporary, if he was in the fighting period of his life (since Nature sets limits about her conscription for spiritual fields, as the state does in physical warfare), will ever forget what was somewhat vaguely called the "Transcendental Movement" of thirty years ago? Apparently set astir by Carlyle's essays on the Signs of the Times, and on History, the final and more immediate impulse seemed to be given by *Sartor Resartus*.[1] At least the republication in

1. In 1836, Emerson saw an American edition of Carlyle's *Sartor Resartus* through the press, and this startling work, which blends the satire and scatology of Swift with the metaphysics of Kant, was, as Lowell states, the "immediate impulse" of the American transcendental movement. Abraham à Sancta Clara,

Boston of that wonderful Abraham à Sancta Clara sermon on
Falstaff's text of the miserable forked radish gave the signal for a
sudden mental and moral mutiny. *Ecce nunc tempus acceptabile!*[2] was
shouted on all hands with every variety of emphasis, and by voices
of every conceivable pitch, representing the three sexes of men,
women, and Lady Mary Wortley Montagues.[3] The nameless eagle
of the tree Ygdrasil[4] was about to sit at last, and wild-eyed enthusiasts rushed from all sides, each eager to thrust under the mystic
bird that chalk egg from which the new and fairer Creation was to be
hatched in due time. *Redeunt Saturnia regna,*[5]—so far was certain,
though in what shape, or by what methods, was still a matter of
debate. Every possible form of intellectual and physical dyspepsia
brought forth its gospel. Bran had its prophets, and the presartorial
simplicity of Adam its martyrs, tailored impromptu from the tar-pot
by incensed neighbors, and sent forth to illustrate the "feathered
Mercury," as defined by Webster and Worcester.[6] Plainness of
speech was carried to a pitch that would have taken away the breath
of George Fox; and even swearing had its evangelists, who answered

mentioned in the following sentence, was an Austrian divine (1644–1709) whose
real name was Ulrich Megerle, and who was famous for his grotesque humor.

2. "Behold now, the time is ripe."

3. English writer and bluestocking (1689–1762). Lowell is suggesting that
liberated women had much to do with the movement. He was not fond of Margaret
Fuller, who might very well be called the "American Lady Mary."

4. In northern mythology, the world tree that connects heaven, earth, and hell.
The eagle at the top and the serpent at the bottom are constantly striving, and the
hatching of the egg would bring about a millennium. In the remainder of this
paragraph, Lowell, rational and classical, shows how little sympathy he had with
food faddists, nudists, language reformers, revolutionary economists, and utopian
socialists, all of whom feel the lash of his wit. These matters were, of course, peri-
pheral to the transcendental movement, but they were far more in the public eye,
and were popularly identified with it. An analogous modern phenomenon is the
situation of existentialism as a serious philosophical idea. For every intelligent
exponent, a Sartre or a Heidegger, one can find dozens of popularizers and de-
basers; the use of drugs and extreme sexual freedom are to modern ideas what the
use of laxatives and extreme sexual freedom were to the transcendentalists.

5. "The reign of Saturn resumes" (Virgil, *Eclogue* I'', 6). That is, the golden age
returns.

6. Joseph Emerson Worcester (1784–1865) rivaled Noah Webster as a lexicog-
rapher.

a simple inquiry after their health with an elaborate ingenuity of imprecation that might have been honorably mentioned by Marlborough in general orders. Everybody had a mission (with a capital M) to attend to everybody else's business. No brain but had its private maggot, which must have found pitiably short commons sometimes. Not a few impecunious zealots abjured the use of money (unless earned by other people), professing to live on the internal revenues of the spirit. Some had an assurance of instant millennium so soon as hooks and eyes should be substituted for buttons. Communities were established where everything was to be common but common sense. Men renounced their old gods, and hesitated only whether to bestow their furloughed allegiance on Thor or Budh. Conventions were held for every hitherto inconceivable purpose. The belated gift of tongues, as among the Fifth Monarchy men,[7] spread like a contagion, rendering its victims incomprehensible to all Christian men; whether equally so to the most distant possible heathen or not was unexperimented, though many would have subscribed liberally that a fair trial might be made. It was the pentecost of Shinar.[8] The day of utterances reproduced the day of rebuses and anagrams, and there was nothing so simple that uncial letters and the style of Diphilus the Labyrinth[9] could not turn it into a riddle. Many foreign revolutionists out of work added to the general misunderstanding their contribution of broken English in every most ingenious form of fracture. All stood ready at a moment's notice to reform everything but themselves. The general motto was:—

> And we'll *talk* with them, too,
> And take upon 's the mystery of things
> As if we were God's spies.[10]

Nature is always kind enough to give even her clouds a humorous lining. I have barely hinted at the comic side of the affair, for the material was endless. This was the whistle and trailing fuse of the shell, but there was a very solid and serious kernel, full of the most

7. A sect of English fanatics of Cromwell's time who believed that Christ's reign (the Fifth Monarchy) was imminent.

8. See *Genesis*, 11:1–8; the tower of Babel.

9. Attic Stoic philosopher, third century B.C.

10. *King Lear*, V. iii. 14–17.

deadly explosiveness. Thoughtful men divined it, but the generality suspected nothing. The word "transcendental" then was the maid of all work for those who could not think, as "Pre-Raphaelite" has been more recently for people of the same limited housekeeping. The truth is, that there was a much nearer metaphysical relation and a much more distant esthetic and literary relation between Carlyle and the Apostles of the Newness, as they were called in New England, than has commonly been supposed. Both represented the reaction and revolt against *Philisterei*, a renewal of the old battle begun in modern times by Erasmus and Reuchlin, and continued by Lessing, Goethe, and, in a far narrower sense, by Heine in Germany, and of which Fielding, Sterne, and Wordsworth in different ways have been the leaders in England. It was simply a struggle for fresh air, in which, if the windows could not be opened, there was danger that panes would be broken, though painted with images of saints and martyrs. Light, colored by these reverend effigies, was none the more respirable for being picturesque. There is only one thing better than tradition, and that is the original and eternal life out of which all tradition takes its rise. It was this life which the reformers demanded, with more or less clearness of consciousness and expression, life in politics, life in literature, life in religion. Of what use to import a gospel from Judaea, if we leave behind the soul that made it possible, the God who keeps it forever real and present? Surely Abana and Pharpar *are* better than Jordan, if a living faith be mixed with those waters and none with these.[11]

Scotch Presbyterianism as a motive of spiritual progress was dead; New England Puritanism was in like manner dead; in other words, Protestantism had made its fortune and no longer protested; but till Carlyle spoke out in the Old World and Emerson in the New, no one had dared to proclaim, *Le roi est mort: vive le roi!* The meaning of which proclamation was essentially this: the vital spirit has long

11. This qualification of the serious side of the transcendental movement is usually ignored by critics who quote long sections of the preceding paragraph. *Philisterei* is Lowell's word for Philistinism. Desiderius Erasmus (1466?–1536) and Johann Reuchlin (1455–1522) were early humanists. Abana and Pharpar are rivers in Damascus. See *2 Kings*, 5:12.

since departed out of this form once so kingly, and the great seal has been in commission long enough; but meanwhile the soul of man, from which all power emanates and to which it reverts, still survives in undiminished royalty; God still survives, little as you gentlemen of the Commission seem to be aware of it,—nay, will possibly outlive the whole of you, incredible as it may appear. The truth is, that both Scotch Presbyterianism and New England Puritanism made their new avatar in Carlyle and Emerson, the heralds of their formal decease, and the tendency of the one toward Authority and of the other toward Independency might have been prophesied by whoever had studied history. The necessity was not so much in the men as in the principles they represented and the traditions which overruled them. The Puritanism of the past found its unwilling poet in Hawthorne, the rarest creative imagination of the century, the rarest in some ideal respects since Shakespeare; but the Puritanism that cannot die, the Puritanism that made New England what it is, and is destined to make America what it should be, found its voice in Emerson. Though holding himself aloof from all active partnership in movements of reform, he has been the sleeping partner who has supplied a great part of their capital.

The artistic range of Emerson is narrow, as every well-read critic must feel at once; and so is that of Aeschylus, so is that of Dante, so is that of Montaigne, so is that of Schiller, so is that of nearly every one except Shakespeare; but there is a gauge of height no less than of breadth, of individuality as well as of comprehensiveness, and, above all, there is the standard of genetic power, the test of the masculine as distinguished from the receptive minds. There are staminate plants in literature that make no fine show of fruit, but without whose pollen, quintessence of fructifying gold, the garden had been barren. Emerson's mind is emphatically one of these, and there is no man to whom our esthetic culture owes so much. The Puritan revolt had made us ecclesiastically and the Revolution politically independent, but we were still socially and intellectually moored to English thought, till Emerson cut the cable and gave us a chance at the dangers and the glories of blue water. No man young enough to have felt it can forget or cease to be grateful for the mental and moral *nudge* which he received from the writings of his high-minded and brave-spirited countryman. That we agree with him, or that he always agrees with himself, is aside from the question; but that he arouses in us something that we are the better for having awakened, whether that something be of opposition or assent, that he speaks always to what is highest and least selfish in us, few Americans of the generation younger than his own would be disposed to deny. His oration before the Phi Beta Kappa Society at Cambridge, some thirty years ago, was an event without any former parallel in our literary annals, a scene to be always treasured in the memory for its picturesqueness and its inspiration. What crowded and breathless aisles, what windows clustering with eager heads, what enthusiasm of approval, what grim silence of foregone dissent! It was our Yankee version of a lecture by Abelard, our Harvard parallel to the last public appearances of Schelling.[12]

I said that the Transcendental Movement was the protestant spirit of Puritanism seeking a new outlet and an escape from forms and creeds which compressed rather than expressed it. In its motives, its preaching, and its results, it differed radically from the doctrine of Carlyle. The Scotchman, with all his genius, and his humor gigantesque as that of Rabelais, has grown shriller and shriller with years, degenerating sometimes into a common scold, and emptying very unsavory vials of wrath on the head of the sturdy British Socrates of worldly common sense. The teaching of Emerson tended much more exclusively to self-culture and the independent development of the individual man. It seemed to many almost Pythagorean[13] in its voluntary seclusion from commonwealth affairs. Both Carlyle and Emerson were disciples of Goethe, but Emerson in a far truer sense; and while the one, from his bias toward the eccentric, has degenerated more and more into mannerism, the other has clarified steadily toward perfection of style,—exquisite fineness of material, unobtrusive lowness of tone and simplicity of fashion, the most high-bred garb of expression. Whatever may be said of his thought, nothing

12. Pierre Abelard (1079–1142), French scholastic philosopher, and Friedrich Wilhelm Joseph von Schelling (1775–1854), German philosopher. This is, of course, enormous praise of Emerson and his "American Scholar" address of 1837.

13. Pythagoras, sixth century B.C. philosopher, cultivated a strict religious asceticism.

can be finer than the delicious limpidness of his phrase. If it was ever questionable whether democracy could develop a gentleman, the problem has been affirmatively solved at last. Carlyle, in his cynicism and his admiration of force in and for itself, has become at last positively inhuman; Emerson, reverencing strength, seeking the highest outcome of the individual, has found that society and politics are also main elements in the attainment of the desired end, and has drawn steadily manward and worldward. The two men represent respectively those grand personifications in the drama of Aeschylus, Βία and Κράτος.[14]

Among the pistillate plants kindled to fruitage by the Emersonian pollen, Thoreau is thus far the most remarkable; and it is something eminently fitting that his posthumous works should be offered us by Emerson, for they are strawberries from his own garden. A singular mixture of varieties, indeed, there is;—alpine, some of them, with the flavor of rare mountain air; others wood, tasting of sunny roadside banks or shy openings in the forest; and not a few seedlings swollen hugely by culture, but lacking the fine natural aroma of the more modest kinds. Strange books these are of his, and interesting in many ways,—instructive chiefly as showing how considerable a crop may be raised on a comparatively narrow close of mind, and how much a man may make of his life if he will assiduously follow it, though perhaps never truly finding it at last.

I have just been renewing my recollection of Mr. Thoreau's writings, and have read through his six volumes in the order of their production. I shall try to give an adequate report of their impression upon me both as critic and as mere reader. He seems to me to have been a man with so high a conceit of himself that he accepted without questioning, and insisted on our accepting, his defects and weaknesses of character as virtues and powers peculiar to himself. Was he indolent, he finds none of the activities which attract or employ the rest of mankind worthy of him. Was he wanting in the qualities that make success, it is success that is contemptible, and not himself that lacks persistency and purpose. Was he poor, money was an unmixed evil.

---

14. Strength and Power, the two characters in *Prometheus Bound* who bind Prometheus to the rock. The only difference between the two characters is that *Bia* is wordless in the drama, while Kratos communicates, that is, takes a human part.

Did his life seem a selfish one, he condemns doing good as one of the weakest of superstitions. To be of use was with him the most killing bait of the wily tempter Uselessness. He had no faculty of generalization from outside of himself, or at least no experience which would supply the material of such, and he makes his own whim the law, his own range the horizon of the universe. He condemns a world, the hollowness of whose satisfactions he had never had the means of testing, and we recognize Apemantus behind the mask of Timon.[15] He had little active imagination; of the receptive he had much. His appreciation is of the highest quality; his critical power, from want of continuity of mind, very limited and inadequate. He somewhere cites a simile from Ossian,[16] as an example of the superiority of the old poetry to the new, though, even were the historic evidence less convincing, the sentimental melancholy of those poems should be conclusive of their modernness. He had none of the artistic mastery which controls a great work to the serene balance of completeness, but exquisite mechanical skill in the shaping of sentences and paragraphs, or (more rarely) short bits of verse for the expression of a detached thought, sentiment, or image. His works give one the feeling of a sky full of stars,—something impressive and exhilarating certainly, something high overhead and freckled thickly with spots of isolated brightness; but whether these have any mutual relation with each other, or have any concern with our mundane matters, is for the most part matter of conjecture,—astrology as yet, and not astronomy.

It is curious, considering what Thoreau afterwards became, that he was not by nature an observer. He only saw the things he looked for, and was less poet than naturalist. Till he built his Walden shanty, he did not know that the hickory grew in Concord. Till he went to Maine, he had never seen phosphorescent wood, a phenomenon early familiar to most country boys. At forty he speaks of the seeding of the pine as a new discovery, though one should have

15. In Shakespeare's *Timon of Athens*, Apemantus appears even surlier than the misanthrope, Timon.

16. James Macpherson published a series of poems in 1761–1765 which he said were transcriptions from the Welsh bard Ossian, possibly of the third century A.D. They were, of course, a hoax.

thought that its gold-dust of blowing pollen might have earlier drawn his eye. Neither his attention nor his genius was of the spontaneous kind. He discovered nothing. He thought everything a discovery of his own, from moonlight to the planting of acorns and nuts by squirrels. This is a defect in his character, but one of his chief charms as a writer. Everything grows fresh under his hand. He delved in his mind and nature; he planted them with all manner of native and foreign seeds, and reaped assiduously. He was not merely solitary, he would be isolated, and succeeded at last in almost persuading himself that he was autochthonous. He valued everything in proportion as he fancied it to be exclusively his own. He complains in *Walden* that there is no one in Concord with whom he could talk of Oriental literature, though the man was living within two miles of his hut who had introduced him to it.[17] This intellectual selfishness becomes sometimes almost painful in reading him. He lacked that generosity of "communication" which Johnson admired in Burke. De Quincey tells us that Wordsworth was impatient when any one else spoke of mountains, as if he had a peculiar property in them. And we can readily understand why it should be so: no one is satisfied with another's appreciation of his mistress. But Thoreau seems to have prized a lofty way of thinking (often we should be inclined to call it a remote one) not so much because it was good in itself as because he wished few to share it with him. It seems now and then, as if he did not seek to lure others up "above our lower region of turmoil," but to leave his own name cut on the mountain peak as the first climber. This itch of originality infects his thought and style. To be misty is not to be mystic. He turns commonplaces end for end, and fancies it makes something new of them. As we walk down Park Street, our eye is caught by Dr. Winship's dumb-bells, one of which bears an inscription testifying that it is the heaviest ever put up at arm's length by any athlete; and in reading Mr. Thoreau's books we cannot help feeling as if he sometimes invited our attention to a particular sophism or paradox as the biggest yet maintained by any single writer. He seeks, at all risks, for perversity of thought, and revives the age of *concetti*[18] while he fancies himself

17. That is, Emerson.
18. Conceits; that is, literary mannerisms.

going back to a pre-classical nature. "A day," he says, "passed in
the society of those Greek sages, such as described in the 'Banquet'
of Xenophon, would not be comparable with the dry wit of de-
cayed cranberry-vines and the fresh Attic salt of the moss-beds."
It is not so much the True that he loves as the Out-of-the-Way.
As the Brazen Age shows itself in other men by exaggeration of
phrase, so in him by extravagance of statement. He wishes always
to trump your suit and to *ruff* when you least expect it. Do you love
Nature because she is beautiful? He will find a better argument in
her ugliness. Are you tired of the artificial man? He instantly dresses
you up an ideal in a Penobscot Indian, and attributes to this creature of his otherwise-mindedness as peculiarities things that are
common to all woodsmen, white or red, and this simply because he
has not studied the pale-faced variety.

This notion of an absolute originality, as if one could have a
patent-right in it, is an absurdity. A man cannot escape in thought,
any more than he can in language, from the past and the present.
As no one ever invents a word, and yet language somehow grows by
general contribution and necessity, so it is with thought. Mr.
Thoreau seems to me to insist in public on going back to flint and
steel, when there is a match-box in his pocket which he knows very
well how to use at a pinch. Originality consists in power of digesting
and assimilating thoughts, so that they become part of our life and
substance. Montaigne, for example, is one of the most original of
authors, though he helped himself to ideas in every direction. But
they turn to blood and coloring in his style, and give a freshness of
complexion that is forever charming. In Thoreau much seems yet to
be foreign and unassimilated, showing itself in symptoms of indigestion. A preacher-up of Nature, we now and then detect under the
surly and stoic garb something of the sophist and the sentimentalizer.
I am far from implying that this was conscious on his part. But it is
much easier for a man to impose on himself when he measures only
with himself. A greater familiarity with ordinary men would have
done Thoreau good, by showing him how many fine qualities are
common to the race. The radical vice of his theory of life was that he
confounded physical with spiritual remoteness from men. A man is
far enough withdrawn from his fellows if he keep himself clear of

their weaknesses. He is not so truly withdrawn as exiled, if he refuse to share in their strength. "Solitude," says Cowley, "can be well fitted and set right but upon a very few persons. They must have enough knowledge of the world to see the vanity of it, and enough virtue to despise all vanity." It is a morbid self-consciousness that pronounces the world of men empty and worthless before trying it, the instinctive evasion of one who is sensible of some innate weakness, and retorts the accusation of it before any has made it but himself. To a healthy mind, the world is a constant challenge of opportunity. Mr. Thoreau had not a healthy mind, or he would not have been so fond of prescribing. His whole life was a search for the doctor. The old mystics had a wiser sense of what the world was worth. They ordained a severe apprenticeship to law, and even ceremonial, in order to the gaining of freedom and mastery over these. Seven years of service for Rachel were to be rewarded at last with Leah. Seven other years of faithfulness with her were to win them at last the true bride of their souls. Active Life was with them the only path to the Contemplative.

Thoreau had no humor, and this implies that he was a sorry logician. Himself an artist in rhetoric, he confounds thought with style when he undertakes to speak of the latter. He was forever talking of getting away from the world, but he must be always near enough to it, nay, to the Concord corner of it, to feel the impression he makes there. He verifies the shrewd remark of Sainte-Beuve, "On touche encore à son temps et très-fort, même quand on le repousse."[19] This egotism of his is a Stylites pillar after all, a seclusion which keeps him in the public eye. The dignity of man is an excellent thing, but therefore to hold one's self too sacred and precious is the reverse of excellent. There is something delightfully absurd in six volumes addressed to a world of such "vulgar fellows" as Thoreau affirmed his fellow men to be. I once had a glimpse of a genuine solitary who spent his winters one hundred and fifty miles beyond all human communication, and there dwelt with his rifle as his only confidant. Compared with this, the shanty on Walden Pond has something the air, it must be confessed, of the Hermitage of La

19. "Even he who rejects his time still touches it, and strongly." Charles Augustin Sainte-Beuve (1804–1869) was a French critic.

Chevrette.[20] I do not believe that the way to a true cosmopolitanism carries one into the woods or the society of musquashes. Perhaps the narrowest provincialism is that of Self; that of Kleinwinkel[21] is nothing to it. The natural man, like the singing birds, comes out of the forest as inevitably as the natural bear and the wildcat stick there. To seek to be natural implies a consciousness that forbids all naturalness forever. It is as easy—and no easier—to be natural in a salon as in a swamp, if one do not aim at it, for what we call un-naturalness always has its spring in a man's thinking too much about himself. "It is impossible," said Turgot,[22] "for a vulgar man to be simple."

I look upon a great deal of the modern sentimentalism about Nature as a mark of disease. It is one more symptom of the general liver-complaint. To a man of wholesome constitution the wilderness is well enough for a mood or a vacation, but not for a habit of life. Those who have most loudly advertised their passion for seclusion and their intimacy with Nature, from Petrarch down, have been mostly sentimentalists, unreal men, misanthropes on the spindle side, solacing an uneasy suspicion of themselves by professing contempt for their kind. They make demands on the world in advance proportioned to their inward measure of their own merit, and are angry that the world pays only by the visible measure of performance. It is true of Rousseau, the modern founder of the sect, true of Saint Pierre, his intellectual child, and of Châteaubriand,[23] his grandchild, the inventor, we might almost say, of the primitive forest, and who first was touched by the solemn falling of a tree from natural decay in the windless silence of the woods. It is a very shallow view that affirms trees and rocks to be healthy, and cannot see that men in communities are just as true to the laws of their organization and destiny; that can tolerate the puffin and the fox, but not the fool and the knave; that would shun politics because of its demagogues, and

20. Rousseau's house on Mme Epinay's estate.
21. German proverbial expression, a "little corner," a trifle.
22. Pseudonym of Anne Robert Jacques, Baron de l'Aulne (1727–1781), French writer and politician.
23. Bernardin de Saint-Pierre (1737–1814) and René de Chateaubriand (1768–1848), French Romantic writers.

snuff up the stench of the obscene fungus. The divine life of Nature is more wonderful, more various, more sublime in man than in any other of her works, and the wisdom that is gained by commerce with men, as Montaigne and Shakespeare gained it, or with one's own soul among men, as Dante, is the most delightful, as it is the most precious, of all. In outward nature it is still man that interests us, and we care far less for the things seen than the way in which they are seen by poetic eyes like Wordsworth's or Thoreau's, and the reflections they cast there. To hear the to-do that is often made over the simple fact that a man sees the image of himself in the outward world, one is reminded of a savage when he for the first time catches a glimpse of himself in a looking-glass. "Venerable child of Nature," we are tempted to say, "to whose science in the invention of the tobacco-pipe, to whose art in the tattooing of thine undegenerate hide not yet enslaved by tailors, we are slowly striving to climb back, the miracle thou beholdest is sold in my unhappy country for a shilling!" If matters go on as they have done, and everybody must needs blab of all the favors that have been done him by roadside and river-brink and woodland walk, as if to kiss and tell were no longer treachery, it will be a positive refreshment to meet a man who is as superbly indifferent to Nature as she is to him. By and by we shall have John Smith, of No. –12 –12th Street, advertising that he is not the J. S. who saw a cow-lily on Thursday last, as he never saw one in his life, would not see one if he could, and is prepared to prove an alibi on the day in question.

Solitary communion with Nature does not seem to have been sanitary or sweetening in its influence on Thoreau's character. On the contrary, his letters show him more cynical as he grew older. While he studied with respectful attention the minks and wood-chucks, his neighbors, he looked with utter contempt on the august drama of destiny of which his country was the scene, and on which the curtain had already risen. He was converting us back to a state of nature "so eloquently," as Voltaire said of Rousseau, "that he almost persuaded us to go on all fours," while the wiser fates were making it possible for us to walk erect for the first time. Had he conversed more with his fellows, his sympathies would have widened with the assurance that his peculiar genius had more appreciation, and his writings a larger circle of readers, or at least a warmer one, than he dreamed of. We have the highest testimony[24] to the natural sweetness, sincerity, and nobleness of his temper, and in his books an equally irrefragable one to the rare quality of his mind. He was not a strong thinker, but a sensitive feeler. Yet his mind strikes us as cold and wintry in its purity. A light snow has fallen everywhere in which he seems to come on the track of the shier sensations that would elsewhere leave no trace. We think greater compression would have done more for his fame. A feeling of sameness comes over us as we read so much. Trifles are recorded with an over-minute punctuality and conscientiousness of detail. He registers the state of his personal thermometer thirteen times a day. We cannot help thinking sometimes of the man who

> Watches, starves, freezes, and sweats—
> To learn but catechisms and alphabets
> Of unconcerning things, matters of fact,

and sometimes of the saying of the Persian poet, that "when the owl would boast, he boasts of catching mice at the edge of a hole." We could readily part with some of his affectations. It was well enough for Pythagoras to say, once for all, "When I was Euphorbus at the siege of Troy"; not so well for Thoreau to travesty it into "When I was a shepherd on the plains of Assyria." A naïve thing said over again is anything but naïve. But with every exception, there is no writing comparable with Thoreau's in kind, that is comparable with it in degree where it is best; where it disengages itself, that is, from the tangled roots and dead leaves of a second-hand Orientalism, and runs limpid and smooth and broadening as it runs, a mirror for whatever is grand and lovely in both worlds.

George Sand says neatly, that "Art is not a study of positive reality" (*actuality* were the fitter word), "but a seeking after ideal truth." It would be doing very inadequate justice to Thoreau if we left it to be inferred that this ideal element did not exist in him, and that too in larger proportion, if less obstrusive, than his nature-

24. Mr. Emerson, in the Biographical Sketch prefixed to the *Excursions*. [Lowell's note.]

worship. He took nature as the mountain-path to an ideal world. If the path wind a good deal, if he record too faithfully every trip over a root, if he botanize somewhat wearisomely, he gives us now and then superb outlooks from some jutting crag, and brings us out at last into an illimitable ether, where the breathing is not difficult for those who have any true touch of the climbing spirit. His shanty-life was a mere impossibility, so far as his own conception of it goes, as an entire independency of mankind. The tub of Diogenes had a sounder bottom. Thoreau's experiment actually presupposed all that complicated civilization which it theoretically abjured. He squatted on another man's land; he borrows an axe; his boards, his nails, his bricks, his mortar, his books, his lamp, his fish-hooks, his plough, his hoe, all turn state's evidence against him as an accomplice in the sin of that artificial civilization which rendered it possible that such a person as Henry D. Thoreau should exist at all. *Magnis tamen excidit ausis.*[25] His aim was a noble and a useful one, in the direction of "plain living and high thinking." It was a practical sermon on Emerson's text that "things are in the saddle and ride mankind," an attempt to solve Carlyle's problem (condensed from Johnson) of "lessening your denominator." His whole life was a rebuke of the waste and aimlessness of our American luxury, which is an abject enslavement to tawdry upholstery. He had "fine translunary things" in him. His better style as a writer is in keeping with the simplicity and purity of his life. We have said that his range was narrow, but to be a master is to be a master. He had caught his English at its living source, among the poets and prose-writers of its best days; his literature was extensive and recondite; his quotations are always nuggets of the purest ore: there are sentences of his as perfect as anything in the language, and thoughts as clearly crystallized; his metaphors and images are always fresh from the soil; he had watched Nature like a detective who is to go upon the stand; as we read him, it seems as if all-out-of-doors had kept a diary and become its own Montaigne; we look at the landscape as in a Claude Lorraine glass;[26] compared with his, all other books of similar aim, even

25. "He failed in great attempts, however."
26. A tinted glass to bring out the colors of a landscape, as used by Lorraine (1600–1682), French landscape painter.

White's *Selborne*,[27] seem dry as a country clergyman's meteorological journal in an old almanac. He belongs with Donne and Browne and Novalis;[28] if not with the originally creative men, with the scarcely smaller class who are peculiar, and whose leaves shed their invisible thought-seed like ferns.

Works, II, 131–153.

27. Gilbert White (1720–1793) wrote *The Natural History . . . of Selborne* (1789).

28. Novalis was the pseudonym of Baron Friedrich von Hardenberg (1772–1801), German Romantic poet.

Literature and International Copyright

This excerpt is the major portion of an address delivered by Lowell at an International Copyright League meeting in Chickering Hall, New York, November 28, 1887. At the end of his life he expended much effort in this one cause, chairing meetings like the one from which this excerpt is taken, lobbying for a copyright treaty in Washington, and organizing readings by writers for the cause. Like most American men of letters of this period, he spared no effort, and had the peculiar pleasure of living to see the one great legal stride made during the nineteenth century toward equality of opportunity for American writers when the first copyright treaty was signed into law in March, 1891.

The speech is divided in two parts. The first is a retrospective review of the American literary situation when Lowell was a young man, especially in comparison with the situation in 1887. The second part is a consideration of the logic favoring an international copyright treaty. It is possible that Lowell, like many American literary men, may have overestimated the effect a copyright treaty would have. But surely he was correct in his suggestion that it is better that America does not allow "the shaping of its thought, and therefore of its character" to be done by another people.

When I was beginning life, as it is called,—as if we were not always beginning it!—the question of "Who reads an American book?" still roused in the not too numerous cultivated class among us a feeling of resentful but helpless anger. The pens of our periodical writers fairly sputtered with rage and many a hardly suppressed imprecation might be read between their lines. Their position was, in truth, somewhat difficult. We had had Jonathan Edwards, no doubt; and people were still living who thought Barlow's *Hasty*

Pudding[1] a lightsome *jeu d'esprit*, and who believed that Dwight's *Conquest of Canaan* was a long stride towards that of Posterity and the conversion of the heathen. We had had Freneau who wrote a single line,

The hunter and the deer a shade,[2]

which had charmed the ear and cheated the memory of Scott (I think it was) till he mistook it for his own. We had the "Star-spangled Banner" and two or three naval ballads which to my ear have the true rough and ready tone. Philip Cooke[3] of Virginia had written a few graceful and musical lyrics. We had "McFingal,"[4] as near its model as any imitation of the inimitable can be, but far indeed from that intricate subtlety of wit which makes *Hudibras* a metaphysical study as well as an intellectual delight. We had in *The Federalist* a mine of political wisdom by which even Burke might have profited, and whose golden veins are not yet exhausted, as foreign statists and jurists are beginning to discover. But of true literature we had next to nothing. Of what we had, Duyckinck's scholarly *Cyclopaedia of American Literature* gives us an almost too satisfactory notion. Of what we had not, there was none to tell us, for there were no critics. We had no national unity, and therefore no national consciousness, and it is one of the first conditions of a virile and characteristic literature that it should feel solid and familiar earth under its feet. New England had indeed a kind of unity, but it was a provincial unity, and those hardy commonwealths that invented democracy were not and could not yet be quite in sympathy with the new America that was to adopt and expand it. Literature

1. Joel Barlow (1754–1812) wrote his best and best-known poem, *Hasty Pudding*, in 1796. It is a mock pastoral in praise of American cornmeal pudding. The reference below is to Timothy Dwight (1752–1817) and his biblical epic *The Conquest of Canaan* (1785).

2. From Freneau's "The Indian Burying Ground." It was not Scott, but Campbell who appropriated the line for his poem "O'Connor's Child."

3. Philip Pendleton Cooke (1816–1850) published only one volume of poems, *Froissart Ballads and Other Poems* (1847).

4. A burlesque epic begun in 1775 and completed in 1782 by John Trumbull (1750–1831).

thrives in an air laden with tradition, in a soil ripe with immemorial culture, in the temperature, steady and stimulating, of historic associations. We had none of these. What semblance we had of them was English, and we long continued to bring earth from the mother country to pot our imported plants with, as the crusaders brought home that of Palestine to be buried in.

And all this time our native oak was dropping its unheeded acorns into the crannies of the rock where by and by their sturdy roots would make room for themselves and find fitting nourishment.

Never was young nation on its way to seek his fortune so dumfounded as Brother Jonathan when John Bull, presenting what seemed to his startled eyes a blunderbuss, cried gruffly from the roadside, "Stand, and deliver a literature!" He was in a "pretty fix" as he himself would have called it. After fumbling in all his pockets, he was obliged to confess that he had left a beautiful one at home which he would have fetched along—only it was so everlasting heavy. If he had but known it, he carried with him the pledge of what he was seeking in that vernacular phrase "fix," which showed that he could invent a new word for a new need without asking leave of anybody.

Meanwhile the answer to Sydney Smith's scornful question was shaping itself. Already we had Irving, who after humorously satirizing the poverty of our annals in his *Knickerbocker*, forced to feel the pensive beauty of what is ancient by the painful absence of it, first tried to create an artificial antiquity as a substitute, and then sought in the Old World a kindlier atmosphere and themes more sympathetic with the dainty and carefully shaded phrase he loved. He first taught us the everliving charm of style, most invaluable and most difficult of lessons. Almost wholly English, he is yet our earliest classic, still loved in the Old Home and the New. Then came Cooper, our first radically American author with the defects of style that come of half-culture, but a man of robust genius who, after a false start, looked about him to recognize in the New Man of the New World an unhackneyed and unconventional subject for Art. Brockden Brown had shown vivid glimpses of genius, but of a genius haunted by the phantasms of imagination and conscious of the substantial realities they mocked only as an opium eater might be. His models were lay figures, shabby from their long service in the studios of Godwin and the Germans. Cooper first studied from the life and it was the *Homo Americanus* with our own limestone in his bones, our own iron in his blood, that sat to him. There had been pioneers before him, like Belknap and Brackenridge,[5] who had, in woodman's phrase, blazed the way for him, but he found new figures in the forest, autochthonous figures, and on the ocean, whose romance he was the first to divine, he touched a nerve of patriotic pride that still vibrates. I open upon my boyhood when I chance on a page of his best. In prose we had also Channing who uttered the perceptions, at once delicate and penetrating like root fibres, of a singularly intuitive mind in a diction of sober fervor where the artist sometimes elbows aside the preacher; and Webster, the massive simplicity of whose language and the unwavering force of whose argument, flashing into eloquent flame as it heated, recalled to those who listened and who saw before them one of the most august shapes manhood ever put on, no inadequate image of Pericles. We had little more. Emerson was still letting grow or trying in short flights those wings that were to lift him and us to Heaven's sweetest air. Hawthorne, scarce out of his teens, had given in *Fanshawe* some inkling of his instinct for style and of the direction his maturer genius was to choose, but no glimpse of that creative imagination the most original and profound of these latter days. Our masters of historical narration were yet to come. In poetry we were still to seek. Bryant's "Waterfowl" had begun that immortal flight that will be followed by many a delighted eye long after ours shall have been darkened; Dana had written some verses which showed a velleity for better and sincerer things; Willis was frittering away a natural and genuine gift; Longfellow was preluding that sweet, pure, and sympathetic song which persuaded so many Englishmen that he must be a countryman of theirs. In his case the question certainly became not "Who reads an American book?" but "Who does not read one?" Holmes had written one imperishable poem.

5. Jeremy Belknap (1744–1798) as a writer was primarily a historian, but he also wrote a satirical allegory, *The Foresters*. Hugh Henry Brackenridge (1748–1816) wrote *Modern Chivalry* (1792–1815), the first American picaresque novel.

This was the state of things when I was a boy. That old question, once so cruelly irritating, because it was so cruelly to the point, has long ago lost its sting. When I look round me on this platform, I see a company of authors whose books are read wherever English is read, and some whose books are read in languages that are other than their own. The American who lounges over an English railway bookstall while his train is making up sees almost as many volumes with names of his countrymen on their backs as he sees of native authors. American Literature has asserted and made good its claim to a definite place in the world. Sixty years ago there were only two American authors, Irving and Cooper, who could have lived by their literary incomes and they, fortunately, had other sources of revenue. There are now scores who find in letters a handsome estate. Our literature has developed itself out of English literature, as our political forms have developed themselves out of English political forms, but with a difference. Not as parasitic plants fed from the parent stock, but only as new growths from seeds the mother-tree has dropped, could they have prospered as they have done. And so our literature is a part of English literature and must always continue to be so, but, as I have said, with a difference. What that difference is, it would be very hard to define, though it be something of which we are very sensible when we read an American book. We are, I think, especially sensible of it in the biography of any of our country-men, as I could not help feeling as I read that admirable one of Emerson by Mr. Cabot.[6] There was nothing English in the conditions which shaped the earlier part of Emerson's life. Something Scottish there was, it may be said, but the later life at Concord which was so beautiful in its noble simplicity, in its frugality, never parsimonious and practised to secure not wealth, but independence, that is,—or must we say was?—thoroughly American. Without pretension, without swagger, without the need of proclaiming itself, and with no affectation of that commonness which our later politicians seem to think especially dear to a democracy, it represented whatever was peculiar and whatever was best in the novel inspirations of our soil. These inspirations began to make themselves felt early in our history and I think I find traces of their influence even so long ago as

6. James E. Cabot, *A Memoir of Ralph Waldo Emerson* (2 vols.; Boston, 1887).

The Simple Cobler of Aggawam, published in 1647. Its author, Ward,[7] had taken his second degree at Cambridge and was a man past middle life when he came over to Massachusetts, but I think his book would have been a different book had he written it in England. This Americanism which is there because we cannot help it, not put there because it is expected of us, gives, I think, a new note to our better literature and is what makes it fresh and welcome to foreign ears.

We have developed, if we did not invent, a form of racy popular humor, as original as it is possible for anything to be, which has found ideal utterance through the genius of Mark Twain. I confess that I look upon this general sense of the comic among our people and the ready wit which condenses it into epigram, as one of the safeguards of our polity. If it be irreverent, it is not superstitious; it has little respect for phrases; and no nonsense can long look it in the eye without flinching.

Our literature, whatever its merits or defects, has grown to what it now is—and certainly the growth has been vigorous, even if sometimes the work of the pruning-knife be missed—under many and great obstacles. Obstacle, no doubt, may be a help as well as a hindrance, as the basket set down on an acanthus is fabled to have suggested the Corinthian capital and the old emblem shows how *Virtus sub pondere crescit.*[8] But the obstacles with which our literature had to struggle were almost wholly of the repressive kind, and they were very serious obstacles. Our country, when it was beginning to feel its way, were a congeries of scattered republics with certain deferential rather than dependent relations to a common centre of legislation if not of authority, but with traditions and sympathies narrow and exclusive in their range. Ease of communication had not yet knit us together in material interests, Civil war had not welded us inseparably into a nation with a common pride and a common ideal. We had no Capital to concentrate, to stimulate, to suggest. We had no large reading public. We were. busy with other and more pressing cares. Above all we had to compete with the literature, and in our own language too, of a period in which great events and

7. Nathaniel Ward (1578–1652) came to America in 1633.
8. "Manhood increases under stress."

mighty movements of thought gave to genius the opportunity and to talent the excitement that it needs. And of this literature there was an ample supply and could be had for nothing. Our men of letters had to struggle as best they might against the disheartening competition with reputations already made, with writers alien yet not foreign, for they wrote in the same tongue. They were handicapped as were never authors before, unless we except those of Switzerland and Belgium, and where are the distinctive literatures of those countries? Rousseau it is true was Genevese, but he left Geneva as soon as he could and became a Frenchman. I believe that the only characteristic Belgian literature has been written in Flemish, not in French. Our own literature then, may fairly lay claim to some vigor and vitality when it could assert itself under conditions such as these.

And why was this foreign literature to be had for nothing? Simply because we could not or would not admit that there could be such a thing as foreign property in an idea. I admit that all property is in the last resort the creature of municipal law, and that a thing may be property in one country which is not so in another, nay may be property in Colonies yet not in the mother country, as Granville Sharp[9] demonstrated in the case of the negro in England. I admit also that in all countries maintaining a tariff of duties on foreign goods, those goods are liable to confiscation if introduced in evasion of the law. But in the case of the slave as in that of the smuggler the owner of the property must connive in the fraudulent introduction of his property into the country so confiscating it. In the case of the English author his property is brought over for the express purpose of being confiscated, brought here, too, against his will and in spite of his earnest protest. When we say property in ideas, we use an ambiguous and deceptive phrase, for what we really mean is property in the value that has been given to an idea by a man's own labor or skill or genius. I shall not argue this. I will only say that this form of property, both foreign and domestic, has been admitted by every civilized country in the world except our own. It has been admitted

9. Sharp (1735–1813) defended the Negro James Somerset, establishing the principle in 1772 that a colonial slave becomes free the moment his foot touches English soil.

by countries where, as between us and England, the language was the same, as between Germany and Austria, or partially so as between Belgium and France. It is certainly odd that while to steal a wine I have bought is theft, to steal the book I have made is meritorious. Now the meeting here today is held for the purpose of raising money to promote the aims of a Society formed in the hope of relieving America from a reproach and American authors from an unjust and unwisely imposed burthen. The question whether the present state of things be a reproach or not, I shall not argue, nor whether the burthen thus laid upon our authors be unjust. That this burthen is unwisely imposed will, I think, be plain to every one who asks himself the question whether it be prudent in a nation to allow its literature, or a great part of its literature, to be made for it by another nation, in other words, to allow the shaping of its thought, and therefore of its character, to be done by that other.

Manuscript in the James Russell Lowell Papers, Houghton Library, Harvard University. Used by permission of the Harvard College Library.

Review of Howells's *Venetian Life*

William Dean Howells, who was from Ohio, was the one "western" writer given instant appreciation by the critics of Brahmin New England. As early as his first trip to New England, in 1861, he was made to feel, as he described it in Literary Friends *and* Acquaintances *(1900)"something like the apostolic succession; this is the laying on of hands." Lowell's review of Howells's first prose work (excepting his campaign biography of Lincoln) has the same aura. Here was nothing to shock, nothing to outrage. Howells could be welcomed into the circle of taste without fear that he would introduce any kind of vulgarity.*

Those of our readers who watch with any interest the favorable omens of our literature from time to time, must have had their eyes drawn to short poems, remarkable for subtilty of sentiment and delicacy of expression, and bearing the hitherto unfamiliar name of Mr. Howells. Such verses are not common anywhere; as the work of a young man they are very uncommon. Youthful poets commonly begin by trying on various manners before they settle upon any single one that is prominently their own. But what especially interested us in Mr. Howells was, that his writings were from the very first not merely tentative and preliminary, but had somewhat of the conscious security of matured *style*. This is something which most poets arrive at through much tribulation. It is something which has nothing to do with the measure of their intellectual powers or of their moral insight, but is the one quality which essentially distinguishes the artist from the mere man of genius. Among the English poets of the last generation, Keats is the only one who early showed unmistakable signs of it, and developed it more and more fully until his untimely death. Wordsworth, though in most respects a far profounder man, attained it only now and then, indeed only once

240

perfectly,—in his "Laodamia." Now, though it be undoubtedly true from one point of view that what a man has to say is of more importance than how he says it, and that modern criticism especially is more apt to be guided by its moral and even political sympathies than by esthetic principles, it remains as true as ever that only those things have been said finally which have been said perfectly, and that this finished utterance is peculiarly the office of poetry, or of what, for want of some word as comprehensive as the German *Dichtung*, we are forced to call imaginative literature. Indeed, it may be said that, in whatever kind of writing, it is style alone that is able to hold the attention of the world long. Let a man be never so rich in thought, if he is clumsy in the expression of it, his sinking, like that of an old Spanish treasure-ship, will be hastened by the very weight of his bullion, and perhaps, after the lapse of a century, some lucky diver fishes up his ingots and makes a fortune out of him.

That Mr. Howells gave unequivocal indications of possessing this fine quality interested us in his modest preludings. Marked, as they no doubt were, by some uncertainty of aim and indefiniteness of thought, that "stinting," as Chaucer calls it, of the nightingale "ere he beginneth sing," there was nothing in them of the presumption and extravagance which young authors are so apt to mistake for originality and vigor. Sentiment predominated over reflection, as was fitting in youth; but there was a refinement, an instinctive reserve of phrase, and a felicity of epithet, only too rare in modern, and especially in American writing. He was evidently a man more eager to make something good than to make a sensation,—one of those authors more rare than ever in our day of hand-to-mouth cleverness, who has a conscious ideal of excellence, and, as we hope, the patience that will at length reach it. We made occasion to find out something about him, and what we learned served to increase our interest. This delicacy, it appeared, was a product of the rough-and-ready West, this finish the natural gift of a young man with no advantage of college-training, who, passing from the compositor's desk to the editorship of a local newspaper, had been his own faculty of the humanities. But there are some men who are born cultivated. A singular fruit, we thought, of our shaggy democracy,—as interesting

a phenomenon in that regard as it has been our fortune to encounter. Where is the rudeness of a new community, the pushing
vulgarity of an imperfect civilization, the licentious contempt of
forms that marks our unchartered freedom, and all the other terrible
things which have so long been the bugaboos of European refinement?
Here was a natural product, as perfectly natural as the deliberate
attempt of "Walt Whitman"[1] to answer the demand of native and
foreign misconception was perfectly artificial. Our institutions do
not, then, irretrievably doom us to coarseness and to impatience of
that restraining precedent which alone makes true culture possible
and true art attainable. Unless we are mistaken, there is something
in such an example as that of Mr. Howells which is a better argument for the American social and political system than any empirical
theories that can be constructed against it.

We know of no single word which will so fitly characterize Mr.
Howells's new volume about Venice as "delightful." The artist has
studied his subject for four years, and at last presents us with a series
of pictures having all the charm of tone and the minute fidelity to
nature which were the praise of the Dutch school of painters, but
with a higher sentiment, a more refined humor, and an airy elegance that recalls the better moods of Watteau. We do not remember
any Italian studies so faithful or the result of such continuous
opportunity, unless it be the *Roba di Roma* of Mr. Story, and what
may be found scattered in the works of Henri Beyle.[2] But Mr. Story's
volumes recorded only the chance observations of a quick and familiar eye in the intervals of a profession to which one must be busily
devoted who would rise to the acknowledged eminence occupied by
their author; and Beyle's mind, though singularly acute and penetrating, had too much of the hardness of a man of the world and of

1. Inevitably, Lowell was contemptuous of Whitman. About him he wrote,
"When a man aims at originality he acknowledges himself consciously unoriginal.
. . . The great fellows have always let the stream of their activity flow quietly—if
one splashes in it he may make a sparkle, but he muddies it too" (*Works*, XIV,
319–320). The quotation marks around Whitman's name probably represent this
artificiality.

2. William Wetmore Story (1819–1895), American sculptor and writer, whose
Roba di Roma appeared in 1862; Henri Beyle is the real name of Stendhal (1783–
1842), who wrote many books of travel along with his much better known fiction.

Parisian cynicism to be altogether agreeable. Mr. Howells, during four years of that consular leisure which only Venice could make tolerable, devoted himself to the minute study of the superb prison to which he was doomed, and his book is his "Prigioni."[3] Venice has been the university in which he has fairly earned the degree of Master. There is, perhaps, no European city, not even Bruges, not even Rome herself, which, not yet in ruins, is so wholly of the past, at once alive and turned to marble, like the Prince of the Black Islands in the story. And what gives it a peculiar fascination is that its antiquity, though venerable, is yet modern, and, so to speak, continuous; while that of Rome belongs half to a former world and half to this, and is broken irretrievably in two. The glory of Venice, too, was the achievement of her own genius, not an inheritance; and, great no longer, she is more truly than any other city the monument of her own greatness. She is something wholly apart, and the silence of her watery streets accords perfectly with the spiritual mood which makes us feel as if we were passing through a city of dream. Fancy now an imaginative young man from Ohio, where the log-hut was but yesterday turned to almost less enduring brick and mortar, set down suddenly in the midst of all this almost immemorial permanence of grandeur. We cannot think of any one on whom the impression would be so strangely deep, or whose eyes would be so quickened by the constantly recurring shock of unfamiliar objects. Most men are poor observers, because they are cheated into a delusion of intimacy with the things so long and so immediately about them; but surely we may hope for something like seeing from fresh eyes, and those too a poet's, when they open suddenly on a marvel so utterly alien to their daily vision and so perdurably novel as Venice. Nor does Mr. Howells disappoint our expectation. We have here something like a full-length portrait of the Lady of the Lagoons.

We have been struck in this volume, as elsewhere in writings of the same author, with the charm of *tone* that pervades it. It is so constant as to bear witness, not only to a real gift, but to the thoughtful cultivation of it. Here and there Mr. Howells yields to the temptation of *execution*, to which persons specially felicitous in language are

3. "Prison," here meaning a work completed in prison.

liable, and pushes his experiments of expression to the verge of being unidiomatic, in his desire to squeeze the last drop of significance from words; but this is seldom, and generally we receive that unconscious pleasure in reading him which comes of naturalness, the last and highest triumph of good writing. Mr. Howells, of all men, does not need to be told that, as wine of the highest flavor and most delicate *bouquet* is made from juice pressed out by the unaided weight of the grapes, so in expression we are in danger of getting something like acridness if we crush in with the first sprightly runnings the skins and kernels of words in our vain hope to win more than we ought of their color and meaning. But, as we have said, this is rather a temptation to which he now and then shows himself liable, than a fault for which he can often be blamed. If a mind open to all poetic impressions, a sensibility too sincere ever to fall into maudlin sentimentality, a style flexible and sweet without weakness, and a humor which, like the bed of a stream, is the support of deep feeling, and shows waveringly through it in spots of full sunshine,—if such qualities can make a truly delightful book, then Mr. Howells has made one in the volume before us. And we give him warning that much will be expected of one who at his years has already shown himself capable of so much.

North American Review, CIII (October 1866), 610–613; reprinted in Albert Mordell (ed.), *The Function of the Poet and Other Essays by James Russell Lowell* (Boston and New York: Houghton Mifflin, 1920), pp. 146–152.

Review of Henry James's
Tales and *Sketches*

Like Howells, Henry James represented the kind of literary genius to which Lowell could respond honestly and sympathetically. But as James's genius was greater, so was Lowell's enthusiasm and, it is to be noted, the points of accuracy in his estimate. Indeed, the estimate is quite extraordinarily accurate for the bulk of James's creation, even though it is based upon a consideration of only his two very earliest works, A Passionate Pilgrim and Other Tales *and* Transatlantic Sketches *(1875), while his first novel,* Roderick Hudson, *was still being serialized.*

Whoever takes an interest, whether of mere curiosity or of critical foreboding, in the product and tendency of our younger literature, must have had his attention awakened and detained by the writings of Mr. James. Whatever else they may be, they are not common, and have that air of good breeding which is the token of whatever is properly called literature. They are not the overflow of a shallow talent for improvisation too full of self to be contained, but show everywhere the marks of intelligent purpose and of the graceful ease that comes only of conscientious training. Undoubtedly there was a large capital of native endowment to start from—a mind of singular subtlety and refinement; a faculty of rapid observation, yet patient of rectifying afterthought; senses daintily alive to every esthetic suggestion; and a frank enthusiasm, kept within due bounds by the double-consciousness of humor. But it is plain that Mr. James is fortunate enough to possess, or to be possessed by, that finer sixth sense which we call the artistic, and which controls, corrects, and discontents. His felicities, therefore, are not due to a lucky turn of the dice, but to forethought and afterthought.

Accordingly, he is capable of progress, and gives renewed evidence of it from time to time, while too many of our authors show premature marks of arrested development. They strike a happy vein at starting, perhaps, and keep on grubbing at it, with the rude helps of primitive mining, seemingly unaware that it is daily growing more and more slender. Even should it wholly vanish, they persist in the vain hope of recovering it further on, as if in literature two successes of precisely the same kind were possible. Nay, most of them have hit upon no vein at all, but picked up a nugget rather, and persevere in raking the surface of things, if haply they may chance upon another. The moral of one of Hawthorne's stories is that there is no element of treasure-trove in success, but that true luck lies in the deep and assiduous cultivation of our own plot of ground, be it larger or smaller.[1] For indeed the only estate of man that savors of the realty is in his mind. Mr. James seems to have arrived early at an understanding of this, and to have profited by the best modern appliances of self-culture. In conception and expression he is essentially an artist and not an irresponsible *trouvère*. If he allow himself an occasional carelessness, it is not from incaution, but because he knows perfectly well what he is about. He is quite at home in the usages of the best literary society. In his writing there is none of that hit-or-miss playing at snap-dragon with language, of that clownish bearing-on in what should be the light strokes, as if mere emphasis were meaning, and naturally none of the slovenliness that offends a trained judgment in the work of so many of our later writers, unmistakably clever as they are. In short, he has *tone*, the last result and surest evidence of an intellect reclaimed from the rudeness of nature, for it means self-restraint. The story of Handel's composing always in full dress conveys at least the useful lesson of a gentleman-like deference for the art a man professes and for the public whose attention he claims. Mr. James, as we see in his sketches of travel, is not averse to the lounging ease of a shooting-jacket, but he respects the usages of convention, and at the canonical hours is sure to be found in the required toilet. He does not expect the company to pardon his own indolence as one of the necessary appendages of

1. Lowell is referring specifically to "Peter Goldthwaite's Treasure" (1838), but surely he also has in mind Voltaire's *Candide*.

originality. Always considerate himself, his readers soon find reason to treat him with consideration. For they soon come to see that literature may be light and at the same time thoughtful; that lightness, indeed, results much more surely from serious study than from the neglect of it.

We have said that Mr. James was emphatically a man of culture, and we are old-fashioned enough to look upon him with the more interest as a specimen of exclusively *modern* culture. Of any classical training we have failed to detect the traces in him. His allusions, his citations, are in the strictest sense contemporary, and indicate, if we may trust our divination, a preference for French models, Balzac, De Musset, Feuillet, Taine, Gautier, Mérimée, Sainte-Beuve, especially the three latter.[2] He emulates successfully their suavity, their urbanity, their clever knack of conveying a fuller meaning by innuendo than by direct bluntness of statement. If not the best school for substance, it is an admirable one for method, and for so much of style as is attainable by example. It is the same school in which the writers of what used to be called our classical period learned the superior efficacy of the French small-sword as compared with the English cudgel, and Mr. James shows the graceful suppleness of that excellent academy of fence in which a man distinguishes by effacing himself. He has the dexterous art of letting us feel the point of his individuality without making us obtrusively aware of his presence. We arrive at an intimate knowledge of his character by confidences that escape egotism by seeming to be made always in the interest of the reader. That we know all his tastes and prejudices appears rather a compliment to our penetration than a proof of indiscreetness on his part. If we were disposed to find any fault with Mr. James's style, which is generally of conspicuous elegance, it would be for his occasional choice of a French word or phrase (like *bouder, se reconnait, banal,*[3] and the like) where our English, without being driven

2. Few modern readers would agree with Lowell here that Gautier, Mérimée, and Sainte-Beuve ranked higher than Balzac and De Musset as French models for James, although the more general statement—that James shows a preference for French models over English—is surely correct.

3. *Bouder*: to sulk; *se reconnait*: he recognizes in himself; *banal* as "hackneyed," or "commonplace," has been an English word for some time now, perhaps partly because of James's extensive use of it. The reader who is familiar with James's

to search her coffers round, would furnish one quite as good and surer of coming home to the ordinary reader. We could grow as near surly with him as would be possible for us with a writer who so generally endears himself to our taste, when he foists upon us a disagreeable alien like *abandon* (used as a noun), as if it could show an honest baptismal certificate in the registers of Johnson or Webster. Perhaps Mr. James finds, or fancies, in such words a significance that escapes our obtuser sense, a sweetness, it may be, of early association, for he tells us somewhere that in his boyhood he was put to school in Geneva. In this way only can we account for his once slipping into the rusticism that "remembers of" a thing.

But beyond any advantage which he may have derived from an intelligent study of French models, it is plain that a much larger share of Mr. James's education has been acquired by travel and through the eyes of a thoughtful observer of men and things. He has seen more cities and manners of men than was possible in the slower days of Ulysses, and if with less gain of worldly wisdom, yet with an enlargement of his artistic apprehensiveness and scope that is of far greater value to him. We do not mean to imply that Mr. James lacks what is called knowledge of the world. On the contrary, he has a great deal of it, but it has not in him degenerated into worldliness, and a mellowing haze of imagination ransoms the edges of things from the hardness of over-near familiarity. He shows on analysis that rare combination of qualities which results in a man of the world, whose contact with it kindles instead of dampening the ardor of his fancy. He is thus excellently fitted for the line he has chosen as a story-teller who deals mainly with problems of character and psychology which spring out of the artificial complexities of society, and as a translator of the impressions received from nature and art into language that often lacks only verse to make it poetry. Mr. James does not see things with his eyes alone. His vision is always modified by his imaginative temperament. He is the last man we should consult for statistics, but his sketches give us the very marrow

---

style will sense the correctness of these criticisms, perhaps the more so because of the irony of James's own comment deploring Whitman's "too extensive acquaintance with the foreign languages." But one is less happy about Lowell's strictures on the nominative use of *abandon*.

of sensitive impression, and are positively better than the actual pilgrimage. We are tolerably familiar with the scenes he describes, but hardly knew before how much we had to be grateful for. *Et ego in Arcadia*,[4] we murmur to ourselves as we read, but surely this was not the name we found in our guide-book. It is always *Dichtung und Wahrheit*[5] (Goethe knew very well what he was about when he gave precedence to the giddier sister)—it is always fact seen through imagination and transfigured by it. A single example will best show what we mean. "It is partly, doubtless, because their mighty outlines are still unsoftened that the aqueducts are so impressive. *They seem the very source of the solitude in which they stand*; they look like architectural spectres, and loom through the light mists of their grassy desert, as you recede along the line, with the same insubstantial vastness as if they rose out of Egyptian sands." Such happy touches are frequent in Mr. James's pages, like flecks of sunshine that steal softened through every chance crevice in the leaves, as where he calls the lark a "disembodied voice," or says of an English country-church that "it made a Sunday where it stood." A light-fingered poet would find many a temptation in his prose. But it is not merely our fancies that are pleased. Mr. James tempts us into many byways of serious and fruitful thought. Especially valuable and helpful have we found his *obiter dicta* on the arts of painting, sculpture, and architecture; for example, when he says of the Tuscan palaces that "in their large dependence on pure symmetry for beauty of effect, [they] reproduce more than other modern styles the simple nobleness of Greek architecture." And we would note also what he says of the Albani Antinoüs.[6] It must be a nimble wit that can keep pace with Mr. James's logic in his esthetic criticism. It is apt to spring airily over the middle term to the conclusion, leaving something in the likeness of a ditch across the path of our slower intelligences, which look about them and think twice before taking the leap. Courage! there are always fresh woods and pastures new on the other side. A curious reflection has more than once flashed upon our minds as we lingered with Mr. James over his complex and refined

4. "I too dwell in Arcadia," the *memento mori* of Poussin's most famous painting.
5. *Poetry and Truth.* See p. 212, note 7.
6. Famous antique bust of Antinoüs in the Villa Albani, near Rome.

sensations: we mean the very striking contrast between the ancient and modern traveller. The former saw with his bodily eyes, and reported accordingly, catering for the curiosity of homely wits as to the outsides and appearances of things. Even Montaigne, habitually introspective as he was, sticks to the old method in his travels. The modern traveller, on the other hand, superseded by the guidebook, travels in himself, and records for us the scenery of his own mind as it is affected by change of sky and the various weather of temperament.

Mr. James, in his sketches, frankly acknowledges his preference of the Old World. Life—which here seems all drab to him, without due lights and shades of social contrast, without that indefinable suggestion of immemorial antiquity which has so large a share in picturesque impression—is there a dome of many-colored glass irradiating both senses and imagination. We shall not blame him too gravely for this, as if an American had not as good a right as any ancient of them all to say, *Ubi libertas, ibi patria.*[7] It is no real paradox to affirm that a man's love of his country may often be gauged by his disgust at it. But we think it might fairly be argued against him that the very absence of that distracting complexity of associations might help to produce that solitude which is the main feeder of imagination. Certainly, Hawthorne, with whom no modern European can be matched for the subtlety and power of this marvellous quality, is a strong case on the American side of the question.

Mr. James's tales, if without any obvious moral, are sure to have a clearly defined artistic purpose. They are careful studies of character thrown into dramatic action, and the undercurrent of motive is, as it should be, not in the circumstances but in the characters themselves. It is by delicate touches and hints that his effects are produced. The reader is called upon to do his share, and will find his reward in it, for Mr. James, as we cannot too often insist, is first and always an artist. Nowhere does he show his fine instinct more to the purpose than in leaving the tragic element of tales (dealing as they do with contemporary life, and that mainly in the drawingroom) to take care of itself, and in confining the outward expression of passion within the limits of a decorous amenity. Those who must have their intellectual gullets tingled with the fiery draught of coarse sensation

7. "Where is liberty, there is my homeland."

must go elsewhere for their dram; but whoever is capable of the aroma of the more delicate vintages will find it here. In the volume before us "Madame de Mauves" will illustrate what we mean. There is no space for detailed analysis, even if that were ever adequate to give the true impression of stories so carefully worked out and depending so much for their effect on a gradual cumulation of particulars each in itself unemphatic. We have said that Mr. James shows promise as well as accomplishment, gaining always in mastery of his material. It is but a natural inference from this that his "Roderick Hudson," now going on in the *Atlantic Monthly*, is the fullest and most finished proof of his power as a story-teller. Indeed, we may say frankly that it pleases us the more because the characters are drawn with a bolder hand and in more determined outline, for if Mr. James need any friendly caution, it is against overdelicacy of handling.

Nation, XX (June 24, 1875), 425–427; reprinted in Albert Mordell (ed.), *The Function of the Poet and Other Essays by James Russell Lowell* (Boston and New York: Houghton Mifflin, 1920), pp. 105–114.

Selected Bibliography

WORKS

LOWELL, JAMES RUSSELL. *Lectures on English Poets*. Cleveland: The Rowfant Club, 1897. (Edited by "S.A.J." from the reports in the Boston *Advertiser* of Lowell's Lowell Institute Lectures, January 9 to February 16, 1855.)

————. *The Complete Writings of James Russell Lowell*. Ed. Charles Eliot Norton. 16 vols. Boston and New York: Houghton Mifflin Company, 1904. (The Elmwood Edition, cited in this volume as *Works*.)

————. *The Round Table*. Boston: Richard G. Badger, The Gorham Press, 1913.

————. *The Function of the Poet and Other Essays*. Ed. Albert Mordell. Boston and New York: Houghton Mifflin Company, 1920.

————. *New Letters*. Ed. Mark A. DeWolfe Howe. New York: Harper, 1932.

————. *The Pioneer*. Introduction by Sculley Bradley. New York: Scholars' Facsimiles and Reprints, 1947.

BOOKS ABOUT LOWELL

BEATTY, RICHMOND CROOM. *James Russell Lowell*. Nashville, Tenn.: Vanderbilt Univ. Press, 1942.

BROWNELL, W. C. "Lowell," in *American Prose Masters*. New York: Scribner's, 1909.

DUBERMAN, MARTIN. *James Russell Lowell*. Boston: Houghton Mifflin Company, 1966.

FOERSTER, NORMAN. "Lowell," in *American Criticism*. Boston: Houghton Mifflin Company, 1928.

GREENSLET, FERRIS. *James Russell Lowell*. "American Men of Letters Series." Boston, 1905.

HALE, EDWARD EVERETT, JR. *James Russell Lowell and His Friends*. Boston: Houghton Mifflin Company, 1899.

HOWARD, LEON. *Victorian Knight-Errant: A Study of the Early Literary Career of James Russell Lowell*. Berkeley, Cal.: University of California Press, 1952.

HOWELLS, WILLIAM DEAN. *Literary Friends and Acquaintances*. New York: Harper, 1900.

JAMES, HENRY. "James Russell Lowell," in *Essays in London and Elsewhere*. New York: Harper, 1893.

PRITCHARD, JOHN P. "James Russell Lowell," in *Return to the Fountains*. Durham, N.C.: Duke University Press, 1942.

REILLY, JOSEPH J. *James Russell Lowell as a Critic*. New York: Putnam's, 1915.

SCUDDER, HORACE E. *James Russell Lowell: A Biography*. 2 vols. Boston: Houghton Mifflin Company, 1901.

ARTICLES ABOUT LOWELL

ALTICK, RICHARD D. "Was Lowell an Historical Critic?" *American Literature*, XIV (November 1942), 250–259.

CLARK, GEORGE P. "James Russell Lowell's Study of the Classics Before Entering Harvard," *Jahrbuch für Amerikastudien*, VIII (1963), 205–209.

CLARK, HARRY HAYDEN. "Lowell's Criticism of Romantic Literature," *Publications of the Modern Language Association*, XLI (1926), 209–228.

———. "Lowell—Humanitarian, Nationalist, or Humanist?" *Studies in Philology*, XXVII (1930), 411–441.

FOERSTER, NORMAN. "The Creed of Lowell as Literary Critic," *Studies in Philology*, XXIV (1927), 454–473.

LANGE, ALEXIS F. "James Russell Lowell as a Critic," *California University Chronicle*, VIII (1906), 352–364.

LOMBARD, C. M. "Lowell and French Romanticism," *Revue de Litterature Comparée*, XXXVIII (1964), 582–588.

NICHOLS, E. J. "Identification of Characters in Lowell's *A Fable for Critics*," *American Literature*, IV (1932), 191–194.

ROBERTSON, JOHN M. "Lowell as a Critic," *North American Review*, CCIX (February 1919), 246–262.

TRAUBEL, HORACE L. "Lowell—Whitman: A Contrast," *Poet-Lore*, IV (January 15, 1892), 22–31.

WARREN, AUSTIN. "Lowell on Thoreau," *Studies in Philology*, XXVII (1930), 442–462.

WHITE, WILLIAM. "Two Versions of Lowell's 'Function of the Poet,'" *Philological Quarterly*, XX (1941), 587–596.

Acknowledgments

In the writing and collecting of this book, I have been aided by many people to all of whom I am deeply grateful. I wish particularly to thank Herbert Howe of the Classics Department of the University of Wisconsin for help in identifying, translating, and documenting so many of Lowell's classical allusions; Gerard Sweeney for assistance in indexing; the editor of this series, Paul A. Olson for whole basketsful of suggestions; and my wife, Virginia, for some very constructive criticism.

I am also indebted to the Research Council of the University of Wisconsin for a research grant and travel expenses during the summer of 1968.

HERBERT F. SMITH

INDEX